BARRON'S

IELTS®

STRATEGIES AND TIPS

2ND EDITION

Lin Lougheed
Ed.D., Teachers College
Columbia University

BARRON'S

IELTS® is a registered trademark of University of Cambridge ESOL, the British Council, and IDP Education Australia, which neither sponsor nor endorse these products.

All inquiries should be addressed to:
Barron's Educational Series, Inc.
250 Wireless Boulevard
Hauppauge, New York 11788
www.barronseduc.com

Library of Congress Catalog No.: 2016941126

ISBN: 978-1-4380-7640-9

10%
POST-CONSUMER
WASTE
Paper contains a minimum
of 10% post-consumer
waste (PCW). Paper used
in this book was derived
from certified, sustainable
forestlands.

PRINTED IN THE UNITED STATES OF AMERICA
9 8 7 6 5 4 3 2 1

CONTENTS

IELTS WRITING MODULE

INTRODUCTION

Definitions

STRATEGIES AND TIPS

A **strategy** is a plan. A **tip** is a suggestion. A strategy tells you how to answer a question. A tip will help you answer it quickly.

The IELTS exam is a two-hour exam with four parts and many types of questions in each part. You need to have a plan before you start to answer these questions. You need to have a strategy. There are many possible ways to try to answer a question; you must find the best strategy for you.

The tips in this book will help you make efficient choices. The tips will make you a faster, more proficient test taker. A good test strategy combined with useful tips will improve your efficiency and increase your score on the exam.

IELTS Basic Strategies

Key Words

When you search the Internet, you type a word into the web browser. That word is a **key word**. The browser will search all the web pages on the Internet for that word or a related word.

Similarly, you can use key words to help you on the IELTS. You identify a key word in the questions and answers and then search the passage for that word or a related word.

Key words will help you focus your attention on what is important when you read or when you listen. If you look and listen for a key word or a related word, you will be able to find the answer to the question faster.

Key words can be any part of speech, but they are usually nouns, verbs, and modifiers. They answer the questions: *who, what, when, where, why,* and *how.*

READING

STRATEGY	Identify a key word and scan for the key word or related word in the passage.
TIP	Scan for several key words at the same time.

Multiple-Choice Questions

Before you read the passage, read the multiple-choice questions below. The key words are underlined. Then scan the passage looking for key words or related words. These key words are also underlined. Finally, answer the questions.

*Choose the correct letter, **A**, **B**, or **C**.*

1   The wheel was <u>invented</u>
   A before <u>making of textiles</u>.
   B during the <u>Bronze Age</u>.
   C after <u>3500 BC</u>.

2   The <u>earliest evidence</u> shows wheels being used to
   A make <u>pottery</u>.
   B move <u>carts</u>.
   C run <u>machinery</u>.

3   Wheels were used on <u>toy animals</u> in ancient
   A <u>Poland</u>.
   B <u>Mesopotamia</u>.
   C <u>Mexico</u>.

The wheel is one of the most important technological developments of human civilization. Even so, it wasn't <u>invented</u> until the <u>Bronze Age</u> and was preceded by many other important technological innovations such as <u>making textiles</u>, boats, pottery, and musical instruments.

We tend to think of the wheel as a means of transportation, but its uses go far beyond helping <u>carts</u> and cars roll. In addition to innovations such as water wheels and spinning wheels, wheels in the form of gears and other spin-ning parts are vital components in countless types of <u>machines</u>. In fact, the <u>first recorded use</u> of the wheel was actually a <u>potter's wheel</u>. Clay tablets from ancient <u>Mesopotamia</u> show evidence that potter's wheels were in use as early as <u>3500 BC</u>. This is several hundred years before wheels were first used on chariots for transportation.

It is not certain where the use of wheels on <u>carts</u> and chariots originated. At one time, <u>Mesopotamia</u> was considered to be the birthplace of wheeled transportation, but recent evidence points to Europe as a likely place. Early images of carts have been discovered in <u>Poland</u> and other nearby areas, while linguistic evidence suggests that Ukraine was the place where wheeled <u>carts</u> were first used.

Wherever the wheel originated, its use spread throughout the Middle East and Europe from about 3300 BC on. It did not, however, develop among the ancient cultures of the Americas. Or rather it did, but only in the form of <u>toys</u>. Excavations in <u>Mexico</u> in the 1940s revealed small ceramic dogs and other <u>animals</u> that had wheels for legs, and it is assumed that these were used as children's <u>toys</u>. One possible reason that these cultures did not develop the wheel for transportation is that they did not have any domestic animals that were large enough to pull wheeled wagons.

Explanation

1. **Answer: B.** The second sentence of the first paragraph contains most of the key words in question #1. This sentence tells us that the wheel was invented in the Bronze Age (*...it wasn't invented until the Bronze Age...*), after, not before, sewing and weaving (*...was preceded by...sewing and weaving...*). The key word *3500 BC* appears in the next paragraph, in a different context.
2. **Answer: A.** The key words and related words for question #2 appear in the second paragraph. The phrase *first recorded use* means the same as *earliest evidence*, so we know the answer to the question will be found near it. The phrase *potter's wheel* in the same sentence tells us that the earliest evidence shows wheels being used for making pottery.
3. **Answer: C.** Two of the key words for question #3, *Mesopotamia* and *Poland*, both appear in the third paragraph; however, the key word that the question asks about, *toy animals*, is not in that paragraph. The other answer choice, *Mexico*, appears in the fourth paragraph and the key word *toy animals* also appears there. This is where the wheeled toys of ancient Mexico are described.

Short-Answer Questions

Before you read the passage, read the short-answer questions below. The key words are underlined. Then scan the passage looking for key words or related words. These key words are also underlined. Finally, answer the questions.

Write **NO MORE THAN THREE WORDS AND/OR A NUMBER** for each answer.

1   On what <u>date</u> did the fire <u>begin</u>? ....

2   <u>How many people died</u> in the fire? ....

3   <u>Where</u> did the fire <u>start</u>? ....

One of the worst disasters in the nineteenth-century United States was the Great Chicago Fire of 1871. The fire raged through the city from the evening of <u>October 8</u> until the early hours of <u>October 10</u>, when a rainfall finally helped extinguish it. By that time, the fire had swept through an area of about nine square kilometers, destroying everything in its path: houses, apartment buildings, streets, sidewalks, even lampposts. Property damage was estimated at around 200 million dollars, and over <u>100,000</u> people (out of the city's total <u>population</u> of <u>300,000</u>) were left homeless. <u>Three hundred people lost their lives</u>, a relatively small number for such a large fire.

The <u>first</u> alarm notifying the fire department of the fire was pulled at a <u>pharmacy</u> at 9:40 in the evening. The <u>origin</u> of the fire has been famously traced to <u>Mrs. O'Leary's barn</u>. However, the popular legend that has the fire being <u>started</u> when Mrs. O'Leary's cow kicked over a kerosene lantern is simply not true. A newspaper reporter later admitted to having invented that story for its sensationalistic value. Nevertheless, it was determined that the fire did <u>begin</u> in <u>Mrs. O'Leary's barn</u>, although the exact cause remains unknown. Interestingly enough, <u>Mrs. O'Leary's house</u>, just in front of her barn, escaped damage.

Explanation

1. **Answer: October 8.** There are two dates in the first paragraph: *October 8*, the beginning date of the fire, and *October 10*, the end date.
2. **Answer: Three hundred.** When answering a *How many* question, look for numbers. There are several numbers about people near the end of the first paragraph. Also in the last sentence of that paragraph, we have the phrase *lost their lives*, which means the same as *died*. That is the sentence that tells us the answer to the question.

3. **Answer: Mrs. O'Leary's barn.** When answering a *Where* question, look for places. There are several places mentioned in the second paragraph: a pharmacy, Mrs. O'Leary's barn, and Mrs. O'Leary's house. The second sentence contains key words *origin* (meaning *beginning*) and *Mrs. O'Leary's barn*. The second to the last sentence contains key words *begin* and *Mrs. O'Leary's barn*. Both these sentences state that the fire began in Mrs. O'Leary's barn.

PRACTICE 1 (answers begin on page 213)

Before you look at each passage, read the questions and underline the key words. Then scan the passage and underline the key word or related word. Finally, answer the questions.

Passage 1

Oceans make up over seventy percent of the Earth's surface. But an ocean is more than just a large area of water. Oceans consist of several zones with different conditions, providing habitat for a variety of plant and animal species. The littoral zone is the area where the ocean meets the land. This zone consists of several subzones: land that is only underwater when there are super high tides such as during a storm (the supralittoral zone), the area that is submerged when the tide is high and exposed when the tide is low (the intertidal zone), and the area below the low tide line that is always underwater (the sublittoral zone). Snails, crabs, and small fish as well as various types of seaweed are all inhabitants of this part of the ocean.

The pelagic zone is the area farther out from the shore. This zone covers most of the ocean, excepting the areas close to shore and near the ocean floor. The top 200 meters of this zone is where sunlight is most abundant and is home to the highest diversity of plant and animal species in the ocean. In addition to various seaweeds and fishes, marine mammals such as whales and dolphins also inhabit this area and feed on the abundant plankton.

As you move into the deeper waters, less and less sunlight is able to penetrate the water. In the benthic zone, near the ocean floor, there is no light at all, and photosynthesis cannot take place. Animals that live here are scavengers, getting their nutrition from dead and dying organisms that float down from the upper regions of the water.

Classify the following phrases as describing

    A the littoral zone
    B the pelagic zone
    C the benthic zone

1   the area along the shore .... A ....
2   the area at the bottom of the ocean .... C ....
3   home to crabs and snails .... A ....
4   home to sea mammals .... B ......
5   has the greatest variety of plant and animal types .... B ....
6   inhabitants eat dead animals .... C ....

Passage 2

The use of wheeled carts in the ancient world was limited by the fact that to be truly useful they needed smooth roads. The ancient Romans are renowned for the stone roads they constructed all over Europe, beginning in 312 BC with the Appian Way. This 260-kilometer road connected Rome with the city of Taranto. As more and more territory came under Roman control, roads were built throughout the empire, extending from Rome to what is today Great Britain, Romania, North Africa, and Iraq. These roads facilitated all types of travel, wheeled or not.

Wooden work carts were common throughout Europe for centuries. In fact, they were the major mode of wheeled transportation until the 1500s, when Hungarians began to build coaches. With smooth, finished wood and soft, cushioned seats, coaches provided a much more comfortable ride than rough wooden carts. Their popularity spread across the continent. In the following centuries, various styles of coaches, carriages, and wagons were developed to provide transportation for all types of situations.

Directions

Do the following statements agree with the information given in the passage?

TRUE   *if the statement agrees with the information in the passage*
FALSE   *if the statement contradicts the information in the passage*
NOT GIVEN   *if there is no information about this in the passage*

1   The Appian Way was the first stone road built by the ancient Romans. ..... *True* ....
2   The Appian Way led from Rome to Great Britain. .... *T* ....
3   The Appian Way was the most heavily used Roman road. .... *NG* ......
4   Ancient Roman roads were used only by travelers in wheeled carts. ...... *F* ....
5   The first European coaches were made in Hungary. .... *F* ....

Passage 3

*Choose the correct heading for each section, **A–D**, from the list of headings below.*

List of Headings

i Reasons to Use Wind Power
ii Wind Power in the Twentieth Century
iii Arguments Against Wind Power
iv Wind Power in Early History

---

1   Section **A** ....
2   Section **B** ....
3   Section **C** ....
4   Section **D** ....

A
People have been harnessing the power of the wind for centuries. The first documented use of wind power was in Persia about 1500 years ago, where windmills were used to pump water and grind grain. Windmills may actually have been in use in China earlier than this; however, the first documented use of wind power there was in the thirteenth century, again for pumping water and grinding grain. Windmills were also being used in Europe at the same time and were an important source of power for several centuries. Their use eventually declined in the nineteenth century with the introduction of the steam engine.

B

Throughout the 1900s, the development and use of windmills was focused on the generation of electricity. In the early part of the century, wind-generated electricity was widely used in the Midwestern United States. As the demand for electricity grew and the electrical grid was extended through that part of the country, wind power fell out of use. In the latter part of the century, there was a renewed interest in wind power as an alternative to the use of fossil fuels to generate electricity.

C

In the twenty-first century, the use of wind-generated electricity is growing as many see the benefits of this source of power. In addition to reducing dependency on fossil fuels, wind power is also clean and inexpensive to use. The wind, after all, is free. Wind turbines can be built on open farmland, thus providing the farmer with another source of income. Wind turbines don't occupy a large amount of space, and the land around them can be cultivated.

D

As with anything, however, there are also drawbacks. Although using wind turbines is inexpensive, the initial investment required to construct them is quite high. Wind turbines have to be located where they can capture the wind, often on high mountain ridges or in open areas free of obstacles, such as tall buildings. This means they are usually located away from population centers where the most electricity is needed. So there is the additional cost of installing lines to transmit the electricity to cities. Some people are concerned about the high level of noise spinning wind turbines create. Others are concerned about the effect on wildlife, especially birds, which have been killed by flying into the turbines.

Passage 4

As with anything, however, there are also drawbacks. Although using wind turbines is inexpensive, the initial investment required to construct them is quite high. Wind turbines have to be located where they can capture the wind, often on high mountain ridges or in open areas free of obstacles, such as tall buildings. This means they are usually located away from population centers where the most electricity is needed. So there is the additional cost of installing lines to transmit the electricity to cities. Some people are concerned about the high level of noise spinning wind turbines create. Others are concerned about the effect on wildlife, especially birds, which have been killed by flying into the turbines.

Which **FOUR** disadvantages of wind power are mentioned in the passage?

A   Wind turbines can cause harm to animals.
B   Wind turbines in a rural landscape can spoil the scenery.
C   The best wind turbine sites are usually far from cities.
D   It costs a lot to build wind turbines.
E   Wind speed is not reliable.
F   Wind turbines are very noisy.
G   Wind turbines don't generate as much electricity as fossil fuel power stations do.

Passage 5

Psychologist Jean Piaget identified four stages in the intellectual development of children, from birth to about twelve years of age. He identified the ages at which most children pass through each stage and the concepts and abilities they develop. While he acknowledged that children may go through each stage at different rates or at somewhat different ages, he was firm in his belief that the cognitive development of all children always follows the same sequence.

According to Piaget, children from birth to around two years of age are in the sensorimotor stage of development. During this stage, children learn how objects can be manipulated. They learn that their actions can have an effect on objects. They experiment by touching, holding, or throwing things or by putting them in their mouths and seeing what results. Initially, infants are concerned only with things that are directly before their eyes. During this stage, they develop the concept of object permanence. They learn that things continue to exist even when out of sight.

The preoperational stage is the period from around two to seven years of age. Children in this stage are able to think symbolically. They develop their use of language. They are also very egocentric, assuming that everyone else shares their same point of view. Another characteristic of this stage is animism—the belief that inanimate objects can think and feel in the same way the child does. Thus, a child might feel sorry for a broken toy, for example.

*Choose the correct letter, **A**, **B**, or **C**.*

1 Piaget believed that all children
   A learn at the same pace.
   B develop cognitive abilities in the same order.
   C pass through twelve stages of development.

2 During the sensorimotor stage, infants learn by
   A manipulating objects.
   B focusing only on what they can see.
   C being touched and held by their parents.

3 Children in the preoperational stage
   A have very limited use of language.
   B are interested in other people's viewpoints.
   C believe that things have thoughts and feelings.

LISTENING

STRATEGY	Read the questions before you listen. Identify a key word, and then listen for the key word or related word in the passage.
TIP	Pay attention to the words following the key word or related word.

Complete Notes

Before you listen to the audio, read the incomplete notes below. The key words have been underlined for you. Then listen to the audio and follow along with the audio text. (You will not see the text during the test. This is only for strategy practice.) As you listen to the audio, note the underlined key words or related words.

Complete the notes below.
    Write **NO MORE THAN THREE WORDS** for each answer.

Apartments

Luxury Towers   Parkview Apartments   Main Street Apartments
top floor apartment: * ground floor apartments have a   * smallest and most 5 ....
    * has a 1 .... 3 ....
all apartments: * one available
    * large living room   4 ....
    * separate 2 ....
    * eat-in kitchen

 Audio Text

Woman: Our agency has quite a few apartments listed in your price range. So a lot will depend on which part of the city you are interested in.

Man: I'd prefer not to be too far from downtown, or at least close to the subway.

Woman: That gives us several options. You may like Luxury Towers. There are several vacant apartments there now. There is one on the top floor that has a view that's quite spectacular. You can see the harbour very clearly from there.

Man: Great. How big is the apartment?

Woman: All the apartments in the building are quite spacious, and in addition to a large living room, each also has a separate dining room as well as an eat-in kitchen.

Man: I'd definitely like to visit Luxury Towers. But I'd like to look in other buildings, too.

Woman: Parkview Apartments will have some vacancies soon. All the ground floor apartments there have a small patio, which is a very nice feature.

Man: Will any of the ground floor apartments be vacant soon?

Woman: Yes, there will be one available next month. Now, if you'd like to be right downtown, I can show you some apartments on Main Street.

Man: Yes, I'd like to see them.

Woman: They're the smallest apartments I have to show you, but despite that, they're also the most expensive, because of the location, you know.

Man: I think it's still worth looking at.

Explanation

1. **Answer: view.** The categories of the notes *Luxury Towers* and *top floor* are key words. Listen for the answer to question 1 in the discussion of the top floor apartment in Luxury Towers. The words right before the blanks are also key words. For question 1, the key word is *has,* so listen for the answer near that word.

2. **Answer: dining room.** Question 2 comes under the category of *all apartments*, so listen for the answer to that question during the discussion of all apartments in Luxury Towers. Then listen for the key word *separate.* The speaker mentions a separate dining room.

3. **Answer: small patio.** The key words *Parkview Apartments* and *ground floor apartments* signal in which part of the conversation to listen for the answer to this question. Listen for the exact answer near the key word that comes right near the blank, in this case, *have.* The speaker says: *All the ground floor apartments there have a small patio….*

4. **Answer: next month.** Listen for the key word *available.* The speaker says: *…there will be one available next month.*

5. **Answer: expensive.** In the discussion of Main Street Apartments, listen for the key word *most.* The speaker says: *…they're also the most expensive….*

Multiple-Choice Questions

Before you listen to the audio, read the multiple-choice questions below. The key words have been underlined for you. Then listen to the audio and follow along with the audio text. (You will not see the text during the test. This is only for strategy practice.) As you listen to the audio, note the underlined key words or related words.

1 <u>Theory X and Theory Y</u> explain
   A <u>employees' behavior</u>.
   B <u>managers' perceptions</u>.
   C <u>psychologists' motivation</u>.

2 According to <u>Theory X</u>, workers
   A <u>enjoy their jobs</u>.
   B seek out <u>more responsibility</u>.
   C <u>need</u> constant <u>supervision</u>.

3 According to <u>Theory Y</u>, workers
   A <u>motivate themselves</u>.
   B <u>avoid decision making</u>.
   C prefer a <u>hierarchical workplace</u>.

<u>Theory X</u> and <u>Theory Y</u> are theories of motivation in the workplace developed by social <u>psychologist</u> Douglas McGregor in the 1960s. They describe how <u>managers</u> may <u>perceive</u> their employees rather than how <u>employees</u> actually <u>act</u>.

A <u>Theory X</u> manager assumes that <u>workers</u> are not <u>motivated</u> and <u>dislike their jobs</u>. Therefore, they have to be controlled and <u>supervised</u> every step of the way or they will not carry out their duties. They <u>avoid responsibility</u> or taking on any extra work. Workplaces that ascribe to Theory X are <u>hierarchical</u> with many levels of managers and <u>supervisors</u> to keep the workers under control.

<u>Theory Y</u> describes the opposite situation. This theory assumes that <u>employees</u> are <u>self-motivated</u> and <u>enjoy their work</u>, that they want greater responsibility and <u>don't need a lot of supervision</u>. Theory Y managers believe that their employees want to do well at work and that, given the right conditions, they will. In a Theory Y workplace, even lower-level employees are involved in <u>decision making</u>.

Explanation

1. **Answer: B.** This question asks what Theory X and Theory Y are about, which is explained at the beginning of the talk. The last sentence of this part of the talk answers the question. It tells us that these theories are about manager's perceptions (related word: *perceive*), not about how employees act (related word: *behavior*).

2. **Answer: C.** The second part of the talk describes Theory X. According to this theory, workers have to be supervised. We know that choice A is wrong because the talk says the opposite (related word: *dislike*). Workers enjoying their jobs is part of the Theory Y description in the next part of the talk. We know that choice B is wrong because the talk says the opposite: Workers avoid responsibility. Workers seeking out responsibility is part of the Theory Y description.

3. **Answer: A.** The third part of the talk describes Theory Y. Theory Y describes employees as self motivated (related words: *workers, motivate themselves*). Choice B contains key words *decision making*. These are discussed near the end of the talk, but the speaker says that employees are involved in this, not that they *avoid* it. Choice C key word *hierarchical* is part of the discussion of Theory X.

(Track 4)
PRACTICE 2 (answers begin on page 218)

Before you listen to the audio, read the questions. Underline the key words. Then listen to the audio and pay attention to the key words and related words. Answer the questions as you hear the answers.

Passage 1

Label the map below.
    Write **NO MORE THAN TWO WORDS** for each answer.

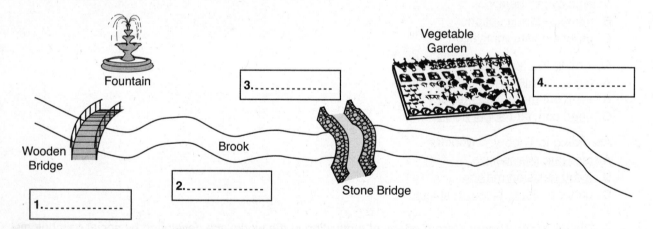

Passage 2

What will the students include in their presentation?
A   They definitely will include this.
B   They might include this.
C   They will not include this.

*Write the correct letter, **A, B,** or **C**.*
1   a guest speaker ....
2   charts and graphs ....
3   photographs ....
4   interview transcripts ....
5   their questionnaire ....

In the answer key on page 218, you will find the key words for the map, the questions, and the audio text underlined. Use the answer key to practice your key word strategies.

Passage 3

Complete the table below.
Write **NO MORE THAN TWO WORDS** for each answer.

Advantages	Disadvantages
People will be more likely to recycle because the system is so **1**	Some residents are angry because they **2** .... the system.
It costs little to **3** .... recyclables from residences.	The cost of building the **4** .... is high.

Passage 4

Complete the form below.
Write **NO MORE THAN THREE WORDS AND/OR A NUMBER** for each answer.

Piano Rentals Unlimited

Client Information Form

Name: Patricia **1** ....

Address: **2** ....

Instrument requested: *upright piano* ....

Delivery date: **3** ....

Length of rental: **4** ....

Payment method: **5** ....

Passage 5

Choose **FOUR** letters, **A–G**.
Which **FOUR** things should trip participants bring from home?

A bicycles
B water bottles
C maps
D food
E hats
F tents
G cameras

IELTS Basic Tips

There are some basic tips that will help you in all sections of the IELTS.

Directions

Always read the directions carefully. Do exactly what the question asks. Pay special attention to the number of words you can write. Do not write more than the number of words specified.

Guessing

Answer every question. If you don't answer a question, you will receive no point for that question. But if you guess, you have a chance of getting the right answer.

Time

Keep moving through the questions. Don't take too much time with a question. You can come back later. If you don't know an answer, guess.

Question/Answer Sequence

The questions follow the order of the passage, talk, or conversation, but the answer options do not. The answer options might be in a different order.

Spelling

Spelling is important. All words must be spelled correctly. Check your answers to make sure the words are spelled correctly. A good study practice is to listen to the audio recordings in this book and write what you hear. Then check your spelling in the audio transcript section.

IELTS Study Contract

You must make a commitment to study English. Sign a contract with yourself. A contract is a formal agreement to do something. You should not break a contract—especially a contract with yourself.

- Print your name below on line 1.
- Write the time you will spend each week studying English on lines 4–8. Think about how much time you have to study everyday and every week, and make your schedule realistic.
- Sign your name and date the contract on the last line.
- At the end of each week, add up your hours. Did you meet the requirements of your contract?

IELTS STUDY CONTRACT

I, ... , promise to study for the IELTS. I will begin my study with *Barron's IELTS Strategies and Tips*, and I will also study English on my own.

I understand that to improve my English I need to spend time on English.

I promise to study English .... a week.

I will spend .... hours a week listening to English.
I will spend .... hours a week writing English.
I will spend .... hours a week speaking English.
I will spend .... hours a week reading English.

This is a contract with myself. I promise to fulfill the terms of this contract.

_____   _____
Signed   Date

Self-Study Activities

Here are some ways you can improve your English skills on your own. Check the ones you plan to try. Add some of your own ideas.

Internet Based Self-Study Activities

LISTENING

.... Podcasts on the Internet
.... News websites: CNN, BBC, NBC, ABC, CBS
.... Movies in English
.... You Tube
.... Lectures on the Internet
....
....

WRITING

.... Write e-mails to website contacts
.... Write a blog
.... Leave comments on blogs
.... Post messages in a chat room
.... Use Facebook and MySpace
....
....

SPEAKING

.... Use Skype to talk to English speakers
....
....

READING

.... Read news and magazine articles online
.... Do web research on topics that interest you
.... Follow blogs that interest you
....
....

Other Self-Study Activities

LISTENING

.... Listen to CNN and BBC on the radio

.... Watch movies and TV in English

.... Listen to music in English

....

....

SPEAKING

.... Describe what you see and do out loud

.... Practice speaking with a conversation buddy

....

....

WRITING

.... Write a daily journal

.... Write a letter to an English speaker

.... Make lists of the things you see everyday

.... Write descriptions of your family and friends

.... Summarize news items or sports events that you've read about online

....

....

READING

.... Read newspapers and magazines in English

.... Read books in English

....

....

Examples of Self-Study Activities

Whether you read an article in a newspaper or on a website, you can use that article in a variety of ways to improve your vocabulary while you practice reading, writing, speaking, and listening in English.

- Read about it.
- Paraphrase and write about it.
- Give a talk or presentation about it.
- Record or make a video of your presentation.
- Listen to or watch what you recorded. Write down your presentation.
- Correct your mistakes.
- Do it all again.

PLAN A TRIP

Go to *www.cntraveler.com*

Choose a city, choose a hotel, go to that hotel's website and choose a room, and then choose some sites to visit (*reading*). Write a report about the city. Tell why you want to go there. Describe the hotel and the room you will reserve. Tell what sites you plan to visit and when. Where will you eat? How will you get around?

Now write a letter to someone recommending this place (*writing*). Pretend you have to give a lecture on your planned trip (*speaking*). Make a video of yourself talking about this place. Then watch the video and write down what you said. Correct any mistakes you made and record the presentation again. Then choose another city and do this again.

SHOP FOR AN ELECTRONIC PRODUCT

Go to *www.cnet.com*

Choose an electronic product and read about it (*reading*). Write a report about the product. Tell why you want to buy one. Describe its features.

Now write a letter to someone recommending this product, or think of a problem you might have with this type of product and write a letter of complaint to the company. Don't send the letter, this is just an exercise (*writing*). Pretend you have to give a talk about this product (*speaking*). Make a video of yourself talking about this product. Then watch the video and write down what you said. Correct any mistakes you made and record the presentation again. Now choose another product and do this again.

DISCUSS A BOOK OR A CD

Go to *www.amazon.com*

Choose a book or record or any product. Read the product description and reviews (*reading*). Write a report about the product. Tell why you want to buy one or why it is interesting to you. Describe its features.

Now write a letter to someone recommending this product (*writing*). Pretend you have to give a talk about this product (*speaking*). Make a video of yourself talking about this product. Then watch the video and write down what you said. Correct any mistakes you made and record the presentation again. Then choose another product and do this again.

DISCUSS ANY SUBJECT

Go to *http://simple.wikipedia.org/wiki/Main_Page*

This website is written in simple English. Pick any subject and read the entry (*reading*).

Write a short essay about the topic (*writing*). Give a presentation about it (*speaking*). Record the presentation. Then watch the video and write down what you said. Correct any mistakes you made and record the presentation again. Choose another topic and do this again.

DISCUSS ANY EVENT

Go to *http://news.google.com*

Google News has a variety of links. Pick one event and read the articles about it (*reading*).

Write a short essay about the event (*writing*). Give a presentation about it (*speaking*). Record the presentation. Then watch the video and write down what you said. Correct any mistakes you made and record the presentation again. Now choose another event and do this again.

REPORT THE NEWS

Listen to an English language news report on the radio or watch a news program on TV (*listening*). Take notes as you listen. Write a summary of what you heard (*writing*).

Pretend you are a news reporter. Use the information from your notes to report the news (*speaking*). Record the presentation. Then watch the video and write down what you said. Correct any mistakes you made and record the presentation again. Now listen to another news program and do this again.

EXPRESS AN OPINION

Read a letter to the editor in the newspaper (*reading*). Write a letter in response in which you say whether or not you agree with the opinion expressed in the first letter. Explain why (*writing*).

Pretend you have to give a talk explaining your opinion (*speaking*). Record yourself giving the talk. Then watch the video and write down what you said. Correct any mistakes you made and record the presentation again. Now read another letter to the editor and do this again.

REVIEW A BOOK OR MOVIE

Read a book (*reading*). Think about your opinion of the book. What did you like about it? What didn't you like about it? Who would you recommend it to and why? Pretend you are a book reviewer for a newspaper. Write a review of the book with your opinion and recommendations (*writing*).

Give an oral presentation about the book. Explain what the book is about and what your opinion is (*speaking*). Record yourself giving the presentation. Then watch the video and write down what you said. Correct any mistakes you made and record the presentation again. Now read another book and do this again.

You can do this same activity after watching a movie (*listening*).

SUMMARIZE A TV SHOW

Watch a TV show in English (*listening*). Take notes as you listen. After watching, write a summary of the show (*writing*).

Use your notes to give an oral summary of the show. Explain the characters, setting, and plot (*speaking*). Record yourself speaking. Then watch the video and write down what you said. Correct any mistakes you made and record the presentation again. Now watch another TV show and do this again.

LISTEN TO A LECTURE

Listen to an academic or other type of lecture on the Internet. Go to any of the following or similar sites and look for lectures on topics that are of interest to you:

http://lecturefox.com

http://podcasts.ox.ac.uk

http://freevideolectures.com

http://www.ted.com/talks

Listen to a lecture and take notes as you listen. Listen again to check and add to your notes (*listening*). Use your notes to write a summary of the lecture (*writing*).

Pretend you have to give a lecture on the same subject. Use your notes to give your lecture (*speaking*). Record yourself as you lecture. Then watch the video and write down what you said. Correct any mistakes you made and record the lecture again. Now listen to another lecture and do this again.

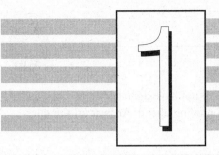

IELTS LISTENING MODULE

OVERVIEW

In this chapter, you will learn and practice specific strategies based on the various types of questions you may see in the Listening Module. Although each of the question types is presented here in the context of one of the four sections of the Listening Module, most of them can appear in any section of the module. In this chapter you will also practice the key word strategies you learned in the first chapter of the book. At the end of this chapter, you will find a Strategy Review that is similar to the actual IELTS Listening test.

GENERAL STRATEGIES

Listening for Words
Listening for Numbers

SPECIFIC STRATEGIES

SECTION 1—CONVERSATION

Complete a Form
Complete a Table
Choose Answers from a List

SECTION 2—TALK

Complete Sentences
Label a Diagram, Plan, or Map
Give a Short Answer

SECTION 3—DISCUSSION

Choose Answer from Multiple Choices
Label a Diagram
Match Words and Phrases

SECTION 4—TALK OR LECTURE

Classify Words or Statements
Complete Notes
Complete a Flowchart

STRATEGY REVIEW

LISTENING MODULE

Listening Tip

Nothing is repeated in the Listening Module. If you miss an answer, you will not have a chance to go back and listen for the answer again. Don't waste time worrying about it. Just keep moving ahead. Answer all the questions that you can.

General Strategies

Listening for Words

STRATEGY	Use the questions to focus your attention on the key words as you listen. (See pages 1–11 for a discussion and activities on Key Words.)
TIP	Key words are often stressed. Listen for words that are stressed.

PRACTICE 1 (answers on page 222)

Here are the directions for the exercises Audio 1–4. For each audio exercise, look at the questions and circle the key words. Then read the script once and make predictions about the words in the gaps, but don't complete them yet. Next, read the script again as you listen to the audio and complete the gaps. Finally, answer the questions.

(Track 5) *Audio 1*

Choose TWO letters.

Which **TWO** things are included in the price of the hotel room?

A   breakfast
B   use of an exercise room
C   use of a swimming pool
D   afternoon tea
E   movies

Script

Woman:	A room for two people is two hundred fifty dollars a night.
Man:	That seems a bit high.
Woman:	The rooms are very comfortable. And we serve **1** .... to all our guests every morning from seven to nine.
Man:	That sounds nice. Do you have an **2** ....?
Woman:	No, but there is a club across the street you can use, for a **3** .... We do have our own **4** ...., which guests can use **5** ....
Man:	Oh, that's good. I'll certainly use that. Do you serve other meals besides breakfast?

Woman: Yes, we serve three meals a day, plus **6**.................. . The menu and **7**.......................... are available on our website if you'd like to see them.

Man: Oh, OK. I'll take a look at it.

Woman: You might also like to know that each room has a large screen TV, and for an **8**.................... you can order **9**.................. .

Audio 2

Choose the correct letter, A, B, or C.

1 Where will they have lunch?
 A in the park
 B by the river
 C near the museum

2 What will they do immediately after lunch?
 A visit the museum
 B take a walk
 C go shopping

Script

Welcome to Urban Tours. We'll begin our tour today with a bus ride through **1**................, which is known for its landscaping and gardens. We'll spend an hour walking through the park's Central Flower garden, which is in full bloom this time of year. Then we'll get back on the bus and ride over the **2**................ and on to the **3**................ . Before visiting the museum, we'll enjoy **4**................ at Shell's Café, located just **5**................, and then take a **6**................ through the neighborhood to view some historic buildings. Then we'll enjoy a special **7**................ of the museum, and we'll have an hour or two after that to visit the nearby **8**................ where you can make any **9**................ you want before returning to the hotel.

Audio 3

What does Bob say about his classes?

Choose your answers from the box.

A It's his favorite class.
B It's not interesting.
C It's very difficult.
D It's too big.

1 chemistry ....
2 math ....
3 psychology ....

Script

Man: I have a really tough schedule this semester.

Woman: You're taking some **1**................. classes, aren't you?

Man: It's not that so much, but I think I chose the wrong courses. My **2**................., for example, has way **3**................. in it.

Woman: Really?

Man: Yeah. It's impossible to ask a question or get any attention from the instructor because of that.

Woman: What about your **4**.................? You were really looking forward to taking that.

Man: I was, but, like I said, I chose the wrong class. I never knew **5**................. could be **6**................. .

Woman: That's too bad. So I guess you feel like this semester is a complete waste.

Man: Actually, no. Believe it or not, I'm really enjoying my **7**................. . I like it **8**................. of all my classes.

Audio 4

Track 8

Which features are characteristic of which animal?

Choose the correct letter.

A	Rabbit
B	Hare

1   Its babies are blind.   ....

2   It lives in groups.   ....

3   It lives above ground.   ....

4   Its diet consists of woody plants.   ....

5   Its diet consists of soft vegetation.   ....

Script

Although rabbits and hares are very similar in appearance, they are different animals with different characteristics. We can say that the differences start at birth. **1**................ are able to defend themselves, at least to some degree, because they **2**................ when they are born. When **3**................, however, they **4**................ and so are completely helpless. Unlike hares, rabbits stick together, living with other rabbits in colonies. They live in **5**................, which provide a safe place to hide from predators. Hares, on the other hand, live most of their lives as loners. They stay **6**................ and are able to avoid predators because they are such good runners. Hares and rabbits also have different **7**................. . Hares tend to favor bark, twigs, and other **8**................ while rabbits prefer **9**................, leaves, and stems.

Listening for Numbers

STRATEGY   Be familiar with the different ways to express numbers.

TIP   Make a note whenever you hear a number. Note that in a long number the intonation rises and then falls at the last number.

↑↑↓ ↑↑↓ ↑↑↑↓
505-475-3948

Whether the number is an identification number, a date, or a price, there are a variety of ways the number can be said.

Dates: November 24, 2013
       November twenty-fourth, two thousand thirteen
       November twenty-four, twenty thirteen

Price: $13.33
       Thirteen dollars and thirty-three cents
       Thirteen thirty three

Time: 2:45
       Two forty-five
       Quarter to three
       A quarter to three

Decimals: 3.75
       Three point seven five
       Three and three-fourths
       Three and three-quarters

Telephone numbers / Credit card numbers / ID numbers:
       +1 505 475-3948
       Plus one five-o-five four seven five, three nine, four eight.
       Plus one five zero five, four seventy-five, thirty-nine forty-eight

PRACTICE 2 (answers on page 223)

Write the numbers, dates, and times you hear.

1	9 ....
2	10 ....
3	11 ....
4	12 ....
5	13 ....
6	14 ....
7	15 ....
8	

Specific Strategies

SECTION 1—CONVERSATION

Complete a Form

STRATEGY   Pay attention to the words before and after the gap. Listen, in this example, for these
words: *Name* and *Address,* which appear before the gap.

  (Name:) **1** .... Jones

  (Address:) 154 **2**................

TIP   The order of the gaps in the form will follow the conversation.

PRACTICE 1 (answers on page 223)

Circle the key words around the gaps. Then listen to the conversation and complete each form.
Write **NO MORE THAN THREE WORDS AND/OR A NUMBER** for each answer.

Conversation 1

Argyle Car Rentals

Name: William **1** ....

Address: 17 North Cameron Street, Compton

License Number: **2** ....

Insurance Company: **3** ....

Type of car: **4** ....

Pick up date: **5** ....

Payment method: credit card

Conversation 2

Ticket Order Form

Name: Petronella Jones

Show date: **1** ...., March 10

Show time: **2** ....

Number of tickets: **3** ....

Seat location: **4** ....

Notes: **5** .... discount

pick up __ mail X̲

Conversation 3

Sanditon Hotel
Reservation Form

Guest name: **1** .... Wiggins

Arrival date: June 23

Length of stay: **2** ....

Room type: **3** ....

Room preferences: **4** .... view

Credit card number: **5** ....

Conversation 4

Westfield Language Academy
Student Registration Form

Name: Ronald McGraw

Address: **1** ....

Phone: **2** ....

Course title: **3** ....

Days: **4** ....

Payment method: **5** ....

Conversation 5

Student Employment Office

Name: Shirley Chang

Address: PO Box **1** .... , Bradford

Date available: **2** ....

Job type: **3** ....

Previous experience: **4** ....

Skills: **5** ....

Complete a Table

STRATEGY	Read the headings in the table and decide what you are listening for.
TIP	The missing words will be the same as the other words in the column.

CLASS SCHEDULE			
↓ **Classroom**	↓ **Course**	↓ **Days**	↓ **Time**
Room 10	1	Monday, Wednesday	10:30–11:30 AM
Room 25	Chemistry	2	1:00–2:30 PM
Room 45	Physics	Wednesday, Friday	3 ....

If the gap appears in a column of course titles, the missing word is a course title. If the gap appears in a column of days, the missing word is a day of the week. If the gap appears in a column of time, the missing word is a time of day.

PRACTICE 2 (answers on page 223)

(Track 11)

Circle the headings. Guess the type of word you will provide. Then listen to the conversation and complete the table.
Write **NO MORE THAN THREE WORDS AND/OR A NUMBER** for each answer.

Conversation 1

Westfield Language Academy—Spring Schedule

Course Title	Days	Cost	Ages
1	Monday and Wednesday	$575	Adults over 18
Advanced Spanish	Tuesday	2 $	Adults over 18
Beginning Chinese	3	$325	Children 4 ....
Beginning French	5	$325	Children 6–10

Conversation 2

City Arts Center—Calendar of Events

Date	Time	Event	Ticket Price	Location
August 10	10 AM–8 PM	1	$35	Circle Theater
August 11	9 AM–5 PM	Crafts Fair	$5	2 ....
August 17	8 PM	Play: *Romeo and Juliet*	3 $	Starlight Theater
August 24	4 .... PM	5	$18	Rigby Hall

Conversation 3

Student Employment Office—Job Listings

Employer	Job	Start date	Salary
Restaurant	1	October 15	$18/hour
Clothing store	Bookkeeper	2	$21/hour
3	Receptionist	October 23	4 $........./hour
5	Administrative Assistant	November 2	$13/hour

Conversation 4

Argyle Car Rentals

Vehicle Type	Maximum # of Passengers	Rental Fee (per day)	Special Features
Compact car	four	1 $	Roof rack
Mid-size car	2	$50	3 ....
4	eight	$75	DVD player
Small truck	four	$85	5 ....

Conversation 5

Tours

Place	Activity	Length	Transportation
Art museum	view paintings	two hours	1 ....
National Park	2	four hours	bus
3	visit monuments	4 .... hours	walking
Grover Mansion	house tour	two hours	5 ....

Choose Answers from a List

STRATEGY	Circle the key words and paraphrase them.
TIP	If you make notes, write the notes in a column for each speaker.

Focus your attention on the subject of the conversation. The words in the activity and the words spoken in the conversation might not be exactly the same. You should listen for words or phrases with similar meanings.

Which **TWO** activities is the guest interested in?

List	Related Words
A water sports	swimming, boating, water skiing
B hikes	walks, climbs
C learn crafts	sew, knit, make, build
D observe wildlife	watch birds, animals, bears
E learn to cook	prepare meals, food

PRACTICE 3 (answers on page 223)

(Track 12)

Circle the key words and write related words for the key words. Then listen to the conversation. Make notes. Answer the questions.

Conversation 1

*Choose **TWO** letters.*

Which **TWO** activities does the Language Academy offer?

List	Related Words
A cooking classes	....
B social gatherings	....
C movies	....
D outdoor activities	....
E book groups	....

Conversation 2

*Choose **TWO** letters.*

Which **TWO** things did Amanda do during her homestay?

List	Related Words
A took trips	....
B spoke Chinese	....
C met people	....
D tried new food	....
E celebrated a holiday	....

Conversation 3

*Choose **TWO** letters.*

Which **TWO** things will Lee do during the summer?

List	Related Words
A visit relatives	....
B study	....
C relax	....
D walk in the mountains	....
E read	....

Conversation 4

*Choose **TWO** letters.*

Which **TWO** things are included in the condo fee?

List	Related Words
A landscaping	....
B parking garage	....
C apartment maintenance	....
D exercise room	....
E trash removal	....

Conversation 5

*Choose **TWO** letters.*

Which **TWO** things does Mary say she likes about her job?

List	Related Words
A her co-workers	....
B the manager	....
C her salary	....
D the location	....
E her schedule	....

SECTION 2—TALK

Complete Sentences

STRATEGY	Circle the key words and pay attention to the words around the gaps. Note the grammatical form of the words around the gap.
TIP	Determine what kind of word is needed to complete the gap: a noun, modifier, verb, or preposition?

Track 13 **PRACTICE 1** (answers on page 224)

Circle the key words and note the grammatical forms of the words around the gaps. Write the grammatical form needed to complete each gap. Listen to the talk and complete the sentences.
Write **NO MORE THAN THREE WORDS AND/OR A NUMBER** for each answer.

Talk 1

1 .... of Tapei 101 began in 1999.

2 The building has .... underground stories.

3 The building has the world's .... elevators.

Talk 2

1 Tourists like to visit the .... in Washington, DC.

2 The Stone House is the .... building in the city.

3 Office workers often like to .... by the river.

Talk 3

1 One skating rink is used as a .... in the summertime.

2 .... use the path around the reservoir.

3 The park roads are closed to automobiles on ....

Talk 4

1 Construction of Green Acres began in ....

2 The .... are located near the shopping complex.

3 Children often .... behind the Community Center building.

Talk 5

1 Grover Mansion was first used as a ....

2 The .... is found in the basement.

3 In the summer, the Grover family usually .... on the porch.

Label a Diagram, Plan, or Map

STRATEGY	Look at the words that are on the diagram, plan, or map. Use these words to focus your listening.
TIP	Listen for direction or location words. These will help you identify specific spots on the plan or map. Listen carefully for the starting point so you can follow the conversation.

Useful expressions for direction or location

in the middle	behind
above	in front of
to the left (right) of	past
around the corner from	beyond
at the bottom of the map	on the other side
north, south, east, west	across
next to	on the corner of

Track 14

PRACTICE 2 (answers on page 224)

Look at the diagrams and read what you will have to do. You may be asked to match labels with letters on the diagram. Or, you may be asked to write labels for different points on the diagram. Do NOT write more words than required. Listen to the conversation and label the plan, diagram, or map.

Talk 1

Label the plan below.
*Write **NO MORE THAN TWO WORDS AND/OR A NUMBER** for each answer.*

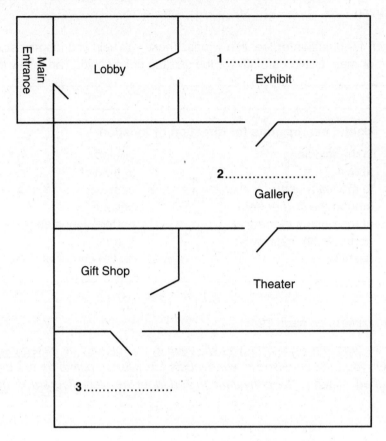

Talk 2

*Look at the map below. Choose the correct letter, **A–D**.*

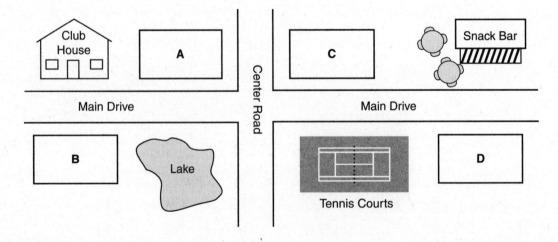

1   parking lot ....
2   swimming pool ....
3   picnic area ....
4   sports area ....

Talk 3

Label the plan below. Write **NO MORE THAN TWO WORDS AND/OR A NUMBER** for each answer.

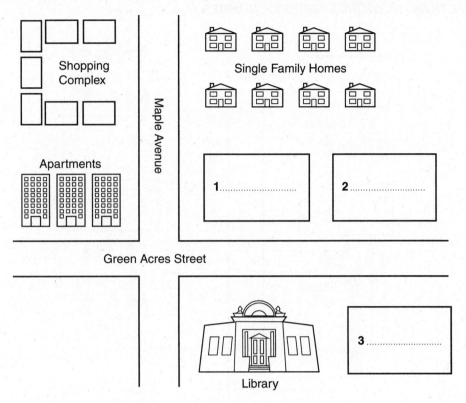

Talk 4

Look at the map below. Choose the correct letter, **A–D.**

1   benches ....
2   storage shed ....
3   fish pond ....
4   flower garden ....

Talk 5

Label the map below.
Write **NO MORE THAN TWO WORDS AND/OR A NUMBER** *for each answer.*

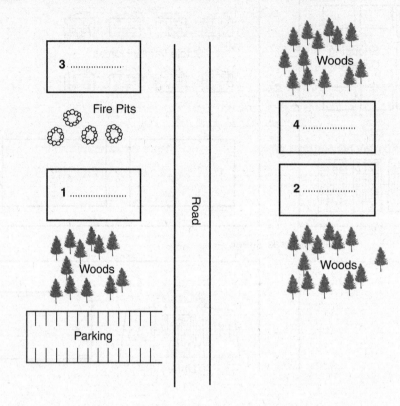

Give a Short Answer

STRATEGY	Circle the question words and the key words to determine the kind of answer you need to give.
TIP	The order of the answers follows the talk.

If you see the question word *who*, you will listen for a name or an occupation. You will listen to something that refers to a person. Study the following lists to learn the type of answer required by a question word.

Question Word	Type of Answer
Who	person or name
What	thing
Where	place
When	time
Why	reason
How much/long	quantity
How often	time

(Track 15)

PRACTICE 3 (answers on page 225)

Circle the question words and the key words. Listen to the talk and answer the questions. Write **NO MORE THAN THREE WORDS AND/OR A NUMBER** *for each answer.*

Talk 1

1　When will the first film be shown?

　　...

2　How much does it cost to see one film?

　　...

Talk 2

1　What is in front of the house?

　　...

2　What time will the tour bus leave?

　　...

Talk 3

1   When will the snack bar start selling food?

....

2   Where can club members buy a complete meal?

....

Talk 4

1   How often do buses leave the mall to go downtown?

....

2   Where can you catch the downtown bus?

....

Talk 5

1   How long will the hike last?

....

2   What can people do at the pond?

....

SECTION 3—DISCUSSION

Choose an Answer from Multiple Choices

STRATEGY	Listen for details.
TIP	A speaker may correct himself or herself. Pay attention to the possible changes in opinions or facts.

To focus on the details, circle the key words in the question or statement and the key words in the multiple-choice options. Listen for these words (or similar words) in the discussion. Listen carefully because a speaker may alter what she or he says.

Examples
Speaker:
I left on June 23. No, it was the 24th. I arrived on the 23rd, but returned on the 24th.

PRACTICE 1 (answers on page 225)

Circle the key words. Listen to the audio and answer the questions.

Conversation 1

1 What does the student say about the Introductory Spanish class?
   A He took it already.
   B It's too easy.
   C His schedule doesn't have room for it.

2 Why does the woman suggest Intermediate Spanish?
   A A foreign language class is required.
   B The schedule is convenient.
   C It's preparation for the student's trip to Mexico.

3 What class will the student take on Monday and Wednesday afternoons?
   A Intermediate Spanish
   B European History
   C Latin American History

Conversation 2

1 What has the woman not done yet?
   A chosen a research topic
   B made a resource list
   C spoken about her project with the professor

2 What does she have to include as part of her project?
   A interviews
   B photographs
   C charts and graphs

3   When is the project due?
   A   in two weeks
   B   next month
   C   the end of the semester

Conversation 3

1   People originally grew knotweed
   A   as a screen for hiding structures.
   B   for its attractive flowers.
   C   to repel bees.

2   The best way to get rid of knotweed is to
   A   cover the ground with plastic.
   B   apply herbicides.
   C   dig up the roots.

3   Knotweed can be used as
   A   food.
   B   medicine.
   C   rat poison.

Conversation 4

1   Why is the professor meeting with the student?
   A   To discuss her classwork
   B   To give her the semester grade
   C   To help her plan the next assignment

2   The professor wants the student to
   A   improve her attendance.
   B   turn her assignments in on time.
   C   participate more in class discussions.

3   According to the professor, what aspect of the student's recent paper needs improvement?
   A   the organization
   B   the clarity
   C   the conclusion

Conversation 5

1   What kind of school did Martha work at?
    A   elementary school
    B   middle school
    C   high school

2   What did Martha enjoy most about her student teaching?
    A   working in small groups
    B   planning lessons
    C   taking field trips

3   What does Martha say about the school where she worked?
    A   The staff was supportive.
    B   The building was modern.
    C   The textbooks were outdated.

Label a Diagram

STRATEGY	Try to label the diagram without hearing the audio. This will focus your attention on what you need to listen for.
TIP	Pay attention to the directions. Do not write more words than required.

Track 17 **PRACTICE 2** (answers on page 226)

Listen to the audio and label the missing parts of the diagram.
Write **NO MORE THAN TWO WORDS** for each answer.

Conversation 1

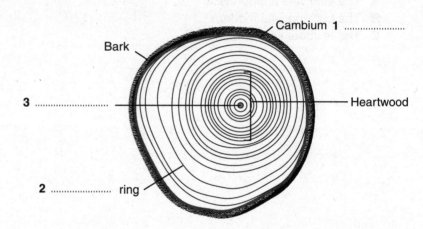

Cambium **1** ....

Bark

3 ....

Heartwood

2 .... ring

Conversation 2

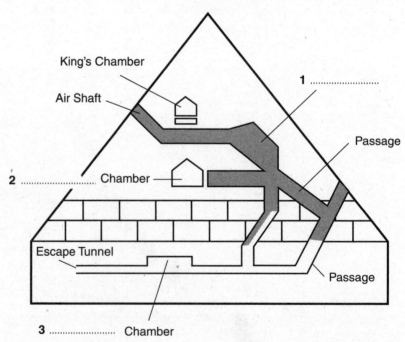

King's Chamber

Air Shaft

1 ....

Passage

2 .... Chamber

Escape Tunnel

Passage

3 .... Chamber

Conversation 3

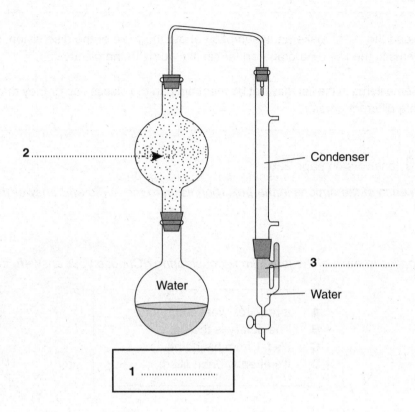

Conversation 4

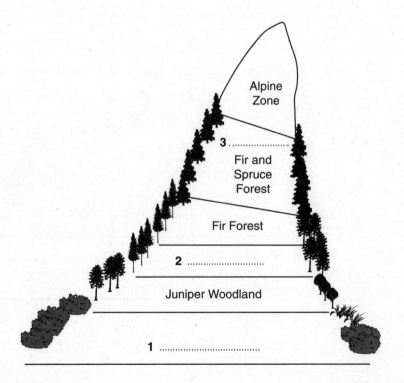

Match Words and Phrases

STRATEGY	Read the list to make an assumption about the topic of the discussion. Paraphrase the items in the list to be prepared for similar words in the discussion.
TIP	Some items in the list may not be mentioned in the discussion or they may be mentioned in a different order.

PRACTICE 3 (answers on page 226)

Paraphrase each of the options in the box. Then listen to the audio and answer the questions.

Conversation 1

Which statement applies to each of the jobs Jim is considering? Choose your answers from the box.

A	It requires weekend hours.
B	The salary is too low.
C	It's far from his home.
D	It's already been filled.

Paraphrases:

A ....

B ....

C ....

D ....

1   office assistant ....

2   cafeteria server ....

3   bookstore cashier ....

Conversation 2

What does Elizabeth do in each one of her classes? Choose your answers from the box.

A	Write papers.
B	Give a presentation.
C	Go on field trips.
D	Read a lot.

Paraphrases:

A ....

B ....

C ....

D ....

1 Economics ....

2 Sociology ....

3 Geology ....

Conversation 3

What does the man say about each of the colors used in ancient Egyptian art? Choose your answers from the box.

A	Represented rage
B	Used for objects in a line
C	Used in pictures of the gods
D	Represented stones

Paraphrases:

A ....

B ....

C ....

D ....

1 blue ....

2 red ....

3 alternating colors ....

Conversation 4

What does the woman say about each of the Hawaiian Islands? Choose your answers from the box.

A	It's the most urban island.
B	It has the most volcanoes.
C	It's the oldest island.
D	It continues to grow.

Paraphrases:

A ....

B ....

C ....

D ....

1   The Big Island ....

2   Oahu ....

3   Kauai ....

Conversation 5

What does the professor say about each of the class assignments? Choose your answers from the box.

A	It is not required.
B	It is the most important assignment.
C	It is due at the end of next month.
D	It should be done with a study partner.

Paraphrases:

A ....

B ....

C ....

D ....

1   the final exam ....

2   the research paper ....

3   the textbook articles ....

SECTION 4—TALK OR LECTURE

Classify Words or Statements

STRATEGY	Read the categories and then read the words quickly. Try to determine a link between a category and a word before you listen. But remember, write what the speaker says, not what you think.
TIP	You may use the categories more than once.

Track 19 **PRACTICE 1** (answers on page 226)

Draw lines between the categories and the words. Then listen to the audio and see if your assumptions were correct.

Talk 1

Which features are characteristic of which type of wetland?
Choose the correct letter.

Wetlands
A Marsh
B Swamp
C Bog

1 acidic water ....

2 grasses ....

3 shrubs ....

4 mosses ....

5 trees ....

Talk 2

Which architectural styles can be described in the following ways?
Choose the correct letter.

Architectural Styles
A Bec River
B Puuc
C East Coast

1 developed in the late classic period ....

2 developed in the post classic period ....

3 used columns on the entrances ....

4 used geometric designs on the walls ....

5 used decorative towers ....

Talk 3

Which TV watching habits are characteristic of which age group?
Choose the correct letter.

Age Groups

A   Teenagers
B   Younger Adults
C   Older Adults

1   average 3–4 hours of TV daily   ....

2   average 5–6 hours of TV daily   ....

3   average 6–7 hours of TV daily   ....

4   prefer news and information programs   ....

5   prefer entertainment programs   ....

Complete Notes

STRATEGY	Circle the key words in the notes provided. Try to guess the focus of the talk or lecture. The notes are just notes. They are not necessarily sentences. They may not include prepositions, articles, verbs, or other grammatical clues.
TIP	The notes follow the order of the talk. If you miss one gap, jump to the next one.

(Track 20) **PRACTICE 2** (answers on page 226)

Circle the key words in the notes below. Then listen to the audio and complete the notes. Write **NO MORE THAN THREE WORDS** for each answer.

Talk 1

Colorblindness

- Colorblindness: the inability to **1** ....
- The most common form is **2** .... colorblindness.
- Causes:
  - genes
  - **3** ....
  - exposure to chemicals

Talk 2

The Llama

The Inca people **1** .... the llama in 4000 BC.
In ancient Inca society, llama wool was worn by **2** ....
A **3** .... in AD 562 caused many llamas to die of starvation and disease.

Talk 3

Small Business Success

Start with a **1** ....
Use as much of your own **2** .... as you can.
Hire **3** .... people.

LISTENING MODULE

Complete a Flowchart

STRATEGY	Circle the key words in the chart. Ask yourself what the chart is about and try to complete the chart without listening. This will make you a careful listener.
TIP	Notice the grammar of the words in the chart. The words you write in the gap should match the grammar of the other words.

Track 21

PRACTICE 3 (answers on page 227)

Look at the missing words. Write what grammatical form you need to complete each gap. Then listen to the audio and complete the chart.
Write **NO MORE THAN THREE WORDS** for each answer.

Talk 1

Dragonfly Lifecycle

The female dragonfly lays her eggs
1 .... or under the water.

Nymphs hatch out of the eggs and live under the water for months or years.

The fully grown nymph leaves the
2 .... and climbs a plant.

The nymph sheds **3**........................ . It lives as an adult for several weeks or months.

Talk 2

Indirect Solar Water Heater

The antifreeze solution is **1** .... in the solar collector.

The antifreeze solution moves through a
2 .... and heats the water.

The heated water is kept in a **3** .... until it is used.

Talk 3

Secure Attachments

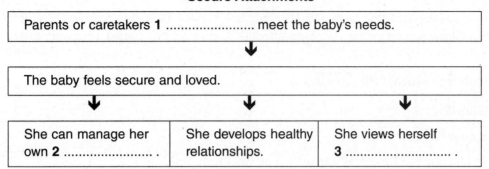

Parents or caretakers **1** .... meet the baby's needs.

⬇

The baby feels secure and loved.

⬇   ⬇   ⬇

| She can manage her own **2** .... | She develops healthy relationships. | She views herself **3** .... |

STRATEGY REVIEW

An answer sheet can be found on page 285. You may find it useful to make copies and use it for the Strategy Reviews. Alternatively, you can write your answers directly on the book pages. (Answers are on page 227.)

SECTION 1—QUESTIONS 1–10

Questions 1–4

Complete the form below.

Write **NO MORE THAN TWO WORDS AND/OR A NUMBER** *for each answer.*

Lakeside Rentals

Name: *Gregory Thornton*

Address: Box 7, **1**........................, Connecticut

No. in group **2**.........................

Arrival date **3**.........................

Length of stay **4**.........................

Questions 5–8

Complete the table below.

Write **NO MORE THAN ONE WORD AND/OR A NUMBER** *for each answer.*

Name	No. of Bedrooms	Special Features	Weekly Rental
5 .... Cottage	2	porch	$700
Maple Cottage	2	lake view	**6** $.................
Hemlock Cottage	3	**7**	$925
Spruce Cottage	**8**	garden	$900

Questions 9–10

Choose **TWO** *letters,* **A–E**.

Which TWO activities is Mr. Thornton interested in?

A   water skiing
B   paddling a canoe
C   horseback riding
D   tennis
E   hiking

SECTION 2—QUESTIONS 11–20

Questions 11–12

Choose the correct letter, **A**, **B**, or **C**.

11 When is the zoo closed?
   A all holidays
   B the first Monday of the month
   C the final week of the year

12 What benefit do groups of ten or more get?
   A a lower entrance fee
   B free entrance to the zoo
   C entrance before opening time

Questions 13–17

Label the map below.

Write the correct letter, **A–F**, next to questions 13–17.

13 education building   ....

14 picnic area   ....

15 water birds   ....

16 small mammal house   ....

17 reptile house   ....

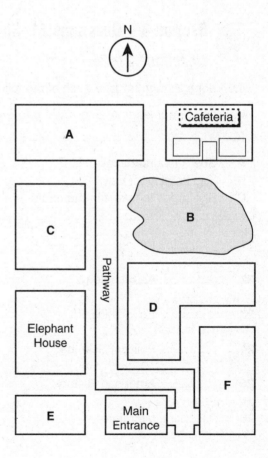

Questions 18–20

*Choose the correct letter, **A**, **B**, or **C**.*

18 The zoo currently has programs for children aged
   A 4–5.
   B 6–10.
   C 12–13.

19 Children are allowed to
   A feed the animals.
   B pet the animals.
   C groom the animals.

20 Teachers are required to
   A provide reading materials.
   B develop a test.
   C remain with their students.

SECTION 3—QUESTIONS 21–30

Questions 21–26

When does Samantha take each of the following classes?

*Write the correct letter, **A**, **B**, or **C**, next to questions 21–26.*

A	She has already taken it.
B	She is taking it now.
C	She plans to take it in the future.

21 .... Biology

22 .... Anthropology

23 .... Economics

24 .... Political Science

25 .... American History

26 .... Literature

Questions 27–30

*Choose the correct letter, **A**, **B**, or **C**.*

27 How does Samantha get to class every day?
   A on foot
   B by bus
   C in a car

28 Where is Samantha working now?
   A in an office
   B in a bookstore
   C in a cafeteria

29 What does Samantha say about this semester?
   A It's difficult.
   B It's boring.
   C It's fun.

30 What will Samantha do during the summer?
   A travel
   B study
   C work

SECTION 4—QUESTIONS 31–40

Complete the notes below.

Write **NO MORE THAN TWO WORDS** for each answer.

DOLPHINS AND PORPOISES

True whales don't have **31** ....
A killer whale is the biggest **32** ....
Porpoises are less than **33** .... long.

Nose
A dolphin's is **34** ....
A porpoise's is **35** ....

Teeth
A dolphin's are shaped like **36** ....
A porpoise's are shaped like **37** ....

Dorsal Fin
A dolphin's is **38** ....
A porpoise's is straight.

Other Information
There are just six **39** .... of porpoises.
Dolphins make **40** .... to talk with each other, while porpoises do not.

IELTS READING MODULE

OVERVIEW

In this chapter, you will learn and practice specific strategies based on the various question types. These strategies will introduce you to the types of questions on the Reading Module. You will learn how to answer these questions quickly and correctly. Most of the reading passages in this chapter are shorter than the actual reading passages you will see on the IELTS. They are intended to give you focused practice with the strategies. In the Strategies Review section, you will read passages that are the same length as the passages on the IELTS.

In this chapter, you will review the basic IELTS strategies that you learned in the first chapter of this book. You will learn how these strategies apply directly to the Reading Module.

At the end of this chapter, you will find a Strategy Review that is similar to the actual IELTS Reading test.

STRATEGIES

Matching	Matching Information
Short Answer	Choosing Answers from a List
True, False, Not Given and Yes, No, Not Given	Classifying Information
Labeling a Diagram	Completing Notes and Summaries
Completing Sentences	Completing Tables and Flowcharts
Matching Sentence Endings	Multiple Choice
Choosing Headings	

STRATEGY REVIEW

Reading Tip

Time is not your friend on the reading test. You must read quickly and diligently to answer all the questions. There are forty questions in the Reading Module. You have one hour to read three passages and answer forty questions.

When you take practice tests, pay attention to how long you spend on each section of the Reading Module. Divide your time and use the time limits in the chart below as a goal. Generally, the passages go from easiest to hardest, so it is better to spend less time on the first passages and more time on the last one.

Passage	Total Time	Skim the Passage	Scan for Answers
1	18	1 minute	1 minute/question
2	20	1 minute	1 minute/question
3	22	1 minute	1 minute/question

You will have to work hard to keep this pace. However, if you work at this rate, you will have extra time to answer questions that are more difficult.

Complete the Answer Sheet as you work. You will not have time to transfer your answers at the end.

Strategies

Matching

DIRECTIONS *Look at the following place names (Questions 1–3) and the list of meanings below.*

Match each place name with the correct meaning.

*Write the correct letter, **A–E**, in boxes 1–3 on your answer sheet.*

STRATEGY Scan the passage looking for words, dates, or phrases from the questions. When you find one, read the entire sentence. Is there a related term or paraphrase in the list? If not, read the sentence that comes before or after.

TIP Don't just match identical words. Be sure to understand the context.

PRACTICE (answers on page 228)

Paragraph 1

Read the paragraph. Match each place name (Questions 1–3) with the correct meaning.

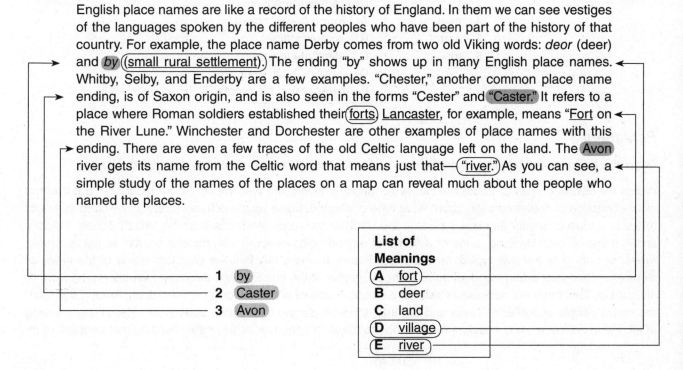

English place names are like a record of the history of England. In them we can see vestiges of the languages spoken by the different peoples who have been part of the history of that country. For example, the place name Derby comes from two old Viking words: *deor* (deer) and *by* (small rural settlement). The ending "by" shows up in many English place names. Whitby, Selby, and Enderby are a few examples. "Chester," another common place name ending, is of Saxon origin, and is also seen in the forms "Cester" and "Caster." It refers to a place where Roman soldiers established their forts. Lancaster, for example, means "Fort on the River Lune." Winchester and Dorchester are other examples of place names with this ending. There are even a few traces of the old Celtic language left on the land. The Avon river gets its name from the Celtic word that means just that—"river." As you can see, a simple study of the names of the places on a map can reveal much about the people who named the places.

1 by
2 Caster
3 Avon

List of Meanings
A fort
B deer
C land
D village
E river

> **Reading Tip**
>
> Scan for the key word *by*. The reference is *small rural settlement*. The paraphrase for a *small rural settlement* is *village*.
> Scan for the key word *Caster*. The reference is *forts* in the next sentence.
> Scan for the key word *Avon*. The reference is *river* in the same sentence.

Paragraph 2

Read the paragraph. Match each plant family (Questions 4–6) with the correct characteristics.

Although it may seem overwhelming at first, learning to identify wild flowers is not necessarily complicated. The easy way to start is by learning the common characteristics of the different plant families. Members of the mint family are easily recognizable by the four-sided shape of their stems. Mints also have opposite leaves and tubular-lipped flowers. Plants of the carrot family bloom in compound umbels—umbrella-shaped clusters. They are also characterized by hollow flower stalks. Members of the rose family include much more than the familiar garden rose. Apples, strawberries, and raspberries, for example, are all members of the rose family. Plants in this family have opposite leaves, flowers with five petals, and their stems may or may not be thorny.

		List of Characteristics	
4	mint	A	round flower stalks
5	carrot	B	square stems
6	rose	C	alternate leaves
		D	flowers in clusters
		E	five-petaled blossoms

Paragraph 3

Read the paragraph. Match each shelter type (Questions 7–9) with the correct description.

Words for different types of traditional Native American shelters are well known in our language, but there is often confusion or misinformation about what type of shelters these words actually refer to. The word *wigwam* refers to a type of shelter that was typical in the northeastern part of what is now the United States. It was a small, dome-shaped dwelling made of a frame of arched poles covered with materials such as grass, brush, reeds, or bark. The *tipi* was typical on the Great Plains. It was a tall, tent-like structure made of the hides of bison stretched over a framework of poles lashed together at the top. Perhaps the most misunderstood word of all is *igloo*. This does not necessarily refer to a house made of snow, although it often does. Among the Inuit, the native people of northern Alaska and Canada, the word simply means *house* and can refer to any dwelling at all: a sod house, a wood shack, a modern house made of concrete, or any other building that people live in.

		List of Descriptions	
7	wigwam	A	a tall tent covered with animal skins
8	tipi	B	a concrete building
9	igloo	C	Inuit word for any type of house
		D	small, round, covered with plant material
		E	a log cabin

Short Answer

DIRECTIONS *Answer the questions below.*
*Write **NO MORE THAN THREE WORDS** for each answer.*
Write your answers in boxes 1–3 on your answer sheet.

STRATEGY	Scan the passage looking for key words found in the question and read for the answer to *who, what, when, where, or how long.*
TIP	Do not write more than the suggested numbers of words. If the directions say ***"NO MORE THAN THREE WORDS"*** write ONLY three words or less. DO NOT WRITE FOUR WORDS. You will be penalized.

The *Wh-* word at the beginning of the question tells you what type of specific detail to look for. If you see the question word *who*, you will look for a name or an occupation. You will look for something that refers to a person. Study the following lists to learn what to look for.

First word	Look for…
Who	person
What	place, object, emotion
When	time
Where	location
Why	reason
Which	place, person, object
How many	quantity
How long	time, distance

PRACTICE (answers on page 228)

Read the paragraphs and answer the questions.
*Write **NO MORE THAN THREE WORDS** for each answer.*

Paragraph 1

A marathon is a type of running race. Its name comes from a legend about the Persian-Greek war. According to the story, a soldier named Phidippides ran from the battlefield in Marathon to Athens, a distance of approximately 26 miles, to carry news about victory. When the first modern Olympics were held in Athens in 1896, the idea of the marathon running race was brought up as a means of popularizing the event. At those games, the marathon was just under 25 miles. In 1908 at the London Olympics, the length of the marathon was changed to 26 miles. At the Paris Olympics in 1924 the official length of the marathon was finally established at 26.2 miles, and that is as it remains to this day.

1   How long is a marathon race now? ....

2   What two places did Phidippides run between? ....

3   Where were the Olympics held in 1908? ....

Paragraph 2

The answer to the question, "Which was the first novel written in English?" depends on how one defines the term "novel." There are a number of works that have tried to claim this honor. Probably the earliest is *Le Morte d'Arthur*, written by Thomas Malory, published in 1485. However, many do not count this as a novel since it is not an original story but a retelling of legends. John Bunyan's 1678 work *Pilgrim's Progress* is another claimant to the title, but because it is allegorical in nature, it also doesn't fit most definitions of "novel." *Pamela*, written by Samuel Richardson in 1740, is widely considered to be the first English language novel. It is written in the form of letters between the characters, as many early novels were.

4   Who wrote *Le Morte d'Arthur*? ....

5   Why isn't *Pilgrim's Progress* considered to be a novel? ....

6   Which novel is generally accepted to be the first English novel? ....

Paragraph 3

The word penguin often brings to mind playful black and white animals sliding on the ice. However, not all of the seventeen species of penguin live in icy parts of the world. In fact, some live in areas where it is quite warm. The Galapagos penguin, for example, lives near the equator. Four penguin species live in the region of Antarctica. The rest are distributed around different areas of the world, in cold, temperate, or tropical zones, but all in the southern hemisphere. There are no native penguins in the northern hemisphere. Penguins live off seafood—shrimp, krill, squid, and different kinds of fish, depending on the species of penguin.

7   How many species of penguin are there in the world? ....

8   Where do all penguins live? ....

9   What do penguins eat? ....

True, False, Not Given and Yes, No, Not Given

These two question types are very similar to each other. The True/False question is concerned with facts in a passage; the Yes/No question is concerned with an author's opinion or attitude.

DIRECTIONS	*Do the following statements agree with the information given in the passage? In Boxes 1–4 on your answer sheet write*
TRUE	*if the statement agrees with the information in the passage*
FALSE	*if the statement contradicts the information in the passage*
NOT GIVEN	*if there is no information about this in the passage*
DIRECTIONS	*Do the following statements agree with the views of the writer in the passage? In Boxes 1–4 on your answer sheet write*
YES	*if the statement agrees with the views of the writer*
NO	*if the statement contradicts the views of the writer*
NOT GIVEN	*if it is impossible to say what the writer thinks about this*

STRATEGY	Scan the passage for words that match the key words in the statement. The statements may be paraphrases of similar statements in the passage. If there is no similar statement in the passage, the answer is NOT GIVEN.
TIP	Pay attention to adjectives and adverbs (modifiers). A modifier in a question may be the opposite of the modifier in the passage.

PRACTICE 1 (answers on page 228)

True/False/Not Given

Read the paragraphs and write TRUE, FALSE, or NOT GIVEN next to each statement that follows. For each statement, underline the sentence or sentences in the paragraph where you found the answer. If you cannot find a sentence to underline, the answer is NOT GIVEN.

Paragraph 1

Deep in the Guatemalan rainforest lies Tikal, one of the most important archeological sites of the ancient Mayan civilization. The site contains more than 3,000 buildings, constructed between 600 BC and AD 900. The ancient city was an important ceremonial center with temples, palaces, and a central plaza, as well as numerous dwelling places scattered around the area. Much of the site has been excavated and restored, making it a popular attraction for tourists and students of the ancient Maya. However, many structures are still covered under a thick layer of jungle growth and have yet to be excavated. At its height, Tikal was home to a population of about 90,000. Archeologists have excavated the remains of cotton, tobacco, beans, pumpkins, and peppers, as well as tools used to grow these crops, showing that this was an agricultural society.

1   All of the buildings at Tikal have been excavated. ....

2   Tikal was the home of the most important Mayan king. ....

3   The ancient inhabitants of Tikal were farmers. ....

Paragraph 2

The Hawaiian Islands are a chain of volcanic islands stretching along a line of about 1500 miles in the Pacific Ocean. The chain consists of eight major islands, the largest being the island of Hawaii, as well as some 124 smaller islands and islets. The islands were formed by the movement of the Pacific Plate over a volcanic hot spot. In the late eighteenth and early nineteenth centuries, the islands were known to Europeans as the Sandwich Islands. This was the name given to them by Captain Cook when he first visited the area in 1778. He called them this in honor of the fourth Earl of Sandwich, who had provided the financial backing for Cook's expeditions. By the 1840s, the name Sandwich Islands had largely fallen out of use.

4   Several of the volcanoes on the Hawaiian Islands are still active. ....

5   There are a total of eight islands in the Hawaiian Island chain. ....

6   Captain Cook named the islands after his financial backer. ....

PRACTICE 2 (answers on page 228)

Yes/No/Not Given

Read the paragraph and write YES, NO, or NOT GIVEN next to each statement that follows. For each statement, underline the sentence or sentences in the paragraph where you found the answer. If you cannot find a sentence to underline, the answer is NOT GIVEN.

Paragraph 1

The dangers of driving while using a cell phone are hard to ignore. Statistics from 2009 show close to 1,000 people in the United States killed in traffic accidents where use of a cell phone was reported as a factor in the accident. Note that these numbers show only reported information. The number of traffic deaths caused by distracted drivers with cell phones is likely a good deal higher. Statistics also show that it is the 30- to 39-year-old age group that has the highest number of cell phone-related traffic deaths, rather than the under 20 age group, as would be expected. Cell phone use while driving is more common among women than among men and more common in the southern part of the country than in the north.

1   The reported number of traffic accident deaths caused by cell phone use is much lower than the actual number. ....

2   It is generally assumed that drivers under 20 are more often involved in cell-phone related traffic accidents than older drivers are. ....

3   Laws regarding using a cell phone while driving are too strict. ....

Paragraph 2

The Learning Styles Model and the Multiple Intelligences Theory both provide frameworks for teachers working to organize their classrooms and lessons to maximize the learning experience for all their students. Both these approaches recognize that children learn differently, and they can be used effectively together in the classroom. The Learning Styles Model identifies five areas that influence learning: environment, emotions, social, physical, and psychological. It then looks at different factors within these areas. The environment, for example, can affect learning in terms of sound (some children learn better in a quiet environment while others prefer noise), light (some children prefer a brightly lit environment while others feel better in softer light), and other factors. Social influences include such things as whether a child prefers to work alone or with others, with or without the guidance of an adult, with a routine or in a variety of ways.

4   The Learning Styles Model is a more effective tool than the Multiple Intelligences Theory. ....

5   Light and noise levels can affect how children learn. ....

6   Most children prefer to work with adult guidance. ....

Labeling a Diagram

DIRECTIONS   *Label the diagram below.*

*Choose **NO MORE THAN TWO WORDS** from the passage for each answer.*

Write your answers in boxes 1–3 on your answer sheet.

STRATEGY	Scan the text for key words that indicate location: *next to, above, across, edge, center, beneath,* Look for words that indicate geometric patterns: *square, rectangle, bisect.* You don't have to write *a, and,* or *the.*
TIP	Labeling a Diagram questions test your ability to translate words into pictures. When you read, turn words into pictures in your head, then make a simple drawing on paper before you answer the questions.

PRACTICE (answers on page 229)

*Read the paragraphs and label the diagrams. Choose **NO MORE THAN TWO WORDS** from the reading passage for each answer.*

Paragraph 1

The art of carpet weaving is an old Persian tradition. The various motifs that make up the carpet designs often have a symbolic meaning. For example, peacocks represent immortality while peonies symbolize power. Persian carpets usually follow one of three layouts. The medallion layout shows a large decoration in the center of the carpet, often with smaller motifs around it, the whole enclosed by a decorative border. This is probably the most common carpet design. The one-sided layout shows the most predominate design element weighted toward one end of the carpet rather than being placed in the center. The all-over layout shows a pattern distributed all over the surface of the carpet.

1 ....   2 ....   3 ....

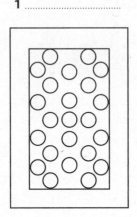  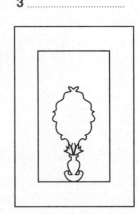

Paragraph 2

Earth is made up of three main parts: the crust, the mantle, and the core. The crust is the outer layer, and the thinnest. It makes up about 0.5 percent of Earth's mass and consists of rocks, such as granite and basalt. It is only about 10 kilometers thick under the oceans and about 30 to 50 kilometers thick under the continents. Beneath the crust is the mantle. We know much less about this layer than we know about the crust since we can't see it. It makes up about 50 percent of Earth's mass. In Earth's interior, we have the core. This is divided into two parts. The *outer core* is liquid. It is about 2,100 kilometers thick and makes up about 30 percent of Earth's mass. The solid *inner core* is about 1,300 kilometers thick and makes up just 2 percent of Earth's mass.

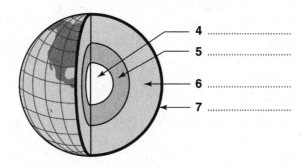

4 ....

5 ....

6 ....

7 ....

Paragraph 3

A cantilever bridge is built with cantilevers—structures that project into space horizontally and are supported on one end only. A cantilever needs to be firmly anchored on its supported side so that its freestanding side can hold up weight. A diving board is a type of a cantilever, and a balcony sticking out from the side of a building is another example. A simple cantilever bridge consists of two cantilever arms extending from opposites sides of a gap (river or other obstacle) and meeting at the center. Most cantilever bridges are balanced cantilevers. In these bridges, an anchor arm and cantilever arm extend in opposite directions from a pier. The other end of the anchor arm is attached to an anchor pier. When the distance to be crossed is longer than can be covered by two cantilever arms, they may be connected in the center by a suspended span.

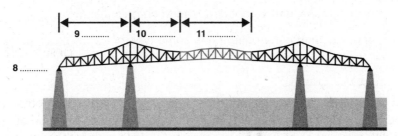

9 ....   10 ....   11 ....

8 ....

Completing Sentences

DIRECTIONS   *Complete the sentences below.*

*Choose **ONE WORD ONLY** from the passage for each answer.*

Write your answers in boxes 1–3 on your answer sheet.

STRATEGY	Try to complete the sentence first, then return to the passage to check your answer. Skim the passage looking for synonyms or paraphrases of words from the sentence. The word that completes the sentence will be the same word in the passage. The grammatical form will be the same.
TIP	Make sure the word you write in the blank matches grammatically.

PRACTICE (answers on page 229)

*Read the paragraph. Fill in each blank with **ONE WORD ONLY** from the paragraph.*

Paragraph 1

The term *insomnia*, from a Latin word meaning *sleepless*, refers to a common sleep disorder where the sufferer has difficulty falling or staying asleep. *Acute insomnia* lasts for just a few days or weeks and is often brought on by a traumatic event, such as job loss or death of a loved one. It happens in situations of temporary stress. *Chronic insomnia* is long term. It is usually defined as insomnia that lasts for a month or longer. Clinical depression, constant stress, and chronic pain are common causes. *Secondary insomnia* is not a disease itself, but is a symptom of some other health condition such as arthritis, cancer, or pain, or it may be caused by a patient's medication. *Primary insomnia*, on the other hand, is a disorder that is not caused by some other medical issue.

1   .... insomnia is a sleep disorder that lasts a short period of time.

2   .... stress is one situation that can lead to chronic insomnia.

3   Secondary insomnia is a sign that the patient has some type of .... problem.

Paragraph 2

Moths and butterflies, animals of the Lepidoptera order, are very similar to each other. However, there are a few characteristics by which you can tell them apart. Generally, butterflies are diurnal, active during the day, and moths are nocturnal, active at night. There are some exceptions to this, though, such as the diurnal buck moth. If you look at a butterfly's antennae, you will notice that they are long and thin with a knob at the end. A moth's antennae, on the other hand, are not thin but feathery. When moths are at rest, they hold their wings out flat, while butterflies at rest hold them up in a vertical position. There are many more species of moths than butterflies. In fact, they make up around 90 percent of the Lepidoptera order.

4   Unlike most other moths, the buck moth is active in the ....

5   Resting butterflies hold their .... vertically.

6   Around 90 percent of Lepidoptera are ....

Paragraph 3

The list of health benefits, both physical and mental, that result from regular exercise is long. Most experts recommend that you get a minimum of thirty minutes of moderate exercise per day, while forty-five minutes or an hour, at least on some days out of every week, is even better. The good news is that you don't have to take your daily exercise all at once. If your goal is sixty minutes a day, you can walk for fifteen minutes in the morning, then do a forty-five minute workout at the gym later on, for example. Weight-bearing exercise, such as walking and running, is important because it strengthens your bones and muscles. Any type of moderate exercise increases the level of endorphins in the brain. These hormones are associated with a better mood, so if you want to feel happier, exercise more. Exercise can also strengthen the immune system, reducing your susceptibility to illness.

7   You should get at least ....*thirty*............. minutes of moderate exercise daily.

8   Walking is an example of a ......*weight-bearing*............. exercise.

9   Endorphins are associated with improved ....*moderate*.... *mood*

Matching Sentence Endings

DIRECTIONS   *Complete each sentence with the correct ending, **A–E**, below.*

*Write the correct letter, **A–E**, in boxes 1–3 on your answer sheet.*

STRATEGY	There are more sentence endings than you will use. Therefore, focus on the sentence beginnings. Identify the key words in them, then skim the text for the key words, synonyms, or paraphrases. After you match a sentence beginning with an ending, read the whole thing to make sure it makes sense.
TIP	The sentence beginnings follow the same order as the information in the text.

PRACTICE (answers on page 229)

Read the excerpt from a reading passage. Complete each sentence that follows with the correct ending from the box. Write the correct letter next to each sentence.

Passage 1

A bog is a type of wetland that gets most of its water from precipitation—rain and snow. This is a source of water that is lacking in the mineral and sediment content of the streams and groundwater that feed other types of wetlands. The result is soil that is low in nutrient content. This, together with the acidity resulting from the peat mosses that cover bogs, creates an environment that is unwelcoming to many life forms.

Few species of animals can survive in the unfriendly conditions of a bog. No fish swim its acidic waters, nor will you find mollusks such as snails, mussels, and crabs, which require calcium to live. On the other hand, a variety of insects thrive in bog conditions, as do a number of species of amphibians that live and/or breed in bogs. Other animals, including snakes and mammals such as raccoons and moose, visit bogs to hunt and feed.

A few highly-specialized plant species have adapted to the conditions of the bog environment. While the soil in a bog may be nutritionally poor, the environment is rich in insect life. Carnivorous plants take advantage of this situation by turning to insects to meet their nutritional needs. Instead of relying on the poor soil for food, they consume the insects and other small animals that inhabit or visit bogs. These plants have developed a variety of ingenious methods to capture their prey. Strong scents lure an insect to a plant, where it is caught in a sticky substance or trapped in some sort of container from which it can't escape. Then the plant feeds itself by digesting the insect over the next few days or weeks.

A	the high level of water in the soil.
B	feeding on the high number of insects.
C	the lack of an important mineral in the water.
D	the content of the soil.
E	hunting and feeding by other animals.
F	the poor soil and acidity of the water.

1   Conditions in a bog are unfavorable to most plant and animal life because of .... F

2   Mollusks are absent from bogs because of ....

3   Carnivorous plants are able to survive in bogs because of ....

Passage 2

Attention-Deficit/Hyperactivity Disorder (ADHD) is a neurological disorder that affects approximately five percent of school-age children. Children with this disorder exhibit behaviors that are incompatible with a typical school setting as they have difficulty doing things that are generally expected of school children, such as sitting still, taking turns, and staying on task for designated periods of time.

ADHD has been divided into three types. Children who have the Predominantly Inattentive type are easily distractible. They have difficulty starting or completing tasks and organizing their activities. They tend to be forgetful and may often lose things they need to complete their schoolwork, such as books, pencils, or homework assignments. While they may not face intellectual difficulties in the content of their school assignments, their behavioral symptoms make completing their school tasks a challenge.

Children who have the Predominantly Hyperactive-Impulsive type have difficulty sitting or engaging in any task quietly. They often fidget and talk excessively. It is difficult for them to wait their turn, and they tend to interrupt others, whether in class or at play. These behaviors make getting along with their peers challenging, and they are often outside the social group at school. Children who have the Predominantly Combined type of ADHD exhibit the symptoms and face the challenges of both the other types of the disorder.

Although any child may exhibit one or more of the behaviors of ADHD from time to time, that does not necessarily mean that the child suffers from the disorder. In fact, most children behave in these ways to one degree or another at some time or other. If a teacher or parent suspects that a child has this disorder, it is important to get a professional evaluation so that the child can receive the proper diagnosis and treatment.

A	are occasionally inattentive or hyperactive.
B	find schoolwork difficult to understand.
C	may have few friends.
D	are only disruptive at school.
E	cannot stay properly focused on their assignments.
F	tend to forget or lose things.

4   Children with Predominantly Inattentive ADHD ....

5   Children with Predominantly Hyperactive ADHD ....

6   The majority of children ....

Choosing Headings

DIRECTIONS The following reading passage has four sections, **A–D**.

Choose the correct heading for each section from the list of headings.

Write the correct number, **i–viii,** in boxes 1–4 on your answer sheet. There are more headings than sections so you will not use them all.

STRATEGY	The heading summarizes the main idea of the paragraph. Read the paragraph and determine the main idea. Then scan the headings and choose one that is similar in meaning.
TIP	The main idea may be stated in the first or second sentence of the paragraph. Cross out the headings as you use them.

PRACTICE (answers on page 229)

Read the excerpt from a reading passage. Choose the correct heading for each section from the list of headings, and write the correct number next to the corresponding letter below.

Passage 1

A

Although the Sonoran Desert of the southwestern United States and northern Mexico is a desert, it does rain there. In fact, for a desert, it is fairly wet, with 3 to 16 inches of rain a year. It is also one of the hotter deserts of North America. The average high temperature is 86 degrees, although temperatures can reach well over 100 degrees in some southern areas. On the other hand, nighttime temperatures can fall to freezing in other parts of the desert.

B

The magnificent saguaro cactus, which can grow as high as fifty feet tall, lives only in the Sonoran Desert, and then only in those parts of the desert where conditions are right. It is found only in elevations below 3,500 feet as it cannot withstand freezing temperatures. This mighty plant is well-adapted to the dry Sonoran climate. In addition to the large taproot, which helps hold it up, it also has a system of roots that spread out just below the surface of the ground, ready to soak up the rain when it does fall. The spines that cover the cactus stem point downward, directing the raindrops toward the base of the plant where the roots are. The stems can absorb and store large amounts of water. The pores of the cactus open only at night, closing up during the sunny daytime to prevent moisture loss.

C

The saguaro provides shelter for a variety of desert birds. Gila woodpeckers and gilded flickers hollow out holes in the sides of the cactus to make their nests. After they abandon their cactus homes, other birds move in and nest in the hollows the woodpeckers created. Screech owls, purple martins, and house finches are among the birds that call the saguaro home.

D

In addition to shelter, the saguaro is also a source of food for many animals. When the cactus reaches sixty or seventy years old, it is finally ready to flower. Each flower blooms for only a day and, during that short time, animals swoop in to take advantage. Long-nosed bats suck up the sweet nectar. Bees, wasps, ants, and butterflies all enjoy a sweet meal from the flower. Later in the season, the fruit and seeds provide nourishment for birds, mice, rats, squirrels, skunks, and foxes. Just about any animal can find something good to eat on a saguaro cactus.

List of Headings

    i   What Is a Desert?

   ii   Grocery Store of the Desert

  iii   Animals of the Sonoran Desert

   iv   A Home for Birds

    v   Conditions in the Sonoran Desert

   vi   The Deserts of North America

  vii   Saguaro Adaptations

 viii   Fruits of the Desert

1   Paragraph A ....

2   Paragraph B ....

3   Paragraph C ....

4   Paragraph D ....

Passage 2

A

Daylight Saving Time—the practice of setting clocks ahead one hour every spring and back one hour every fall—has been in effect in the United States in one form or another since 1918. The establishment of this practice was based on the idea that a longer period of daylight in the evening would lead to reduced electricity consumption. The original Daylight Saving Time period was six months long. During the oil crisis of the 1970s, concerns about energy use motivated the U.S. Congress to lengthen that period to ten months in 1974 and eight months in 1975. The result was a saving of 10,000 barrels of oil a day. However, these changes also meant that people were getting up in the dark on autumn mornings. Therefore, in 1976 the country reverted to an earlier system of beginning Daylight Saving Time on the last Sunday in April. But, this was not the end of efforts to increase energy savings by extending the length of Daylight Saving Time. In 1986, the beginning date was moved to the first Sunday of April resulting in an estimated savings of 300,000 barrels of oil a year. In 2005, the U.S. Congress passed the Energy Policy Act, changing the beginning and end dates of Daylight Saving Time to the second Sunday in March and the first Sunday in November. This change, creating an almost eight-month long Daylight Saving Time period, has been in effect since 2007.

B

A study done by the U.S. Department of Transportation in the 1970s showed that no matter how many months Daylight Saving Time lasts, energy use is reduced by about one percent for each day that it is in effect. This is because household energy use is directly related to the time that people go to bed, since people turn off lights, TVs, and other appliances at bedtime. Since household energy accounts for about 25 percent of the total energy use in the United States, this is significant. More recent studies have cast some doubt on the importance of energy savings stemming from Daylight Saving Time. Not everyone is in agreement, however, and policies regarding Daylight Saving Time have not changed as a result.

C

Reduced energy use has been the major motive for the establishment and continuance of Daylight Saving Time. In addition to this, it has led to other positive results, as well, an important one being improved traffic safety. Several studies have shown a reduction of about one percent in traffic accidents and fatalities during Daylight Saving Time because it reduces the likelihood that people will be driving in the dark. Daylight Saving Time may make our streets safer in other ways, too. One study showed a thirteen percent reduction in violent crime during this time of year. There are also benefits to the retail economy as people are more likely to go out and shop during daylight hours.

D

But there are other sides to the story, centering on issues of convenience, economy, and safety. While some people find changing the clocks twice a year to be a nuisance, for businesses this can represent a significant expense. For many school children and for those who work early morning shifts, extended Daylight Saving Time means getting up in the dark during part of the year and being out on the streets when visibility is low. Nevertheless, the consensus seems to be that the advantages outweigh the disadvantages. People in approximately seventy countries around the world use some form of the system.

List of Headings

i	The Reasons Behind Daylight Saving Time
ii	Effects on Energy Consumption
iii	Negative Aspects
iv	Energy Use in the Home
v	The Expansion of Daylight Saving Time
vi	Effects on Traffic Safety
vii	Advantages of Daylight Saving Time
viii	Daylight Saving Time Around the World

---

5 Paragraph A ....

6 Paragraph B ....

7 Paragraph C ....

8 Paragraph D ....

Matching Information

DIRECTIONS   The reading passage has four paragraphs, **A–D**.

Which paragraph contains the following information?

*Write the correct letter, **A–D**, in boxes 1–6 on your answer sheet.*

You may use any letter more than once.

STRATEGY	Skim the entire passage to get an idea of what it is about. Then for each question, try to predict which paragraph contains the information asked for. Identify the key words in the question and skim the chosen paragraph for key words, synonyms, and paraphrases.
TIP	Read the context of the key words, synonyms, and paraphrases carefully to make sure it contains the information you are looking for.
	For some passages, you may find more than one answer in any one paragraph. If that is the case, the directions will say *You may use any letter more than once.*

PRACTICE (answers on page 229)

Read the passage and answer the questions that follow.

A

With growing concerns about congested roads, air pollution, and petroleum supplies, alternative forms of transportation are receiving increasing attention. People are looking for ways to get around that don't involve driving alone in a car. Carpooling, walking, and use of public transportation systems such as buses and trains are some of the methods people are using in place of the traditional private car. Studies suggest that bicycle riding, in particular, is a form of transportation that is rising in popularity.

B

In cities around the world, bicycles are being seen in the street in increasing numbers. While there are a number of reasons for the bicycle's popularity, this form of transportation has its drawbacks, as well. Bike enthusiasts highlight the fitness aspects, including weight maintenance and strengthening of the heart and immune system, as well as the psychological benefits of mood elevation and stress reduction that regular exercise provides. Enthusiasts also favor the bike over buses and trains because of the freedom it allows them. Rather than making plans around bus or train routes and schedules, bicycles allow riders to go where they want when they want, and because they don't require paying a fare, they are advantageous to those who need to economize.

C

When we look at the rising cost of living in modern society, the bicycle clearly comes out a winner. Bicycles are much less expensive to buy and maintain than a private car. And the cost advantage reaches beyond the interest of the individual as bikes cause much less wear and tear on roads, which are maintained with public money. The bicycle does, however, have its detractors, even including those who support the need for alternative forms of transportation. They point out that not everyone can use a bicycle. It is not suitable, for example, for those with health issues, and its ease of use is dependent on the weather as well as on the distances one must travel. Furthermore, the proliferation of bicycles on city streets that are not designed for them gives rise to safety concerns.

D

Whatever position one may take on the issue, whatever reasons one may cite in favor or against, bicycles are here to stay, and we will be seeing more and more of them in the coming years. There is no question that cities must make room for the bicycle along with other alternative forms of transportation. A good place to start would be with creating bike lanes and off-road bike paths as well as educating the driving public about sharing the road safely with cyclists.

Which paragraph contains the following information? You may use any letter more than once.

1   reasons for opposition to bicycles C
2   a comparison of bicycles with public transportation .... D
3   examples of alternative transportation .... A
4   the health benefits of bicycles .... B
5   the writer's suggestions for the future .... D
6   the economic advantages of bicycles C

Choosing Answers from a List

DIRECTIONS   *Choose **THREE** letters, **A–F**.*

Write the correct letters in boxes 1–3 on your answer sheet.

*Which **THREE** of the following facts about .... are mentioned in the text?*

STRATEGY	Read the instructions carefully and scan the passage looking for the key words in the direction line. Read carefully around those words in the passage. Scan the answer choices quickly and look for key words in each statement. Match the key words in the passage with the key words in the statement. Do not pay attention to pronouns. Look for nouns, verbs, and modifiers.
TIP	It is important to read the instructions carefully and pay attention to the key words in the direction line. After you scan, choose the answers that you remember. Then go back and look for the others.

PRACTICE (answers on page 229)

Passage 1

*Look at the excerpt from a reading passage and the list of facts about hummingbirds that follow. Which **THREE** of the facts are mentioned in the passage? For each fact you identify, underline the sentence or phrase in the paragraph where you found it.*

Researchers studying the behavior of black-chinned hummingbirds in Arizona have made some interesting observations. They found that the hummingbirds who built their nests close to hawks' nests had greater breeding success than hummingbirds who nested elsewhere. Further, it was not just a matter of how close the hummingbird nests were to the hawk nests, but exactly how they were placed.

Hawks are predators, but not of hummingbirds. They do, however, go after Mexican jays which, in turn, prey on hummingbird eggs. Since hawks tend to hunt from above, jays tend to forage even higher up when hawks are in the neighborhood. Hummingbird nests that are built below hawk nests, therefore, are protected because they are out of the jays' range. The researchers found that hummingbird nests located near hawk nests had a survival rate as high as thirty percent, whereas hummingbird nests built farther way had a much lower survival rate—as low as six percent according to one study. Additionally, researchers found that when a hawk nest was abandoned for whatever reason, Mexican jays moved back in and the survival rate of nearby hummingbird nests fell dramatically.

A	Hummingbirds camouflage their nests with lichen.
B	Mexican jays eat hummingbird eggs.
C	Around one third of hummingbird nests that are close to hawk nests survive.
D	A hummingbird nest usually contains two eggs.
E	After the nesting season, black-chinned hummingbirds spend the winter in Mexico.
F	Hawks generally don't hunt hummingbirds.

Passage 2

Look at the excerpt from a reading passage and the list of facts about savant syndrome that follow. Which ***THREE*** *of the facts are mentioned in the passage? For each fact you identify, underline the sentence or phrase in the paragraph where you found it.*

Savant syndrome is a condition in which a mentally disabled individual exhibits exceptional skills in a particular area. Savant syndrome is generally congenital but may also occur following an injury or disease. It is frequently associated with autism, a neurological disorder characterized by difficulties with communication and social skills and, often, cognitive deficits. In fact, over half of savant syndrome cases occur in individuals with that condition, while the rest of the cases are seen in people with other disabilities or injuries to the central nervous system.

The outstanding talents seen in savants usually occur within a limited range of categories: musical performance, artistic abilities, mathematics, and calendar calculation. Savants with musical abilities are known for their exceptional performance skills, often including the ability to play a complicated piece even after hearing it just once. Savants with mathematical talents are able to make complicated mathematical calculations with unusual rapidity. Calendar calculators are able to instantly tell the day of the week that any date, past or future, falls on. These talents are notable not only because they contrast sharply with the savant's mental deficits in most other areas, but also because in many cases they are so much greater than the skill level of the average person.

A	Savant syndrome occurs in about one tenth of individuals with autism.
B	Savants' special abilities are usually seen in only a few types of skill areas.
C	Savants may have more than one special talent.
D	Savants usually have intellectual disabilities.
E	Savant syndrome may be acquired, or an individual may be born with it.
F	The causes of savant syndrome are unclear.

Classifying Information

DIRECTIONS   *Classify the following statements as applying to*

    A   "Topic 1" (for example, Mallard)
    B   "Topic 2" (for example, Black duck)

*Write the correct letter, **A** or **B**, in boxes 1–5 on your answer sheet.*

<table>
<tr><td>STRATEGY</td><td>You will have to determine what characteristics distinguish one topic from the other. You will classify the statements by what makes each different from the other. Scan the passage quickly and circle the word or phrase in Heading A and underline the word or phrase in Heading B. Skim the characteristics; then scan the passage looking for characteristics that match the circled word and those that match the underlined word.</td></tr>
<tr><td>TIP</td><td>The characteristics or ideas to be classified will probably be in the same paragraph as the word in the heading.</td></tr>
</table>

PRACTICE (answers on page 229)

Paragraph 1

Scan the paragraph. Circle all words and phrases that describe mallards. Underline all words and phrases that describe black ducks. Then answer the question that follows.

Mallards are among the most common of wild ducks in North America, and almost anyone can identify the green head, brown breast, and bright yellow bill of the male of this species. Distinguishing the female, however, from the closely related black duck is a little bit trickier. In addition to being similar in appearance, mallards and black ducks occupy similar habitat, although the shyer black duck tends to seek out more secluded areas away from human activity. A quick way to tell whether you are looking at a mallard or a black duck is to check out the color of the bill. The female mallard's is bright orange, while the black duck's is a drab greenish yellow or olive. Both the black duck and the female mallard have brown plumage, but the black duck's is darker in color. In addition, the female mallard has a whitish tail.

Classify the following phrases as describing

    A Mallard
    B Black Duck

1   has a brightly colored bill ....
2   has a drably colored bill ....
3   the male's head is green ....
4   prefers quiet places ....
5   feathers are dark brown ....

Paragraph 2

Scan the paragraph. Circle all words and phrases that relate to Vermont. Underline all words and phrases that relate to New Hampshire. Then answer the question that follows.

One might assume that because of their geographic proximity, agricultural conditions in the neighboring states of Vermont and New Hampshire would be similar. This is not so, however, for several reasons. An important one is differing soil conditions, due to geological history. Vermont at one point formed part of the continental shelf and as a result of marine deposits now has a limey soil. New Hampshire was under deeper ocean where limey deposits did not form. In addition, as a result of lying on a bedrock of granite, soil in New Hampshire is gravelly, so minerals wash out of it more easily. In the 1800s, wool was a major crop in the region. Two million of the region's three million sheep were raised on Vermont's rich agriculture land. These sheep were more productive than sheep in other parts of the region, producing twenty percent more wool per animal than New Hampshire sheep. New Hampshire's acidic soil, however, is just right for oak and pine trees. These provide the best lumber for oceangoing boats, a major product of the state in the nineteenth century.

Classify the phrases as describing

  A Vermont
  B New Hampshire

6 has a higher level of lime in its soil ....
7 lay farther out from the coast at one time ....
8 has a significant amount of gravel in its soil ....
9 raised more sheep than other states in the region ....
10 produced wood for shipbuilding ....

Paragraph 3

*Circle all words and phrases that relate to the classic period. Underline all words and phrases that relate to the transitional period. Put an **X** next to all words and phrases that relate to the rug period.*

The Navajo tradition of weaving has evolved over time, going through several distinct phases that marked changes in styles and materials used. Originally, the Navajo wove blankets, shawls, and dresses for personal use out of the wool of churro sheep. This characterized what is known as the classic period. Following this came the transitional period, starting around 1870, when synthetic dyes came into use. These produced more varied and brighter colors than the vegetable dyes that had been used in the earlier period. At this time, weavers also began to use machine spun cotton for the warp, weaving through it a weft of merino sheep wool, which produced a thicker yarn than the wool of the churro sheep. During the rug period, from about 1900 to 1930, weavers concentrated on producing rugs for the tourist trade instead of on items for personal home use. They wove according to what they believed their customers wanted. Thus, some of the designs of this period were very similar to oriental carpet designs, and the rugs were thicker than earlier ones to match the tourists' perception of what a rug should look like.

Classify the phrases as describing

  A classic period
  B transitional period
  C rug period

11 made for use at home rather than for selling ....
12 colored with dyes made from plants ....
13 made with brightly colored yarns ....
14 patterns looked like oriental rugs ....
15 made partly out of cotton ....
16 sold to tourists ....

Completing Notes and Summaries

DIRECTIONS

Example 1

*Complete the summary using the list of words, **A–I**, below.*

*Write the correct letter, **A–I**, in boxes 1–4 on your answer sheet.*

Example 2

Complete the summary below.

*Choose **NO MORE THAN THREE WORDS** from the passage for each answer.*

Write your answers in boxes 1–4 on your answer sheet.

STRATEGY	Look for what is missing in the notes and summary. First, look for the words that ARE given. Then scan the passage to look for these words. The missing words will be near these words.
TIP	Write only the number of words suggested in the directions.

PRACTICE (answers on page 229)

Paragraph 1

Read the paragraph, then complete the summary using words from the list.

The English word *paper* comes from *papyrus*—the name of a marsh grass used by the ancient Egyptians to make sheets to write on. Strictly speaking, this ancient writing material was not actually paper even though it had the same function. Rather, it was a type of mat formed by strips cut from the plant's stem that were layered and pounded together into a thin sheet. True paper first came from China. It was there that the process was developed of macerating plant fibers in water and drying them in a thin sheet. During the third century AD, knowledge of the papermaking process began to spread through Asia. It didn't reach Europe until the 1100s. Prior to that, Europeans had been writing on parchment, a material made from animal skins.

Summary

A	during	**C**	stems	**E**	leaves	**G**	strips	**I**	pounded
B	layered	**D**	before	**F**	soaked	**H**	mats		

The ancient Egyptians wrote on **1** ....H............ , which they made from the **2** ....C........... of a type of grass. Paper was first developed in China. It was made with plant fibers that had been **3** ....F........... and then formed into sheets. Knowledge of the papermaking process arrived in Europe in the twelfth century. **4** ....D........... that time, Europeans wrote on parchment.

Paragraph 2

Read the paragraph, then complete the summary.
*Choose **NO MORE THAN THREE WORDS** from the passage for each answer.*

In 1947, Norwegian explorer Thor Heyerdahl set out to prove that it would have been possible for ancient South Americans to cross the Pacific Ocean and settle in the Polynesian islands. In order to do this, Heyerdahl built a raft using only material and technology that would have been available to South Americans in pre-Colombian times. He constructed the body of the raft out of balsa logs and pine boards lashed together with rope made from hemp. To this he added a small cabin made of bamboo with a roof of thatched banana leaves. Sails were hoisted on a mangrove wood mast. He gave the completed raft the name *Kon Tiki*, which comes from an old name for an Incan god. A group of just six men, with Heyerdahl as their leader, set sail across the Pacific on Kon Tiki.

Summary

Heyerdahl wanted to show that pre-Colombian South Americans could have **5** .... So he constructed an ocean-going raft with the same **6** .... that the ancient South Americans could have used. He named the completed raft for **7** .... Heyerdahl set out on his journey with a crew of **8** ....

Paragraph 3

Read the paragraph, then complete the notes using words from the list.

The first Europeans to witness the game of lacrosse were French missionaries working in the St. Lawrence valley. It was they who dubbed the game "lacrosse." The game was played in various forms by Native American tribes in the eastern part of North America as well as in the Great Lakes region. Lacrosse games were important events that were played over a period of several days and took place in an area of anywhere from 500 yards to several miles in size. The number of players ranged from the hundreds to the thousands. The game was played by throwing and catching the ball with a stick that had a sort of net at the end, and the only important rule was that a player's hand could not touch the ball. To start a game the ball was thrown up into the air, and the players tried to catch it.

Notes

A	over a large area
B	French missionaries
C	throw the ball
D	Native Americans
E	touch the ball
F	next to a lake

- Lacrosse was originally played by **9** ....
- Lacrosse games took place **10** ....
- Lacrosse players were not allowed to **11** ....

Completing Tables and Flowcharts

DIRECTIONS   *Complete the table below.*

*Choose **NO MORE THAN THREE WORDS** from the passage for each answer.*

Write your answers in boxes 1–4 on your answer sheet.

STRATEGY	As in notes and summaries, you will look for what is missing in the table or flowcharts. First look for the words that ARE given. Scan the passage to look for these words. The missing words will be near these words.
TIP	Write only the number of words suggested in the directions.

PRACTICE (answers on page 230)

Paragraph 1

Read the paragraph. Complete the table using words from the paragraph.
*Write **NO MORE THAN THREE WORDS** for each answer.*

Research points to six different factors that can lead to heart disease. One of the most significant of these is physical inactivity. Heart disease is a condition that develops when plaque, or fatty deposits, build up in the coronary arteries, which carry blood to the heart. This buildup causes these blood vessels to become blocked. It can also lead to the formation of masses of thickened blood, that is, blood clots. Physical activity can reduce the risk of heart disease, not only because inactivity is a risk factor itself but also because of the effect it can have on some of the other risk factors. For example, studies have shown that people who follow a routine of taking daily walks are less likely to develop Type 2 diabetes than people who follow no regular exercise routine.

Cause	Effect
Lack of **1** .... exercise	Heart disease
Plaque deposits increase	**2** .... arteries Formation of **3** ....
Walking regularly	Lower risk of **4** ....

Paragraph 2

Read the paragraph. Complete the table using words from the paragraph.
*Write **NO MORE THAN TWO WORDS** for each answer.*

Geothermal energy refers to technologies that extract heat from the earth to use as energy in homes and businesses. It is attractive as an alternative energy source that reduces our reliance on fossil fuels. Although the high cost of construction can be a deterrent, the low cost of operation once the system is up and running is a great benefit. Another attraction is that geothermal energy systems produce no pollution, in contrast to energy systems that rely on fossil fuels. Unfortunately, it is not an alternative for everyone as a geothermal energy plant can only be built in a location where the proper underground conditions exist—often near hills or mountains.

READING MODULE

Advantage	Disadvantage
5 .... is inexpensive	**6** .... is expensive
Does not create **7**	Location requires suitable **8** ....

Paragraph 3

Read the paragraph. Complete the flowchart using words from the paragraph.
*Write **NO MORE THAN ONE WORD** for each answer.*

Rather than chasing after its dinner as other predators do, web-spinning spiders construct a trap—the web—and wait for dinner to come to them. Spider webs are intricate pieces of weaving that could rival the most beautiful handmade lace. How do these tiny creatures make these elegant structures? The spider starts by standing on a branch and releasing a long thread into the wind. The other end of the thread catches onto another branch, so now it is stretched between two branches like a bridge. The spider then releases another, looser thread as it walks across this bridge. The loose thread sags below to form a V shape. The spider walks to the center of this V and lowers itself down on a new thread, forming the leg of a Y shape. The spider then attaches more threads between the bridge and various anchor points to create a framework. Next, the spider attaches threads radiating out from the center of the web to the edges. Over these, the spider attaches threads in the form of a spiral.

Spider Web

The spider attaches thread between two branches to form a **9** ....

⬇

It releases a second, looser thread that hangs down in the form of a **10** ....

⬇

It attaches more threads to form a framework, then places threads radiating out from the center.

⬇

It lays down the last threads in a **11** .... shape.

Multiple Choice

DIRECTIONS   *Choose the correct letter, **A, B, C,** or **D**.*

Write the correct letter in boxes 1–4 on your answer sheet.

STRATEGY   Scan the reading passage looking for the words, dates, or phrase in the multiple-choice options. Read the sentence where these key words are found. Does that sentence answer the question? Remember the key word may be a synonym, antonym, or paraphrase of the correct answer.

TIP   Read the question and try to guess the answer. Scan the passage for the key words in the answer options. Circle the key words when you find them. Do they match your guess?

The answers to the questions are in sequence. The answer to the first question is in the first part of the passage. The answer to the second question follows that. The answer to the third question follows the answer to the second question.

PRACTICE (answers on page 230)

Read each passage and answer the questions that follow. For each question, choose the correct letter, **A, B, C,** *or* **D**.

Passage 1

Supporting children who struggle with reading is a challenge for teachers. Difficulty with learning to read often leads to issues such as low self-esteem and loss of motivation, which only exacerbates the problem. In order to help children in this situation, some schools and libraries are starting to use specially trained therapy dogs. The process is very simple. The child sits with a dog for a certain period of time and reads aloud to it. The presence of the dog is comforting to the child. Dogs enjoy attention from people, so the child feels like she has an interested listener who won't criticize her. With a therapy dog, the child has the opportunity to practice reading in a positive environment. Any dog, large or small, can be trained to be a reading therapy dog as long as it has a peaceful personality. Most of the dogs and their owners are volunteers who have gone through a special training course.

1   How do dogs help children learn to read?
   A They make sure the child reads for the required amount of time.
   B They give the child something to love and care for.
   C They provide the child with a safe audience.
   D They protect the child from strangers.

2   What kinds of dogs make good therapy dogs?
   A gentle
   B intelligent
   C interesting
   D large

Passage 2

Charles Dickens, a famed British novelist known for his stories depicting the sufferings of the poor in Victorian England, grew up in a family that struggled with poverty throughout his childhood. Dickens, the son of a navy payroll clerk, was born in Portsmouth, England in 1812. Despite his father's steady employment, the family struggled financially. Mrs. Dickens, at one point, hoped to alleviate the family's financial difficulties by setting up a small school, but she was unsuccessful in this endeavor. When Dickens was just twelve years old, his father was imprisoned for debt. As a result, the young Dickens had to leave school and go to work to help support the family. He got a job at a factory that produced blacking, a type of shoe polish.

Fortunately, Dickens' father was soon able to pay off his debts, and Dickens returned to school. However, the family's financial difficulties continued, and he had to leave school again in order to work. This time he got a job as a helper at a newspaper office. Dickens was able to turn this situation to his advantage, and after a short while, began working as a reporter at the London law courts. Eventually, Dickens moved from working as a reporter to publishing a magazine, in which he serialized his first novel, *Oliver Twist*. This story of an orphan boy drew on Dickens' own childhood struggles to survive the challenges of poverty. The novel was popular in both England and the United States.

3   When Dickens was a boy he
    A was put in prison.
    B worked in a factory.
    C planned to join the navy.
    D had a job polishing shoes.

4   As a young man Dickens
    A studied law.
    B started his own school.
    C paid off his father's debts.
    D was employed at a newspaper office.

5   The story of *Oliver Twist* was inspired by
    A an orphanage in Dickens's neighborhood.
    B stories Dickens's father told him.
    C Dickens's experiences as a boy.
    D a childhood friend of Dickens.

STRATEGY REVIEW

An answer sheet can be found on page 285. You may find it useful to make copies and use it for the Strategy Reviews. Alternatively, you can write your answers directly on the book pages. (Answers are on page 230.)

Passage 1

Questions **1–13** are based on Reading Passage 1 below.

The Tipi: Shelter of the Great Plains

Prior to the arrival of masses of European settlers in the latter half of the nineteenth century, bison roamed the Great Plains of North America. It is estimated that at one time their numbers reached sixty million or more. Several of the native tribes living in that part of the world depended on these animals for their living. Most importantly, the bison were a major source of food, but they had other uses beyond that. Their hides provided material for shelter, clothing, and storage containers, while their bones and horns were fashioned into cups, cooking utensils, and many other useful items.

Since bison roamed the plains, the people who depended on them had to roam, too. Some lived a mostly nomadic life, following the movement of the bison herds for much of the year. Others were semi-nomadic, living mainly in villages where they raised crops, and following the bison only at certain times.

Mobility is a primary concern for nomadic peoples. The tribes of the Great Plains needed a type of shelter that could be easily packed up and moved from place to place. This was the tipi, a large conical tent made of hides stretched over long wooden poles. The word *tipi* comes to us from the language of the Lakota people, one of the groups that inhabited the Great Plains. It means "they dwell."

Erecting a tipi and taking it down again when the group moved on was generally the responsibility of women. It took two women working together about one hour to put a tipi up. The first step was to erect three or four sturdy poles to form the basis of the framework on which the tipi hides would be stretched. These were lashed together at the top, then a number of other poles were leaned against them and also tied together at the top. A rope hung down from the top of the poles. This could be pegged to the ground inside the tipi to prevent the wind from carrying the structure away.

Next, a long pole was used to lift the cover into position. The cover was made of bison hides sewn together with sinew. The edges of the cover were pinned together along a seam, and the bottom was pegged to the ground. A door flap was pinned over the entrance, and an opening was left at the top to serve as a smoke hole. The tipi was now ready for the family plus all their belongings—including bedding, clothing, cooking utensils, and weapons—to move in.

A typical tipi was about fifteen feet in diameter. It provided protection from the elements and was warm in the winter and cool in the summer. On particularly hot days, the sides could be rolled up a few feet to allow for ventilation. In cold or rainy weather, a lining could be added for extra protection.

Sometimes the outside of a tipi was decorated, and the different tribes had different traditions regarding this. In general, a tipi was viewed as a sacred place and the decorations reflected this. According to belief, the images came to the artists in dreams, a gift from the spirit world. Designs and symbols represented human experiences, usually war and hunting events, as well as things from the natural world such as animals and celestial bodies, and the ancestors and spirits of the spirit world. Bison horns, hair, and tails; horse hair; and bear claws were some of the items incorporated into tipi decorations.

Before the arrival of the horse, the tribes of the Great Plains used dogs to help carry their belongings from place to place. These always included tipi poles, which were not easily replaceable on the treeless plains. The dogs pulled their loads on a type of sled called a travois. This consisted of two poles with a net or basket tied between them to hold the load. The size of the load that could be dragged by a dog was limited by the animal's relatively small size, so tipi poles were much shorter than they came to be later after the advent of the horse.

By the beginning of the eighteenth century, horses were already spreading throughout the Great Plains, and well before the end of the century they had become the common form of transportation there. This had many repercussions on the lives of the peoples of the Great Plains. One of these was that tipis grew in size. A dog could drag poles not more than six feet long, but a horse could carry longer poles and larger tipi covers. Tipis were now as much as fifteen feet tall.

In addition to larger tipis, horses made it possible for people to carry around more possessions in general. Together with guns, horses also made it easier to follow herds and kill more bison. This was just the beginning of many changes that were to come. Now, the nomadic way of life that had the tipi at its center is a thing of the past.

Questions 1–4

Choose **FOUR** *letters, using the list of words,* **A–H,** *below.*

Write the correct letters in boxes 1–4 on your answer sheet.

Which **FOUR** of the following facts about Native Americans of the Great Plains are mentioned in the text?

A	They hunted with bows and arrows.
B	They were sometimes farmers.
C	They traveled around following animal herds.
D	They decorated their clothing with beads.
E	They relied on bison as their primary food.
F	They gathered wild greens and berries.
G	They located their villages next to rivers.
H	They stored items in containers made of bison skins.

1 ....

2 ....

3 ....

4 ....

Questions 5–8

Label the diagram below.

*Choose **NO MORE THAN TWO WORDS** from the passage for each answer.*

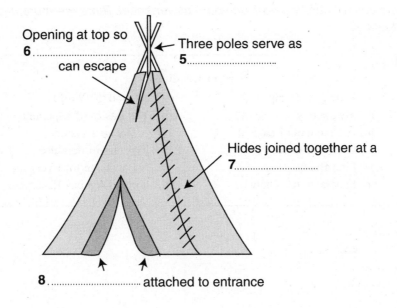

Opening at top so
6 ....
can escape

Three poles serve as
5 ....

Hides joined together at a
7 ....

8 .... attached to entrance

Questions 9–13

Complete the table below.

*Choose **NO MORE THAN THREE WORDS** from the passage for each answer.*

Cause	Effect
There were no trees on the plains.	Tipi poles were not **9** ....
Dogs are small animals and can pull small loads.	Tipi poles were only **10** ....
Horses are large animals and can carry large loads.	Tipi poles became **11**................. People could travel with more **12** ....
Horses can travel far.	People could **13** .... more bison.

Passage 2

Questions **14–27** are based on Reading Passage 2 below.

Questions 14–21

Reading Passage 2 has eight paragraphs, **A–H**. Choose the correct heading for each paragraph from the following list. Write the correct number, **i–xii**, on your answer sheet. There are more headings than sections so you will not use them all.

List of Headings

i	Esperanto Today	vii	Around the World
ii	Vocabulary	viii	The Basics of Esperanto
iii	A Dream not Reached	ix	A Doctor's Vision
iv	Grammar Rules	x	Esperanto Literature
v	First Books	xi	A Language for Everyone
vi	Esperanto in Schools	xii	For and Against Esperanto

14   Paragraph A ....
15   Paragraph B ....
16   Paragraph C ....
17   Paragraph D ....
18   Paragraph E ....
19   Paragraph F ....
20   Paragraph G ....
21   Paragraph H ....

Esperanto

A

Dr. Zamenhof had a dream. He imagined a world where people from different countries and ethnic backgrounds got along with one another. He believed that to create understanding and goodwill among people of diverse backgrounds a common language would be necessary, so he invented one. Today it is known as Esperanto.

B

Dr. Ludwig Lazarus Zamenhof was a Polish ophthalmologist who was born in 1859. He worked on developing his invented language during the 1870s and 1880s. His goal was to have a language that would be accessible to everyone. His first idea was to revive the ancient European languages, Latin and Greek. He quickly realized, however, that these are not simple languages to learn. He also discarded the possibility of focusing on any of the major modern European languages—Russian, German, French, English—for similar reasons. He wanted a language that would be accessible to everyone—simple to learn and not tied to any particular culture or political system.

C

In 1887, Dr. Zamenhof published the first textbook about his new language, *Unua Libro* (First Book). Although Dr. Zamenhof himself had dubbed the language "Lingvo Internacia" (International Language), it came to be known as Esperanto. This was the pseudonym under which he wrote the book and it means "one who hopes." Around this same time, Dr. Zamenhof also published *Fundamenta Gramatiko* (Fundamental Grammar), which explained the sixteen basic grammar rules of the language.

D

Dr. Zamenhof based Esperanto on European languages. The vocabulary is largely rooted in Latin, although English, German, Polish, and Russian roots are also present. The grammar has been described as resembling that of Slavic languages. Dr. Zamenhof focused on keeping the rules of the language uncomplicated. Esperanto has a regular and phonetic spelling system that can be learned very quickly. The grammar is simple and regular with none of the many exceptions to rules that plague learners of other languages. The vocabulary is a system of roots and affixes that can be combined to create new words. Esperanto speakers claim that the basic rules of the language can be learned in just a few hours.

E

In the years immediately following the publication of Dr. Zamenhof's books, interest in Esperanto spread, first through eastern Europe, then to western Europe and the Americas, and eventually to countries all around the world. The first Esperanto World Congress was held in France in 1905, with close to seven hundred people representing twenty different nationalities present. The practice of holding an annual World Congress continues to this day.

F

Esperanto had adherents and detractors both. The Russian writer, Tolstoy, for example, was a huge supporter and learned the language quickly. In general, interest was wide enough to lead to the translation of important literary works into the language as well as the writing of original Esperanto literature. On the other hand, the Russian tsar put a ban on all Esperanto materials, learning the language was discouraged through much of central Europe, and in 1920 the French government banned it from schools. The language that had been developed to be a means of achieving world peace was instead treated with suspicion and fear in many places.

G

Interest in Esperanto waned for a while and was then revived for a brief time during the 1970s. It is currently experiencing another revival through the spread of the Internet. Today it is estimated that between one and two million people have at least some working knowledge of the language. A very small number, around one thousand, speak it as their native tongue. These are generally people who grew up in households where the parents were enthusiastic supporters of Esperanto and decided to make it the language spoken in their home. Books and music continue to be written in the language, and there has even been a movie in Esperanto—*Incubus*, a horror film from 1965 starring William Shatner. Associations of Esperanto speakers exist around the world. Through them, speakers can find each other locally or meet other Esperanto speakers when traveling abroad. Magazines in the language are available and in some places radio and TV stations broadcast Esperanto programs.

H

There have been other invented languages over the years, but none has reached the level of popularity or longevity of Esperanto. Even so, Esperanto has not achieved the goal that Dr. Zamenhof envisioned for it— that of being a means of common understanding among people from all over the world. It remains, instead, a focus of specialized interest among a relatively small number of people.

Questions 22–27

Do the following statements agree with the information given in the passage? In boxes 22–27 on your Answer Sheet write

TRUE   *if the statement agrees with the information in the passage*
FALSE   *if the statement contradicts the information in the passage*
NOT GIVEN *if there is no information about this in the passage*

22   Dr. Zamenhof was trained as an eye doctor.
23   According to Dr. Zamenhof, many European languages were not easy to learn.
24   Dr. Zamenhof took linguistics courses at a Polish university.
25   Dr. Zamenhof named his invented language Esperanto.
26   Many Esperanto words come from Latin roots.
27   Esperanto grammar is similar to that of several western European languages.

Passage 3

Questions **28–40** are based on Reading Passage 3 below.

The Voyages of Christopher Columbus

Christopher Columbus was not alone in his belief that the world was round, but he may have been unique in his determination to open up trade routes to Asia by sailing west. In the 1400s, overland travel from Europe to the gold, silk, and spices of the East was extremely difficult. Political strife, bandits, and harsh desert conditions made most routes practically impassable. Thus arose the motivation of trying to reach that part of the world by sea.

Christopher Columbus, a native of Genoa, Italy, worked for a while as a weaver, his father's trade. He then became a seaman and sailed the Mediterranean. He eventually ended up in Lisbon, Portugal, where his brother worked as a mapmaker, and around 1479, he married a native of that city. Columbus traveled for a time among the Portuguese islands that lay off the west coast of Africa, working as a sugar purchaser. This put him in contact with seamen who talked of islands that they believed lay even further west. Columbus started to dream about sailing west to get to Asia. He tried for years to find financial backing for this journey. At last, the king and queen of Spain agreed to support him in his venture, and he set sail on his first voyage in August of 1492.

In early October, Columbus and his crew landed on a small island in the Bahamas, which Columbus named San Salvador. They explored several more islands in the area, then landed in Cuba on October 28. From there they went on to the island of Hispaniola, landing there in early December. When Columbus returned to Spain in March 1493, he did not bring with him silks and spices from the East. He couldn't report with certainty, either, that he had even found a route to that part of the world, although he believed the islands he had visited might have been off the coast of China or Japan. In any case, he had found new land. The king and queen of Spain rewarded him by appointing him governor general of all the new lands he had found or would find, and he was named Admiral of the Ocean Sea.

Although Columbus had returned from his first trip without the promised cargo of silks and spices, a second voyage was funded. This time he sailed with a fleet of seventeen ships carrying more than one thousand people, who were to establish a Spanish colony. To this end, the ships also carried sheep, pigs, and cattle, the first to be brought to the New World. They left Europe in October of 1493 and landed on the island of Dominica in November. They stayed there briefly, and then went on to visit other islands of the Lesser Antilles before finally landing on Hispaniola. There, Columbus established a colony and served as governor. He also explored other islands of the area, including a return to Cuba and his first visit to Jamaica. He returned to Spain in 1496.

The riches of the East still had not materialized. Nevertheless, in 1498 the king and queen of Spain allowed a third voyage to the New World so that Columbus could carry supplies to the colony on Hispaniola and continue to search for a trade route to the East. This was a trip that was to end in disaster for the explorer. On the last day of July, Columbus and his crew sighted the island of Trinidad for the first time and then spent a couple of weeks exploring the Gulf of Paria, which lies between Trinidad and the coast of South America. They found the mouth of the mighty Orinoco River and realized that this land had to be a continent, not an island. However, they didn't go ashore, but returned to the colony on Hispaniola toward the end of August.

Things were not going well in the colony. The colonists were unruly and, in an attempt to establish order, Columbus had several of them hanged. Needless to say, he was not a popular governor. The Spanish sovereigns had gotten wind of the unrest in the colony and sent Francisco de Bobadilla as their representative to straighten things out. He ended up arresting Columbus and sending him back to Spain in chains. Once back in Spain, Columbus was soon released, but he lost his reputation and several of his honors.

In 1502, Columbus set off on his fourth and final voyage in search of a trade route to the East. During this trip, he explored the coast of Central America for the first time, where he and his crew encountered several native cultures, including some Mayans, and exchanged goods with them. After exploring the area, Columbus and his crew headed back to the colony on Hispaniola. Traveling in ships that had been damaged by storms and termites, they only made it as far as Jamaica before the ships fell apart. There they were forced to stay until they were finally rescued in June of 1504. Columbus returned to Spain never to explore the New World again. He died in 1506.

The history that ensued as a result of Columbus's exploration of the New World has been interpreted from various viewpoints. To some, it meant the introduction of civilization to the New World. Others see it as the beginning of centuries of economic exploitation and oppression. From any viewpoint, however, it cannot be denied that Columbus's travels changed the world.

Questions 28–32

*Complete the summary using the list of words, **A–J**, below.*

A	funds
B	Lisbon
C	buy sugar
D	sailor
E	mapmaker
F	Genoa
G	publicity
H	riches
I	politics
J	find spices

- Fifteenth-century Europeans wanted to travel to Asia because of the **28** .... there.
- Columbus was born in **29** ....
- After he worked in his father's business, Columbus became a **30** ....
- Columbus traveled to Portuguese islands to **31** ....
- The king and queen of Spain gave Columbus **32** .... for his trip.

Questions 33–40

Classify the following events as occurring during Columbus's

    A first voyage
    B second voyage
    C third voyage
    D fourth voyage

33 European domestic animals were transported to the Americas for the first time. ....

34 The crew suffered a shipwreck. ....

35 Columbus's explorations earned him a special title. ....

36 Columbus executed several men. ....

37 The crew saw South America for the first time. ....

38 Columbus discovered Jamaica. ....

39 Columbus traded with Mayans. ....

40 Columbus was imprisoned. ....

IELTS WRITING MODULE

OVERVIEW

In this chapter, you will learn and practice specific strategies based on the two different writing tasks. These strategies will introduce you to the types of topics you will have to address in the writing section. You will learn how to plan, write, and revise your responses to both Task 1 and Task 2. You will review grammar, spelling, and punctuation rules that you will need to know when you write your Task 1 and Task 2 responses. You will also write complete essays in response to sample Task 1 and Task 2 topics.

TASK ONE

GENERAL STRATEGIES

Recognize the Parts of a Graphic
Use the Title

SPECIFIC STRATEGIES

OPENING STATEMENT

Summarize the Information
Describe the Graphic Using Time
Describe the Graphic Using Location
Describe a Process Diagram

DESCRIBING DATA

Ask *Wh-* Questions
Show the Steps in a Process

ANALYZING DATA

Compare and Contrast Data
Summarize Similarities and Differences
Describe Changes and Trends
State Facts

CONCLUSION

State the Purpose

WRITING MODULE

GRAMMAR

Prepositions of Time
Prepositions of Amount
Comparisons
Plurals

Articles
Subject–Verb Agreement
Verb Tenses

SPELLING

CHECK AND REVISE

STRATEGY REVIEW

TASK TWO

SPECIFIC STRATEGIES

INTRODUCTION

Restate the Task
Give Your Opinion
Write a Thesis Statement

BODY

Expand Your Thesis Statement
Introduce Details

CONCLUSION

Summarize Your Opinion

GRAMMAR

Gerunds and Infinitives
Modals
Active and Passive Voice
Relative Pronouns—Subject

Relative Pronouns—Object
Real Future Conditionals
Unreal Conditionals

PUNCTUATION

Apostrophes

CHECK AND REVISE

STRATEGY REVIEW

Plan Your Essay
Write Your Essay
Revise Your Essay

Writing Tip

Pay attention to time when you write your responses to the writing tasks. You will have sixty minutes to complete the writing part of the test. You should allow twenty minutes to plan, write, and revise your response to Task 1. You should allow forty minutes to plan, write, and revise your response to Task 2. When you write your responses to the sample topics in this section, divide your time as follows:

Task 1

Part	Number of Words	Planning and Writing Time
Opening statement	15–20	2–3 minutes
Description of details	25–30	4–5 minutes
Description of trends and features	100–120	12–14 minutes

Task 2

Part	Number of Words	Planning and Writing Time
Introduction	25–40	10 minutes
Body	170–200	20 minutes
Conclusion	25–40	5 minutes +5 minutes to review

TASK 1

SAMPLE GRAPHICS

In Task 1, you will see a graphic. A graphic is a drawing. It can be a chart, graph, table, or diagram.

PIE CHART

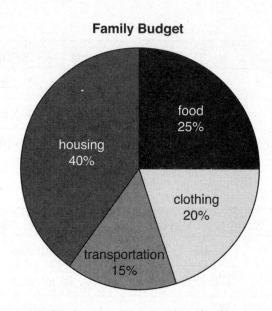

Family Budget

food 25%
housing 40%
clothing 20%
transportation 15%

BAR GRAPH

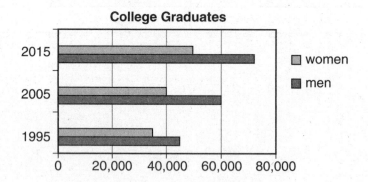

College Graduates

women
men

TABLE

New Cars, 2013

Car Model	Miles per Gallon	Base Price
XT3	40	$32,000
AZ9	32	$25,000
RX34	28	$29,000

DIAGRAM

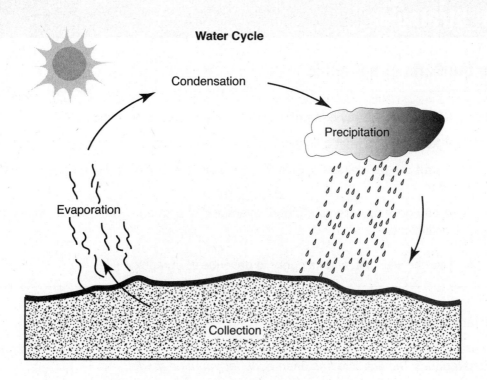

Water Cycle

You will have to do one of the following in Task 1:

- Describe and explain the graphic
- Describe a process
- Describe how something works
- Describe an object or
- Describe an event

You will **NOT** give your opinion about the information. You will write a description about what you see. You will have twenty minutes to write 150 words. Judge your time carefully.

General Strategies

Recognize the Parts of a Graphic

STRATEGY	Know the three key parts of a graphic so you can discuss them.
	A **key** tells you what a line, bar, or color represents.
	A **unit** can be measured. Examples of a unit are percentages, numbers, dates, days, or years.
	A **category** represents a group. Examples of a category are people, cities, regions, or institutions.
TIP	Use the key, unit, and category to describe the graphic.

PRACTICE 1 (answers on page 230)

Charts, graphs, and tables can be divided into units and categories. Look at the following graphics and write the units and categories. The first one has been done for you as a model.

1

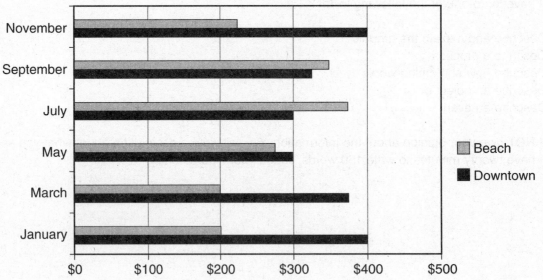

Average Price of a Hotel Room

Key: Beach, Downtown

Units: dollars

Categories: months January, March, May, July, September, November

Key: gray—Beach
black—Downtown

2

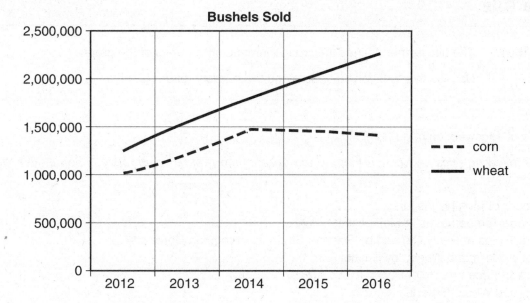

Bushels Sold

Units: ....

Categories: ....

Key: solid line ....

broken line ....

3

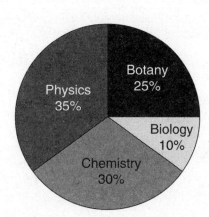

Units: ....

Categories: ....

4

	High	Low
London	73°	60°
Rome	89°	67°
Sydney	60°	45°
Tokyo	82°	66°
Bogota	62°	42°

Units: ....

Categories: ....

Use the Title

STRATEGY	The title further defines the categories and/or the units of the graph.
TIP	Use the title to help you understand the purpose of the graphic.

PRACTICE 2 (answers on page 230)

Read the following titles and match them to the appropriate graphic in Practice 1. Some titles will not be used.

A   Number of Monthly Visitors ....

B   Average Temperatures in Major Cities—July ....

C   Major Fields of Study Chosen by Science Students at Ingman University ....

D   Price of Corn and Wheat, by Bushel ....

E   Average Price of a Hotel Room in Two Areas ....

F   Corn and Wheat Exports ....

Opening Statement

Summarize the Information

> **STRATEGY** In the opening statement, you can describe the graphic by paraphrasing the first sentence of Task 1. The paraphrase will summarize the information in the graphic.
>
> A general description follows the phrase *gives information about....*. Change that general description to a specific description. Ask yourself "What?"
>
> **TIP** Do NOT repeat the Task exactly as written. Paraphrase or restate the task.

PRACTICE 3 (answers on page 230)

Look at the following charts, graphs, or tables and read the first sentence of the Task. Which statement provides a specific description of the task? Choose the description that most closely matches the chart and that adds more information about the phrase in italics. The first exercise is done for you as a model.

1   The graph below gives information about *computer sales* at the XYZ Company.

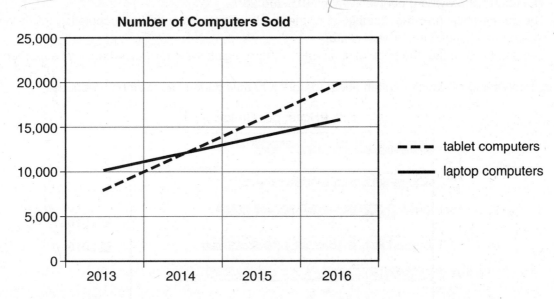

Number of Computers Sold

Ask yourself: What? What kind of computers? What about the number of computers sold? Are they increasing? Are they decreasing?

A The graph shows increases in sales of laptop and tablet computers over a four-year period.
B The graph gives information about computer sales at the XYZ Company.
C The graph shows computer sales over time.

Explanation

Statement **A** is a good opening statement. It provides a complete description and it gives specific information about what the graph shows about computer sales. Computer sales are increasing.

Statement **B** is not a good opening statement. It repeats the task exactly as written.

Statement **C** is incomplete. It includes important information, but it doesn't mention what the graph tells us about computer sales.

2 The charts below show *population distribution* in the northern region in two different years.

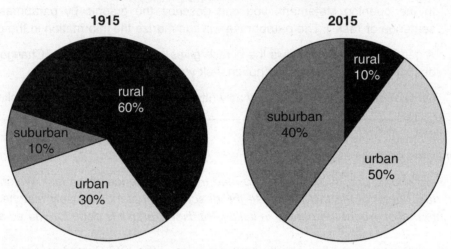

A The charts show where people lived in 1915 and 2015.

B The charts show how the distribution of the rural, urban, and suburban population in the northern region has changed in the past century.

C The charts show that the population of the northern region lives in rural, urban, and suburban areas.

3 The graph below gives information about the *price of milk* during two six-month periods.

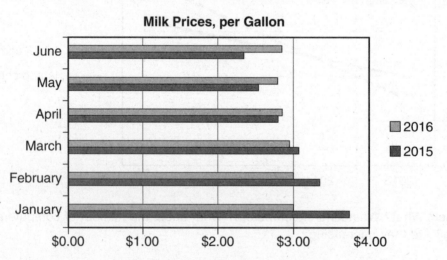

A The graph shows the price of milk at different times.

B The graph compares the average price of a gallon of milk in the first six months of 2015 and 2016.

C The graph shows how much people had to pay for milk recently.

4   The table below shows information about *drivers* and *traffic accidents*.

Drivers Causing Traffic Accidents, by Age

Age Group	15–20 yrs	20–30 yrs	30–40 yrs	40–50 yrs	50–60 yrs	65+ yrs
Percentage of Total Accidents	25%	18%	15%	10%	12%	20%

A The table shows the percentage of traffic accidents caused by drivers in different age groups.
B The table shows that people of different ages cause traffic accidents.
C The table shows how old different drivers are when they have accidents.

Describe the Graphic Using Time

> **STRATEGY**   In the opening statement, add time to the description of the graphic.
>
> You can describe the graphic by restating the first sentence of Task 1 and providing more detail. The detail can be time. Time can be hours, days, years, seasons, or historic periods.
>
> **TIP**   Not all graphs or charts use time. But if time is part of the chart, you should use it in your restatement.

PRACTICE 4 (answers on page 230)

Look at the following charts, graphs, or tables and read the first sentence of the Task. Write a description restating the sentence and adding details about time. The first exercise is done for you as a model.

1   The graph below shows information about museum attendance in two cities *during the year.*

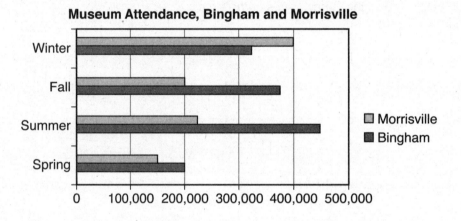

Museum Attendance, Bingham and Morrisville

Ask yourself: When? What are the seasons with the greatest attendance?

A The graph shows the number of people who went to museums last year.
B The graph shows how many people attended museums in each of the four seasons of the year in Bingham and Morrisville.
C The graph shows the changes in museum attendance in Bingham and Morrisville

Explanation

Statement **A** is too general. It does not mention the amount of time or the specific cities covered by the chart.
Statement **B** is a good opening statement. It mentions all the important details—what the chart is about, the places, and the periods of time covered.
Statement **C** is incomplete. It does not mention the time frame covered.

2 The graph below shows the numbers of students that enrolled in Brownsville College *in different years*.

Student Enrollment, Brownsville College

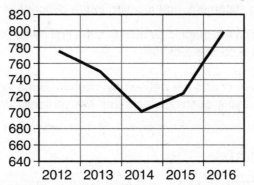

Statement: ....

3 The graph below shows the literacy rates *in the history* of two countries.

Literacy Rates

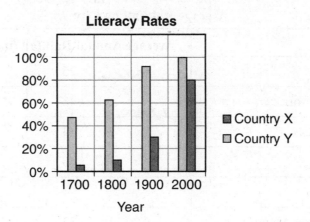

Statement: ....

4 The table below shows the recorded temperature in Oslo, Norway on the *afternoon of August 10*.

Oslo, August 10

Time	Temperature
1:00 PM	21°
2:00 PM	21°
3:00 PM	21°
4:00 PM	20°
5:00 PM	19°
6:00 PM	18°

Statement: ....

Describe the Graphic Using Location

STRATEGY	In the opening statement, add location to the description of the graphic.
	You can describe the graphic by restating the first sentence of Task 1 and providing more detail. The detail can be location.
TIP	Not all graphs or charts are defined by location. But if location is part of the chart, you should use it in your opening statement. Ask yourself: *"Where?"*

PRACTICE 5 (answers on page 231)

Look at the following charts, graphs, or tables and read the first sentence of the Task. Write a description restating the sentence and adding details about location. The first exercise is done for you as a model.

1   The table below shows information about rainfall *in several cities.*

Average Rainfall by City

City	Average Annual Rainfall (inches)
Paris	25
New York	48
Caracas	33
Tokyo	60
Cairo	1
Buenos Aires	33
Sydney	40
Washington, DC	40

Where: Cities in different countries; cities around the world
Ask yourself: Where?

A The table shows the average rainfall in several different cities around the world, in inches.
B The table shows how much rain falls on average in different places.
C The table shows the average rainfall in Paris.

Explanation

Statement **A** is a good opening statement. It is a complete description of the content of the table, including a specific description of the places.
Statement **B** is missing a specific description of the places shown on the table.
Statement **C** is incomplete. It only mentions one of the places covered on the table.

2 The graph below gives information about average housing prices throughout *the city of Plimsburgh*.

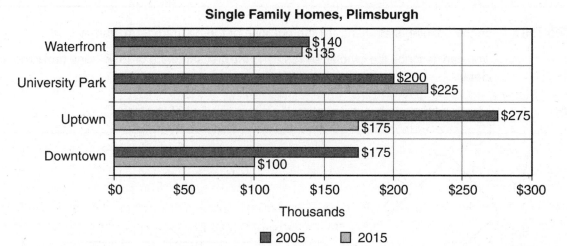

Single Family Homes, Plimsburgh

Statement: ....

3 The table below shows information about the *number of bird species* found in Plimsburgh Park.

Bird Species, Plimsburgh Park

Area	No. of Species Sighted
Lake and shore	17
Woods	26
Field	14
Parking lot	10

Statement: ....

4 The graph below gives information about the population of *several different countries*.

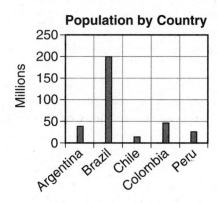

Population by Country

Statement: ....

WRITING MODULE

Describe a Process Diagram

STRATEGY   In the opening statement, tell the purpose of the diagram from start to finish.

You can describe the graphic by restating the first sentence of Task 1 and providing more detail.

TIP   Use synonyms to avoid repeating the exact wording of the task.

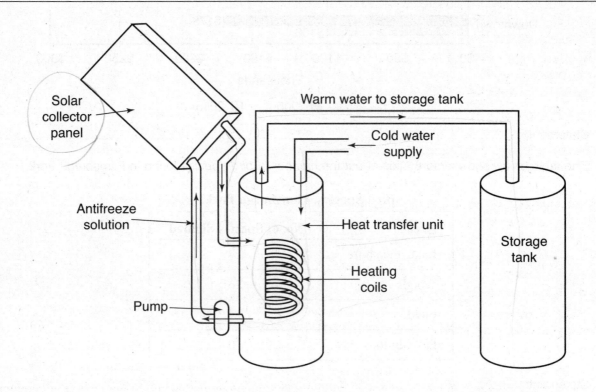

Solar collector panel

Warm water to storage tank

Cold water supply

Antifreeze solution

Heat transfer unit

Heating coils

Pump

Storage tank

Statement: The diagram shows a method for warming water by using an indirect solar water heating system.

PRACTICE 6 (answers on page 231)

Rewrite the opening statement replacing the underlined words with synonyms from the box. Not all the words will be used. This will help you practice finding synonyms when you paraphrase. The first one has been done for you as a model.

Synonyms	
grains	reducing
transportation	vehicles
making	steps
vegetables	removing
introduction	

The diagram below gives information about the <u>shipping</u> of live animals.

1   *The diagram gives information about the transportation of live animals.* ....

The diagram below shows the <u>stages</u> of the brick manufacturing process.

2   .... *steps* .... *e) removing* ....

The diagram below shows the process of <u>extracting</u> juice from sugar cane in order to make granulated sugar.

3   .... *reducing* ....

The diagram below shows the process of manufacturing <u>cars and trucks</u>.

4   .... *vehicles* ....

The diagram below shows the stages in the preparation of <u>fresh produce</u> for market.

5   .... *vegetables* ....

The diagram below shows the process of <u>producing</u> park benches from recycled plastic bottles.

6   .... *making* ....

Describing Data

Ask *Wh-* Questions

STRATEGY	To describe data in the graphics, ask yourself *wh-* questions.
TIP	Do NOT describe everything in the graphic. Describe only the data that relate to the task.

PRACTICE 7 (answers on page 231)

Look at each graphic and answer the questions that follow.
*Write **NO MORE THAN ONE WORD, NUMBER, OR DATE** for each answer. The first one has been done for you as a model.*

Graphic A

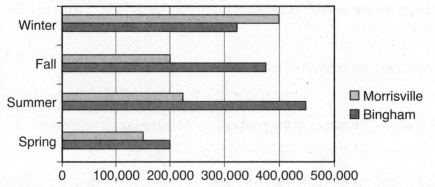

Museum Attendance, Bingham and Morrisville

1 When did museum attendance in Morrisville reach 400,000? *winter* ....

2 How many people attended museums in Bingham in the spring? ....

3 Where was summer museum attendance over 400,000? ....

4 When did Morrisville have its lowest museum attendance? ....

Graphic B

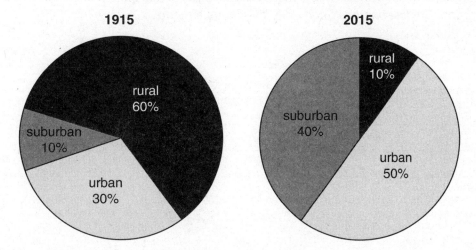

Population Distribution: 1915 and 2015

1915

rural 60%

suburban 10%

urban 30%

2015

rural 10%

suburban 40%

urban 50%

5   How much of the population lived in suburban areas in 1915?   ....

6   When did half the population live in urban areas?   ....

7   Where did only 10% of the population live in 2015?   .... areas

8   Where did over half the population live in 1915?   .... areas

Graphic C

Oslo, August 10

Time	Temperature
1:00 PM	21°
2:00 PM	21°
3:00 PM	21°
4:00 PM	20°
5:00 PM	19°
6:00 PM	18°

9   What was the temperature at 1:00 pm?   ....

10   When did the temperature first start to drop?   ....

11   When was the temperature 18°?   ....

PRACTICE 8 (answers on page 231)

Using your answers and the graphics from Practice 7, write three or four statements to describe the important data of each graph. The first one has been done for you as a model.

Graphic A

1 Museum attendance in Morrisville reached 400,000 in the winter.

2 ....

3 ....

4 ....

Graphic B

5 ....

6 ....

7 ....

8 ....

Graphic C

9 ....

10 ....

11 ....

Show the Steps in a Process

STRATEGY	In a process diagram, show each step in the process.
TIP	Use time words to show the process.

Common words and phrases to show time

first	as soon as	while	begin
next	when	from there	start
then	as	finally	in the beginning
after	at the same time	end	next to the last

PRACTICE 9 (answers on page 231)

Look at the diagram and put the statements in the correct order. Write numbers to show the order in which they should appear.

1   Indirect Solar Water Heating System

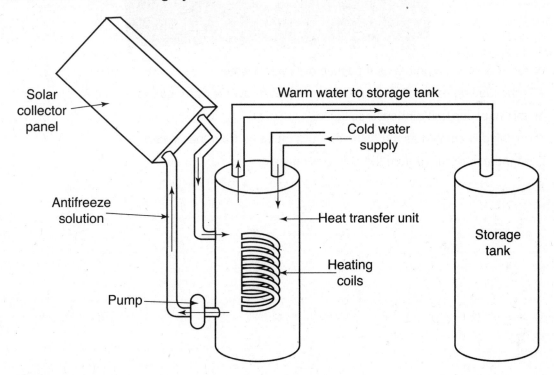

....2....   From there, it goes to the heat transfer unit.

....3....   At the same time, cold water also moves into the heat transfer unit, where it is heated by the warm antifreeze solution.

....1....   First, the antifreeze solution is heated as it moves through the solar collector panel.

....5....   It ends up in a storage tank, where it is held until needed.

....4....   After it is heated, the water moves out of the heat transfer unit.

2   Formation of a Hurricane

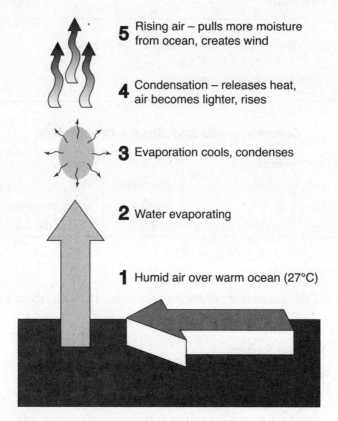

5 Rising air – pulls more moisture from ocean, creates wind

4 Condensation – releases heat, air becomes lighter, rises

3 Evaporation cools, condenses

2 Water evaporating

1 Humid air over warm ocean (27°C)

2....... Water begins to evaporate as it passes over warm water.

1....... A hurricane begins to form when humid air moves over a warm ocean.

4....... As this happens, the air becomes lighter.

5....... Then, wind is created as the rising air pulls moisture from the ocean.

3....... Then, heat is released from the condensing water.

3   Old Field Succession

1   Abandoned field

2   Pioneer species

3   Perennial species

WRITING MODULE

4 Tree saplings

5 Mature forest

..1..... When a field is abandoned, new plants begin to grow there.

..5..... Finally, the trees grow tall and the forest is mature.

..3..... Next, taller perennial flowers and shrubs start growing, and they shade out the annual plants.

..4..... Then, the perennials are shaded out by young trees.

..2..... First, annual plants appear in the sunny field.

Analyzing Data

Compare and Contrast Data

STRATEGY	Compare and contrast data to analyze it.
TIP	Talk about data that change a lot or data that do not change at all.

Common Words and Phrases to Compare/Contrast

Compare	Contrast
both	but
and	although
the same	however
like	on the other hand
similar	while

PRACTICE 10 (answers on page 231)

Look at these graphics. Compare and contrast the descriptions of data by combining the sentences. Use the words in parentheses. The first two have been done for you.

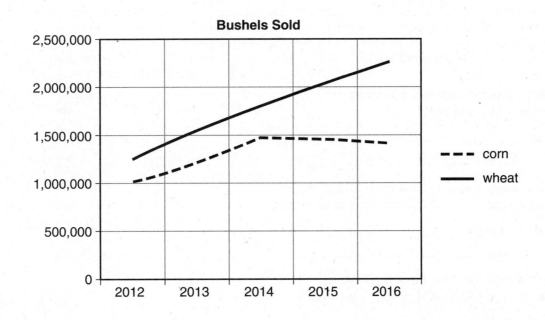

1   In 2016, over two million bushels of wheat were sold.
    Less than 1.5 million bushels of corn were sold.

    (but)

    In 2016, over two million bushels of wheat were sold, but less than 1.5 million bushels of corn were sold.

2   In 2014, just under 1.5 million bushels of corn were sold.
    In 2015, just under 1.5 million bushels of corn were sold.

    (both)

    In both 2014 and 2015, just under 1.5 million bushels of corn were sold.

3   Sales of wheat went up in 2016.
    Sales of corn went down.

    (although)

    ....

Average Rainfall by City

City	Average Annual Rainfall (inches)
Paris	25
New York	48
Caracas	33
Tokyo	60
Cairo	1
Buenos Aires	33
Sydney	40
Washington, DC	40

4   Tokyo's average rainfall is 60 inches.
    Cairo's is only one inch.

    (while)

    ....

5   The average rainfall in Caracas is 33 inches.
    The average rainfall in Buenos Aires is 33 inches.

    (and, the same)

    ....

6   The average rainfall in Paris is 25 inches.
    The average rainfall in New York is 48 inches.

    (however)

    ....

ge rainfall is 40 inches.
, the average rainfall is 40 inches.

data. Wr

k for   sentences about the graph using words from this chart.
the li

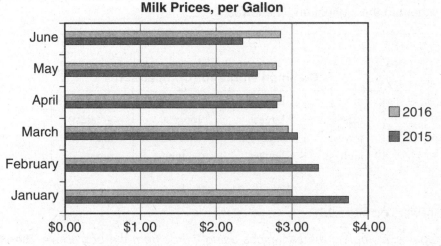

Milk Prices, per Gallon

n of milk cost almost $3.00 in April 2015.
lmost $3.00 in April 2016.

of milk cost almost $4.00 in January 2015.
$3.00 in January 2016.

milk cost almost $4.00 in January 2015.
more than $2.00 in June of the same year.

Summarize Similarities and Differences

STRATEGY   To analyze the data, you will compare the similarities and differences in the [
about the data that are the "most" and those that are the "least."

TIP   In a bar chart, look for the longest and the shortest bars. In a pie chart, loo
biggest and the smallest pieces of the pie. In a line graph, look for the points on
that are the highest and the lowest.

Common Words for Comparison

most	lowest	coldest	oldest
least	largest	longest	greatest
fewest	smallest	shortest	least
highest	hottest	youngest	more

PRACTICE 11 (answers on page 231)

*Look at these graphics. Complete the sentences using words from the box above. The first one
done for you.*

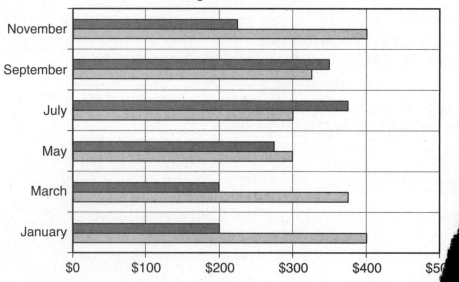

Average Price of a Hotel Room

The **1** <u>lowest</u> price for a hotel room at the beach is $200.

The **2** .... price for a hotel room at the beach is $375.

A hotel room downtown costs the **3** .... in January and November.

A hotel room downtown costs the **4** .... in May and July.

7

Major Fields of Study Chosen by Science Students

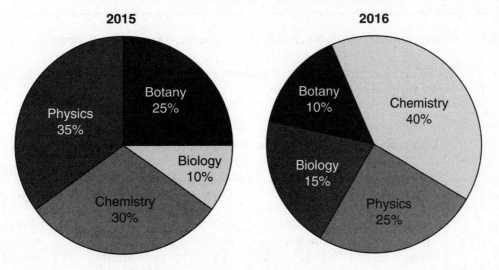

the **5** .... group of students chose to study physics.

he **6** .... group of students chose to study biology.

otany was the **7** .... popular subject.

emistry was the **8** .... popular subject.

8   A gallo
    It cost a
    ....

Drivers Causing Traffic Accidents, by Age

	15–20 yrs	20–30 yrs	30–40 yrs	40–50 yrs	50–60 yrs	65+ yrs
of Total Accidents	25%	18%	15%	10%	12%	20%

9   A gallon o
    It cost just
    ....

10 A gallon of ¡ age group shown is 65+ years.
    It cost a little
                    age group shown is 15–20 years.
    ....
                    0 year-old group caused the **11** .... accidents.
                    ገ year-old group caused the **12** .... accidents.

Describe Changes and Trends

STRATEGY	When you summarize the details of the graphic, think "up" and "down."
TIP	Think "up" and "down," but don't use these words. Use more formal words like those in the boxes below.

Common Words and Phrases to Describe Changes and Trends

Up		Down		Up/Down Modifiers	
Nouns	**Verbs**	**Nouns**	**Verbs**	**Adjectives**	**Adverbs**
increase	increase	decrease	decrease	sharp	sharply
grow	growth	decline	decline	slight	slightly
rise	rise	fall	fall	steady	steadily
jump	jump	drop	drop	rapid	rapidly
strength	strengthen	weakness	weaken	sudden	suddenly
peak	peak	dip	dip	gradual	gradually
			plummet	significant	significantly
				marginal	marginally

Sentence Patterns

There was a <u>steady</u> <u>increase</u> in sales.
              adjective   noun

Sales <u>increased</u> <u>steadily</u>.
        verb   adverb

PRACTICE 12 (answers on page 232)

Look at each graphic and read the statements that follow. Circle the letters of the statements that correctly describe the graphic. There will be **MORE** *than one correct answer for each graphic.*

The graph below shows the numbers of students that enrolled in Brownsville College in different years.

1

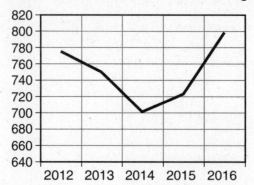

Student Enrollment, Brownsville College

A Student enrollment rose steadily between 2012 and 2016.
B In 2013, there was a sharp drop in student enrollment.
C Student enrollment increased rapidly between 2014 and 2016.
D Student enrollment jumped to 750 in 2013.

2

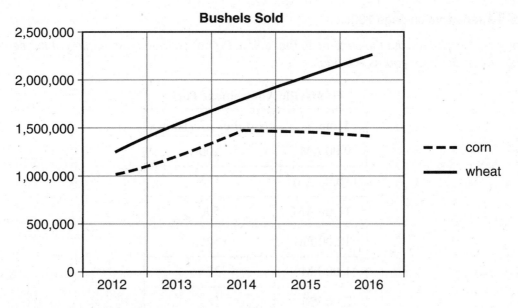

A Corn sales dropped slightly from 2014 to 2016.
B Corn sales declined steadily between 2012 and 2014.
C Wheat sales grew steadily between 2012 and 2016.
D Wheat sales plummeted in 2016.

3

Oslo, August 10

Time	Temperature
1:00 PM	21°
2:00 PM	21°
3:00 PM	21°
4:00 PM	20°
5:00 PM	19°
6:00 PM	18°

A The temperature rose sharply at 6:00 PM.
B There was a slight drop in temperature at 4:00 PM.
C The temperature dipped significantly at 2:00 PM.
D The temperature fell gradually between 1:00 PM and 6:00 PM.

PRACTICE 13 (answers on page 232)

Look at the graphic and rewrite the sentences that follow. Do not change the meaning of the sentences. The first one has been done for you as a model.

Huntsville Amusement Park

Time	Number of Visitors
9:00 AM	100
10:00 AM	175
11:00 AM	500
12:00 PM	525
1:00 PM	375
2:00 PM	185

1 The number of visitors rose slightly between 9:00 AM and 10:00 AM.
There was a *slight rise* in the number of visitors between 9:00 AM and 10:00 AM.

2 The number of visitors jumped suddenly between 10:00 AM and 11:00 AM.
There was a .... in the number of visitors between 10:00 AM and 11:00 AM.

3. There was a marginal increase in the number of visitors between 11:00 AM and 12:00 PM.
The number of visitors .... between 11:00 AM and 12:00 PM.

4 There was a significant drop in the number of visitors between 12:00 PM and 1:00 PM.
The number of visitors .... between 12:00 PM and 1:00 PM.

5 The number of visitors fell sharply between 1:00 PM and 2:00 PM.
There was a .... in the number of visitors between 1:00 PM and 2:00 PM.

WRITING MODULE

State Facts

STRATEGY	Show the examiner that you understand the data by showing the relationships among the data. Determine what happens at the same time, what happens before, and what happens after, what is more or bigger, what is less or smaller.
TIP	Do not give opinions about the graphic. Only give facts.

PRACTICE 14 (answers on page 232)

*Look at the following graphics and read the statements that follow. Write **F** next to the statements that describe facts about the graphic and **O** next to the statements that express opinions. The first one has been done for you.*

Bird Species, Plimsburgh Park

Area	No. of Species Sighted
Lake and shore	17
Woods	26
Field	14
Parking lot	10

1 ..F... The largest number of species is found in the woods

2 .... It seems there are more birds in the woods because it provides a better habitat.

3 .... The parking lot has the smallest number of species.

4 .... I think there are fewer birds in the parking lot because they are afraid of the cars.

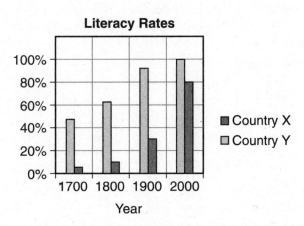

Literacy Rates

5 .... Literacy rates in Country X are lower than in Country Y in every year shown on the graph.

6 .... Literacy rates in both countries have risen in every century since 1700.

7 .... The lower literacy rates in Country X show they have fewer schools.

8 .... In 2000, the literacy rate in Country Y was 20 percent higher than the literacy rate in Country X.

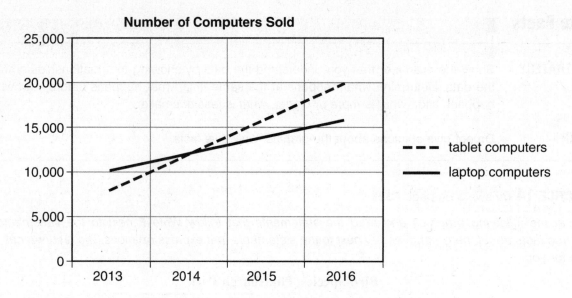

Number of Computers Sold

9 .... Sales of both laptop and tablet computers grew between 2013 and 2016.

10 .... I believe people bought more tablet computers in 2016 because they are cheaper then laptop computers.

11 .... In 2013, sales of laptop computers were higher than sales of tablet computers.

12 .... After 2014, sales of tablet computers grew faster than sales of laptop computers.

Conclusion

State the Purpose

> **STRATEGY** Conclude your Task 1 response with a brief overview that summarizes the trends and tells the purpose of the graph.
>
> **TIP** Ask yourself, "What does this information tell us?"

PRACTICE 15 (answers on page 232)

Look at the following graphics and the statements that follow each one. Choose the statement that best summarizes the trends and tells the purpose of each graphic. The first one is done for you as a model.

1

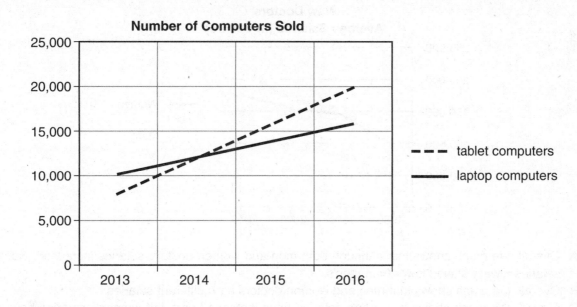

Number of Computers Sold

Ask yourself: What happened to tablet computers? What happened to tablet computers as compared to laptop computers?

A Overall, the graph shows that people buy both laptop and tablet computers.

B Overall, the graph shows that while people continue to buy both types of computers, sales of tablet computers have increased much more than sales of laptop computers.

C Overall, the graph shows that sales of tablet computers used to be lower than sales of laptop computers.

Explanation

Statement **A** is too general. It doesn't tell us anything about the purpose or meaning of the graph.

Statement **B** summarizes the trends of both computers' sales and tells us how they compare—tablet computer sales have increased more than laptop computer sales.

Statement **C** is too specific. It describes just one detail on the graph.

WRITING MODULE

2

Population Distribution: 1915 and 2015

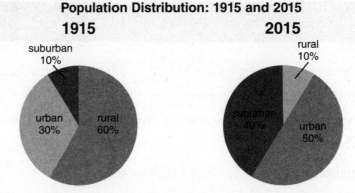

A Generally, these charts show that the population lived in different places in different years.
B Generally, the charts show that a significant number of people lived in rural areas a century ago.
C Generally, the charts show a significant shift of the population from mostly rural areas to mostly urban and suburban areas.

3

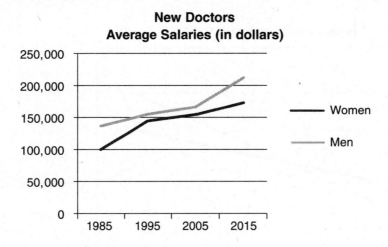

A Overall, the graph shows that although both men and women doctors' salaries increased, women's salaries always stayed lower than men's.
B Overall, the graph shows that men and women doctors earn different salaries.
C Overall, the graph shows that men's salaries have increased and that women's salaries have also increased.

4

Pineapple Cove Beach

Date	Aug 11	Aug 12	Aug 13	Aug 14	Aug 15	Aug 16
High temperature	23	26	28	22	30	27
Number of visitors	525	600	725	475	775	750

A In general, the table shows that temperatures at this time of year can vary significantly.
B In general, the table shows that the number of people visiting the beach changes from day to day.
C In general, the table shows that more people tend to visit the beach when temperatures are higher.

Grammar

This section is a review of grammar that is often a problem for IELTS test takers. This section also has models of answers for Task 1. See how the strategies you learned are shown in these model answers.

Prepositions of Time

Prepositions of time indicate when events happen. They may indicate an exact point in time when something occurs (*in, on, at*), a period of time over which an action takes place (*from…to, between, during*), or the starting or end times of an action (*since, until*).

The restaurant closes at 6:00. (Six o'clock is the exact moment when this action occurs.)

Prices rose until 2012. (Prices rose and then stopped rising in 2012.)

Prices rose between 2008 and 2012. (Prices began to rise in 2008 and continued to rise until 2012.)

The company has been selling this product since 2005. (The company began to sell the product in 2005 and is still selling it.)

Preposition	Use	Example
at	Hour Part of day	At 6:00 At noon; At night
on	Day Date Holiday	On Monday On June 10 On Valentine's Day
in	Month Year Season Part of day	In September In 2013 In the summer In the morning, in the afternoon, in the evening
from…to *between…and*	The start and end point of something	From January to March Between April and August
during	Throughout a period of time	During 2010.
since	The beginning point of something	Since Wednesday
until	Up to a certain time	Until 2:00

PRACTICE 1 (answers on page 232)

Study the graph and the model essay below. Complete the blanks with the prepositions from the box below. Some words may not be used. Some may be used more than once.

in	from	between	until	to	since

The graph below gives information about the numbers of annual visitors to the Marine Museum.

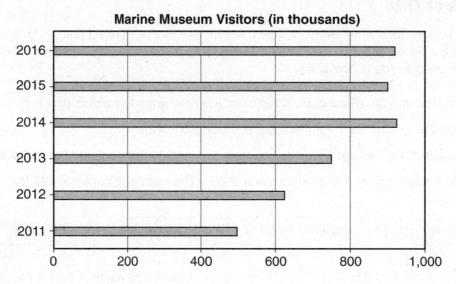

Marine Museum Visitors (in thousands)

Model Essay

The graph shows the number of people who visited the Marine Museum each year, **1** .... 2011 to 2016. The number of annual visitors increased steadily for several years and then started to level off.

2.............. 2011, there were 500,000 visitors to the museum. The following year, the number rose to a little over 600,000. The number of annual visitors continued to rise **3**.............. 2014, when it reached a little over 900,000.

In 2015, there was a change. **4**.............. this year, the number of visitors fell to exactly 900,000. The next year it rose slightly, but was still a little less than it had been in 2014.

5.............. 2011 and 2014, there were large annual increases in the numbers of annual visitors. The small decrease and increase **6**.............. 2015 and 2016 show a leveling off in the numbers of annual visitors to the Marine Museum.

Prepositions of Amount

We use verbs such as *rise, increase, go up, fall, decrease,* and *go down* to talk about changes in amounts on a chart or graph. We use the prepositions *from, to,* and *by* together with these verbs.

Preposition	Use	Example
from	The starting amount	Prices fell from $200.
to	The ending amount	The number rose to over a million.
by	The amount of the change	The cost increased by 25 percent.

PRACTICE 2 (answers on page 232)

Study the graph and model essay below. Complete the blanks with the prepositions from the chart on page 130.

The graph below gives information about population changes in Donner City and its suburbs.

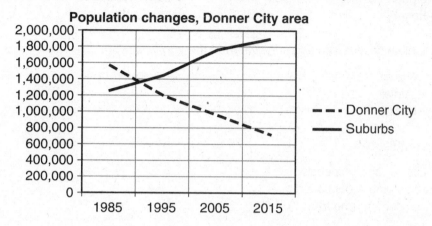

Population changes, Donner City area

Model Essay

This graph shows the changes in the size of the population of Donner City and of the surrounding suburban area over a thirty-year period of time, from 1985 to 2015.

In 1985, the population of Donner City was 1,600,000. At 1,200,000, the population in the suburbs was lower **1**............... 400,000. Over the next thirty years, the population of Donner City fell while the population of the suburbs rose. During that time, the Donner City population decreased **2**............... about 50 percent. In the meantime, the suburban population rose **3**............... almost 2,000,000.

Between 1985 and 1995, the population of Donner City fell **4**............... 1,600,000 **5**............... about 1,200,000. During the same period of time, the population of the suburbs rose **6**............... 1,200,000 **7**............... almost 1,600,000. Over the next ten years, the population in the city fell **8**............... about 200,000 while the suburban population continued to rise and approached 1,800,000.

Overall, this graph shows that the population decreased in the city just as steadily as it increased in the suburbs.

Comparisons

We can compare things in several ways.

More, fewer, less

More indicates a bigger amount.
Fewer and *less* indicate a smaller amount.

      Fewer is used with plural nouns.
      Less is used with non-count nouns.

More people visited the museum in 2010.

The company sold fewer cars last year.
The company made less money last year.

Comparative Adjectives

We form a comparative adjective two ways: (1) by adding *-er* to the end of the adjective or (2) by using the word *more* in front of it.

Add -er to one-syllable adjectives. For words that follow the consonant–vowel–consonant spelling pattern, double the last consonant when adding the -er ending.

small → smaller		high → higher
big → bigger	BUT	cheap → cheaper
hot → hotter		cold → colder

Add -er to two-syllable adjectives ending in -y. Change the y to i.

busy → busier
rainy → rainier
easy → easier

Use *more* for longer adjectives.

expensive → more expensive
populated → more populated
important → more important

PRACTICE 3 (answers on page 232)

Study the table and the model essay below. Complete the blanks with comparative words from the box below. Some words may not be used. Some may be used more than once.

more	higher	fewer	cheaper
less	lower	busier	

The table below gives information about the average number of servings of ice cream sold each day in two different years.

Springer's Café Ice Cream Sales

	April	May	June	July	August	September
2015	15	25	50	55	60	25
2016	25	35	65	80	75	30

The table shows the average number of ice cream servings sold daily for the months of April through September during the years 2015–2016.

Model Essay

The café was **1**............... in 2016 than in 2015. Looking month by month, the average number of servings sold was **2**............... in 2016. For example, in April of 2015, there was an average of 15 servings sold daily, while in April of 2016 the average was 25. In each of the months shown, the average number of servings sold daily is **3**............... for 2015 than it is for the corresponding months in 2016.

In 2015, **4**............... servings were sold in August than in any other month. In 2016, **5**............... servings were sold in July than in any other month. In both years, **6**............... servings were sold in April than in any other month.

Overall the table shows **7**............... sales in 2016 than in 2015. It also shows a significantly **8**............... number of sales in June, July, and August than in the other months.

Plurals

Count nouns are either singular or plural. A singular noun refers to one thing. A plural noun refers to more than one thing.

Most nouns form the plural by adding –*s*:

> year → years
> product → products
> price → prices

Nouns that end in -*s, -z, -ch,* and -*sh* form the plural by adding -*es*:

> watch → watches
> crash → crashes

Nouns that end in a consonant + *y* have a spelling change—change the *y* to *ie*, then add -*s*:

> family → families
> dictionary → dictionaries

Some plural forms are irregular, for example:

> man → men
> woman → women
> person → people
> child → children

PRACTICE 4 (answers on page 232)

Study the graph and the model essay below. Complete the blanks with words from the box below, changing them to the plural form where necessary. All the words will be used more than once.

man	doctor	year
woman	salary	rate

The graph below gives information about new doctors' salaries.

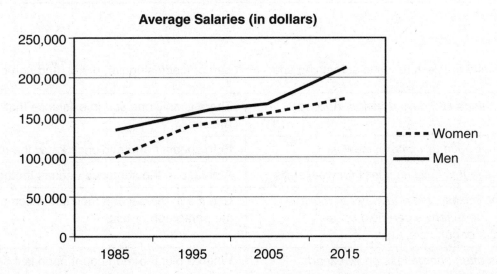

Average Salaries (in dollars)

Model Essay

The chart compares the average **1**............... of men and women who have just become **2**............... over a period of thirty **3**..............., from 1985 to 2015. Women's salaries remained lower than men's throughout the entire period.

In 1985, the average **4**............... of a **5**............... just starting out her career as a **6**............... was $100,000. During that same year, the average salary of a **7**............... in the same situation was a little under $150,000. During the next ten **8**..............., women's salaries increased at a faster **9**............... than men's. In 1995, a woman earned an average salary of just under $150,000 while a man earned a little over that same amount.

The **10**............... of both men and **11**............... continued to increase at a similar rate over the next ten years. Then, between 2005 and 2015, the salaries of **12**............... started increasing at a faster **13**............... . By 2015, **14**............... were earning over $200,000 a year on average, while **15**............... were earning a good deal less than that.

Articles

All singular nouns must be preceded by a determiner. A determiner can be an article: *a/an* or *the*.

A/an

A/an are indefinite articles. They do not refer to any definite or specific item. *A* is used with nouns that begin with consonants. *An* is used with nouns that begin with vowels.

To make concrete, you need a machine to mix sand and water.	This sentence does not refer to any specific machine. It could be any concrete-mixing machine.
Eating an apple every day will improve your health.	You do not need to eat a particular apple to improve your health. Any apple will do.

The

The is a definite article. It refers to something specific. It can precede singular, plural, and non-count nouns.

The sun shines 360 days a year in Arizona.	There is only one *sun* in existence that shines in Arizona.
The teacher gave us some homework.	Both speaker and audience know the reference.
The rooms <u>in this hotel</u> cost less on weekends.	A phrase in the sentence defines the noun.
A machine mixes sand and water to make concrete. The machine can hold up to 250 gallons of concrete.	Use *the* in the second mention of something in the paragraph or text.
(A) Hotels often charge less on weekends. *(B) Rain falls less frequently over desert areas.*	When a plural or non-count noun is indefinite, an article is not required.

PRACTICE 5 (answers on page 232)

Study the diagram and the excerpt from a model essay below. Complete the blanks with a, an, the, or ∅ (to indicate no article is needed). Remember, the first mention of an object in the text is considered indefinite.

The diagram below shows the steps and equipment involved in recycling paper.

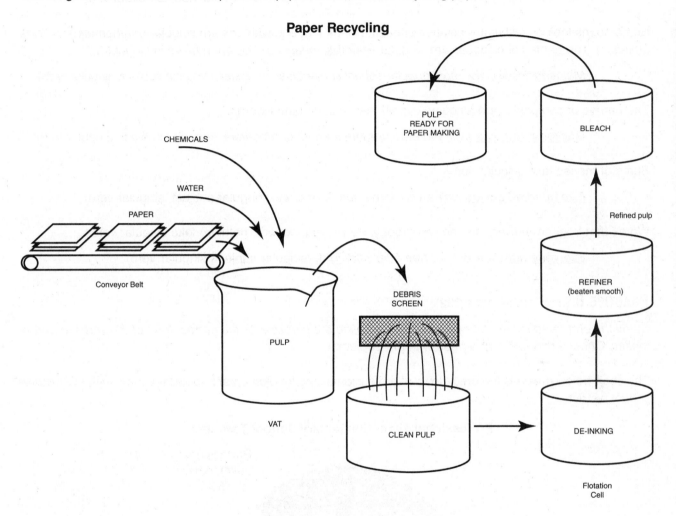

Paper Recycling

Model Essay

1............... bales of **2**............... paper move up **3**............... conveyer belt. They enter **4**............... vat. There,

5............... paper is mixed with **6**............... water and **7**............... chemicals to form **8**............... pulp. Next,

9............... pulp goes through **10**............... screen. **11**............... screen removes debris from **12**............... pulp.

Subject–Verb Agreement

The main verb must agree with the subject of the sentence or clause. If the subject is singular, the verb is singular. If the subject is plural, the verb is plural.

> The *graph* *shows* the cost of different clothing items. (singular subject, singular verb)
> The *graphs* *show* the cost of different clothing items. (plural subject, plural verb)

Non-count nouns always take a singular verb.

> _Milk costs_ more in the winter. (non-count noun, singular verb)

Know the subject of your sentence. Sometimes there might be a phrase or clause between the subject and the verb.

> The _computers_ sold by that company _are_ more expensive. (plural subject, plural verb)

Some nouns look plural but are actually singular. Nouns that end with -_ics_ are singular (_mathematics, politics, athletics_). The names of diseases are singular (_mumps, measles_). The noun _news_ is singular.

> _Mathematics was_ the most popular school subject last semester. (singular subject, singular verb)

The names of companies are singular, even if they include plural words.

> _Intelligent Systems sells_ more computers than its competitors. (singular subject, singular verb)

Sums of money take singular verbs.

> _Five hundred dollars isn't_ a very large sum of money. (singular subject, singular verb)

Words that begin with _every_ and _no_ (everybody, everything, nobody, nothing) take singular verbs.

> _Everyone rides_ the bus for free after midnight. (singular subject, singular verb)

PRACTICE 6 (answers on page 232)

Study the chart and the model essay below. Complete the blanks with the correct form of the verbs in parentheses. Choose the verb that agrees with the subject.

The chart below presents the breakdown of professional time for elementary school teachers in the Wardsville school district.

Professional Time: Elementary School Teachers

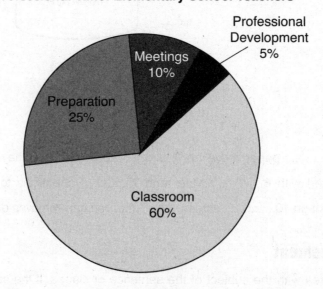

Model Essay

The chart **1**.............. (show/shows) how elementary school teachers in the Wardsville school district **2**.............. (spend/spends) their professional time. Teachers working in elementary school **3**.............. (spend/spends) the largest portion of their time in the classroom. Professional development activities, on the other hand, **4**.............. (take/takes) up the least amount of teachers' time.

An elementary school teacher in Wardsville **5**.............. (spend/spends) a little over half of his or her professional time—60 percent of it—in the classroom. The rest of the time **6**.............. (are/is) taken up with activities such as preparation, meetings, and professional development activities. Preparation **7**.............. (take/takes) up one-fourth of a teacher's professional time. Meetings **8**.............. (take/takes) up 10 percent of it. Professional development activities **9**.............. (account/accounts) for just 5 percent of a teacher's time.

Overall, the chart **10**.............. (show/shows) that teachers **11**.............. (spend/spends) a significant portion of their professional time outside of the classroom. Forty percent of their time—close to half of it—**12**.............. (are/is) spent in other types of activities.

Verb Tenses

You can use a few simple verb tenses to describe the graphics in Writing Task 1.

Use the **simple present tense** to refer to an action or state that is always true.

> The graph _shows_ information about consumer spending in the past decade.
> Houses _cost_ more in Paris than in Bogota.

Use the **present perfect tense** to refer to an action that started in the past and continues to the present.

> Prices _have increased_ more than fifty percent since 2005.
> The number of annual visitors _has fallen_ since they closed part of the museum.

Use the **simple past tense** to describe an action that was completed in the past.

> Prices _increased_ last year.
> Over one million people _visited_ the museum in 2009.

Use the **future tense** to describe an action that will take place in the future.

> Next month, prices _will rise_.
> In the next decade, more people _will leave_ the suburbs to live in the city.

WRITING MODULE

PRACTICE 7 (answers on page 232)

Study the charts and the model essay below. Complete the blanks with the correct form of the verb in parentheses.

The charts below show the allocation of funds in the town budget of Greensboro.

Town Budget for Greensboro

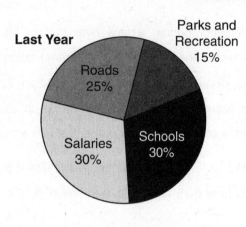

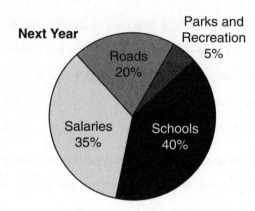

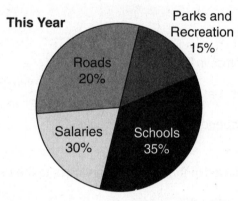

Model Essay

The charts compare the budget of the town of Greensboro in three different years. Last year, the town **1**............... (spend) an equal portion of its budget on schools and salaries. Thirty percent of the budget **2**............... (go) to each of those areas. Spending on roads **3**............... (take) up another 25 percent of the budget, while the smallest amount—15 percent—**4**............... (go) to parks and recreation.

This year, spending on schools **5**............... (increase) 5 percent since last year. Spending on schools **6**............... (remain) the same since last year, while spending on roads **7**............... (decrease) 5 percent.

Next year, the town **8**............... (spend) an even greater portion of its budget on schools—40 percent. Spending on salaries **9**............... (rise) to 35 percent. Spending on roads **10**............... (stay) the same, at 20 percent. Spending on parks and recreation **11**............... (drop) to 5 percent.

The town always **12**............... (spend) more on schools than it does on roads.

Spelling

This section presents some words that are often misspelled by IELTS test takers. This section also has a model essay for Task 1. See how the strategies you learned are shown in the model essay.

Study the following words and make sure you know how to spell them.

Commonly Misspelled Words

almost	chronological	doubled	literacy	reached
although	compared	dramatically	occur	receive
attendance	comparison	education	occurred	salary
before	countries	enough	percentage	several
children	difference	increased	population	similar
career	different	follow	price	temperature

Study the following task and model essay. Find and correct the misspelled words. (answers on page 233)

The graph below shows literacy rates through history in Country X and Country Y.

Summarize the information by selecting and reporting the main features, and make comparisons where relevant.

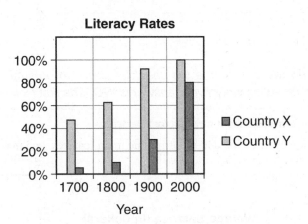

Literacy Rates

The graph gives information about litracy rates in two countrys over a period of sevral centuries, from 1700 until 2000. While the literacy rates in both countrys incresed in each century, the rates in Country Y remained higher than in Country X in every year shown.

In 1700, more than 40 percent of the popalation in Country Y was literate. In Country X, however, a much smaller percenage of the people could read. In fact, the litracy rate was amost zero. Allthough the number of people who could read grew in both contrys over the next centuries, the litrcy rate in Country X remained low. By 1900 only about 30 percent of the people in that country could read, while the litrcy rate in Country Y in the same year was well over 80 percent.

By 2000, the last year shown on the graph, 100 percent of the people in Country Y could read. The litrcy rate in Country X had reeched 80 percent, but this was still low as compard with Country Y.

Check and Revise

(answers on page 233)

As you write your response, ask yourself these questions.

OPENING STATEMENT
- ❑ Did I paraphrase the task?
- ❑ Did I make it more specific?
- ❑ Did I add time and/or location?

DESCRIBING DATA
- ❑ Did I select the important data and features?

ANALYZING DATA
- ❑ Did I interpret the data without giving opinions?

CONCLUSION
- ❑ Did I summarize the trends and state the purpose of the graphic?

LENGTH
- ❑ Did I write at least 150 words?

PRACTICE

Read the following tasks and responses. Use the checklist above to determine if the writer completed the task. Write an analysis of the response where your answer is "NO." The first task is done for you as an example.

1

The graph below gives information about new doctor's salaries.

Summarize the information by selecting and reporting the main features, and make comparisons where relevant.

Write at least 150 words.

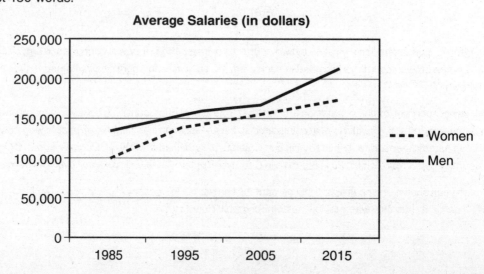

Response

The chart shows how much money doctors earned each year. It shows that men earned more money than women every year.

In 1985, a new woman doctor earned an average salary of $100,000, while the average salary of a man who was a new doctor was almost $150,000. In the next decade, women's salaries increased more quickly than men's. In 1995, a woman earned an average salary of close to $150,000, while a man earned a little more than that, so their salaries were almost equal.

Both men's and women's salaries continued growing. However, between 2005 and 2015, men's salaries started growing more rapidly. In 2015, a man's average salary was more than $200,000. A woman's was around $175,000.

Analysis

The opening statement is incomplete. It doesn't mention the time frame covered by the graph or the detail that the information relates to *new* doctors.

Important information about overall trends and details are included. Comparisons of men's and women's salaries and their different rates of growth are described although some information is missing, for example: How did trends change between 1990 and 2000? Only facts and no opinions are included. There is no conclusion summarizing the trends and stating the purpose of the graph.

At 120 words, this response is 30 words too short.

2

> The table below gives information about the average number of servings of ice cream sold each day in two different years.
>
> Summarize the information by selecting and reporting the main features, and make comparisons where relevant.

Write at least 150 words.

Springer's Café Ice Cream Sales

	April	May	June	July	August	September
2015	15	25	50	55	60	25
2016	25	35	65	80	75	30

Response

The table shows the average number of ice cream servings sold daily at Springer's Café for the months of April through September during the years 2015–2016.

Looking month by month, the average number of servings sold was greater in 2016 than it was in 2015. For example, in April of 2016, the café sold an average of twenty-five daily servings. That is ten more than were sold during the same month in 2015. In each of the months that are shown on the table, the average number of servings sold daily is higher for 2016 than it is for the corresponding months in 2015.

Overall, the table shows higher daily sales in 2016 than in 2015. Also, it shows that there were more sales made in certain months of the year. Probably this is because the weather is warmer during those months so more people want ice cream then.

3

The chart below presents the breakdown of professional time for elementary school teachers in the Wardsville school district.

Summarize the information by selecting and reporting the main features, and make comparisons where relevant.

Write at least 150 words.

Professional Time: Elementary School Teachers

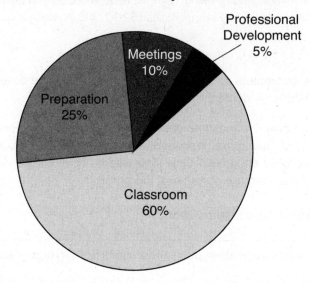

Response

The chart shows how elementary school teachers spend their professional time. These teachers spend the greatest percentage of their professional time in the classroom. On the other hand, they spend the smallest amount of their time participating in professional development activities.

Elementary school teachers spend a little more than half their time (60 percent of it) in the classroom. The rest of their professional time is spent participating in activities such as preparation, meetings, and professional development activities. Twenty-five percent of their time is spent in preparation, ten percent is spent in meetings, and just five percent of their professional time is spent in professional development activities.

What this chart shows is that teachers spend a lot of time involved in activities outside the classroom. I was surprised by this because I think teachers should spend most of their time in class with their students. But these teachers spend almost half their time in other types of activities.

4

> The diagrams below show the process of hurricane formation and the hurricane's structure.
>
> Summarize the information by selecting and reporting the main features, and make comparisons where relevant.

Write at least 150 words.

Formation of a Hurricane

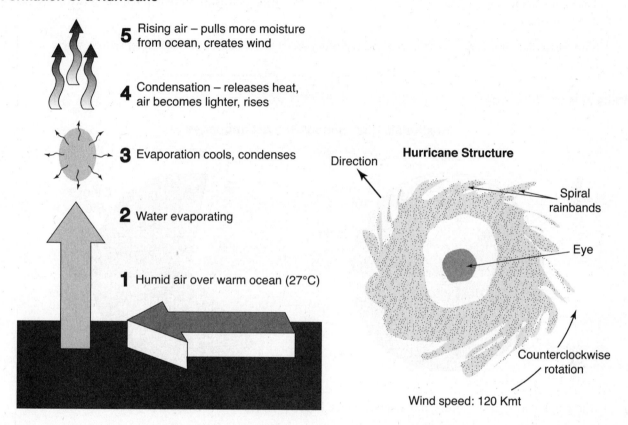

5 Rising air – pulls more moisture from ocean, creates wind

4 Condensation – releases heat, air becomes lighter, rises

3 Evaporation cools, condenses

2 Water evaporating

1 Humid air over warm ocean (27°C)

Hurricane Structure

Direction

Spiral rainbands

Eye

Counterclockwise rotation

Wind speed: 120 Kmt

Response

The diagrams show the process that occurs when a hurricane forms and the structure of the hurricane after it forms. This process takes place over the ocean. A hurricane begins to form when humid air moves over the warm ocean. When this happens, water evaporates from the ocean and rises into the air. As it evaporates and rises, it becomes cool and condenses. The condensation of the rising air releases heat, and this causes the air to become lighter and to rise more. Then, wind is created as the rising air pulls moisture from the ocean. The hurricane forms in a spiral shape, with an eye at the center. Rain bands rotate around the eye as the entire hurricane moves forward.

STRATEGY REVIEW

(answers on page 233)

Read and respond to the following tasks. You should spend about 20 minutes on each task.

1

> The charts below show the native languages spoken by students at Roslindale High School in two different years.
>
> Summarize the information by selecting and reporting the main features, and make comparisons where relevant.

Write at least 150 words.

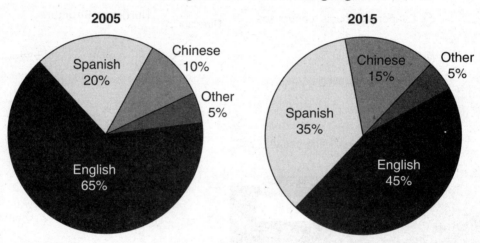

Roslindale High School Native Languages

2

> The graph below gives information about average housing prices throughout the city of Plimsburgh.
>
> Summarize the information by selecting and reporting the main features, and make comparisons where relevant.

Write at least 150 words.

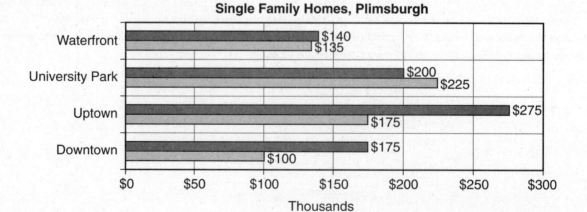

Single Family Homes, Plimsburgh

3

The diagram below shows the steps and equipment involved in recycling paper.

Summarize the information by selecting and reporting the main features, and make comparisons where relevant.

Write at least 150 words.

Paper Recycling

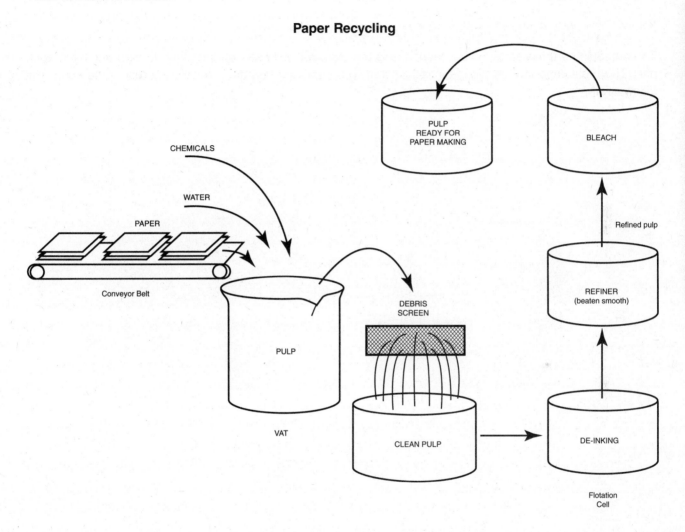

TASK 2

In Task 2, you will be asked for your opinion. Read the task carefully. You may be asked to describe the advantages and disadvantages of something or to discuss two different views of something. Make sure you address all parts of the task.

You will have forty minutes to write 250 words. Judge your time carefully.

There should be three parts to your response to the task. You will need enough time to plan and write each part. The most important part is the introduction. If you plan your introduction well, the rest of the essay will follow easily.

Introduction

Restate the Task

STRATEGY	In the first sentence of the Introduction, you should restate the task.
	You can restate Task 2 by paraphrasing it.
TIP	Spend time planning your essay. Don't just start writing. Read the task carefully. Think about what the task asks you to do and how you will answer it.

PRACTICE 1 (answers on page 234)

Read the following tasks. Paraphrase the task using synonyms for the underlined word or phrases. The first exercise has been done for you.

1

> In some school systems, children start learning at least one foreign language in primary school. In other school systems, foreign language education begins in secondary school.
>
> In your opinion, <u>should</u> children <u>learn</u> foreign languages in schools, and if so, at what age should they begin?

Give reasons for your answer and include any relevant examples from your own knowledge or experience.

Paraphrase

It is important for children to study foreign languages in school.

2

> Some people <u>believe</u> that it is <u>cruel</u> to <u>test</u> drugs and other new products on animals. Others believe that this sort of testing is <u>important and necessary</u> for <u>improving</u> and even saving people's lives.
>
> Discuss both these views and give your own opinion.

Give reasons for your answer and include any relevant examples from your own knowledge or experience.

Paraphrase

....

3

> Traditionally, elderly people have lived with and been cared for by younger family members. In modern society, more and more elderly people are living in special homes for the elderly.
>
> Why do you think families <u>choose</u> to have their <u>elderly relatives</u> live in special homes away from the family? What do you think is the best way for modern families to care for their elderly relatives?

Give reasons for your answer and include any relevant examples from your own knowledge or experience.

Paraphrase

....

4

> Developing an area for tourism changes life in that area in many ways.
>
> What are some of the advantages and disadvantages that tourism can bring to the lives of <u>people who live in the area</u>?

Give reasons for your answer and include any relevant examples from your own knowledge or experience.

Paraphrase

....

5

> Making smoking <u>illegal</u> is the best way to protect people from the <u>harmful effects</u> of tobacco.
>
> To what extent do you agree or disagree?
>
> What other measures do you think might be effective?

Give reasons for your answer and include any relevant examples from your own knowledge or experience.

Paraphrase

....

Give Your Opinion

STRATEGY	In the second sentence of the Introduction, you should give your opinion.
TIP	Your opinion does not have to be the second sentence, but until you get more confidence in writing, keep it the second sentence.

You can use these words and phrases when giving your opinion.

Useful Words and Phrases for Giving Opinions

I think	In my experience
I believe	In my opinion
I feel	It is my belief that
I consider	From my of point of view

PRACTICE 2 (answers on page 234)

Read the second sentence of the following Introductions. Add a word or phrase from the above list to express your opinion. The first exercise has been done for you.

1   It is important for children to study foreign languages in school. It is my belief that they should begin this at a very early age.

2   Some people feel that experimenting with drugs on animals is unkind, while others believe that it is crucial for making people's lives better. ......*I believe*...... this sort of testing is cruel and unnecessary.

3   There are several reasons why families opt to have their older family members live in special homes. ....*I think*............. , however, elderly relatives should stay living with their family whenever possible.

4   Tourism brings both advantages and disadvantages to local residents. ....*From my point of view*.... the benefits it can bring are greater than any drawbacks.

5   I agree that the best way to protect people from the dangers of smoking is to make it against the law. .... this is the only way to get people to stop smoking.
    in my opinion

WRITING MODULE

Write a Thesis Statement

STRATEGY In the third sentence of the Introduction, you should write a thesis statement. This thesis statement tells the reader what ideas you will write to support your opinion.

TIP You should have at least two main ideas. Three would be better, but two are enough.

PRACTICE 3 (answers on page 235)

Read the thesis statements. Which task in Practice 1 best matches the thesis statement? Write the task number in the blank. The first exercise has been done for you.

A ..2.. It may help scientists find ways to cure diseases, but it is painful for the animals and it is not the only way to test drugs.

B ..6.. It would make it extremely difficult to obtain and use tobacco, and it would get people's attention.

C ..1.. Children enjoy language, they learn it best when they are young, and language instruction fits in well with the rest of the primary school curriculum.

D ..3.. It may be difficult for families to find time and energy to care for their elderly relatives, but it is the kinder thing to do and it is also more economical.

E ..4.. Tourism can change the character of a place in undesirable ways, but it gives residents economic opportunities that they wouldn't have otherwise.

Body

Expand Your Thesis Statement

> **STRATEGY**   Use your thesis statement to write a topic sentence for each paragraph. The first sentence of each paragraph of the body of the essay is the topic sentence. The topic sentence shows how you will support your opinion.
>
> **TIP**   You should have at least two paragraphs in the body of your essay. Three would be better, but two are enough. Don't forget to indent.

PRACTICE 4 (answers on page 235)

Read each thesis statement and the sentences that follow it. Which are appropriate topic sentences for the body of the essay? Circle the correct letters. There may be more than one answer. The first exercise has been done for you.

1   Thesis Statement

If smoking were illegal, it would be extremely difficult to obtain and use tobacco, and it would get people's attention.

Topic Sentences

A   A tax on cigarettes would make them too expensive for most people to buy.
Ⓑ   Even if people had cigarettes, it would be hard to find a place to smoke.
Ⓒ   People may choose to have bad habits, but most people won't choose to break the law.
D   Smoking is prohibited in many public places these days.
Ⓔ   If smoking were illegal, then people wouldn't be able to buy cigarettes easily.

2   Thesis Statement

Children enjoy language, they learn it best when they are young, and language instruction fits in well with the rest of the primary school curriculum.

Topic Sentences

A   Everyone knows that childhood is the best time to learn foreign languages.
B   Young children enjoy learning and playing with language.
C   Most children have a large vocabulary by the age of five.
D   Some children are better than others at learning languages.
E   Most of the things children learn in primary school are related to language.

3   *Thesis Statement*

It may be difficult for families to find time and energy to care for their elderly relatives, but it is the kinder thing to do, and it is also more economical.

Topic Sentences

A   Elderly people often need more medical attention than younger people do.
B   Homes for the elderly are very expensive.
C   Elderly people have less energy than younger people do.
D   People who have jobs and children don't have much time to care for elderly relatives.
E   Our elderly relatives deserve to be treated kindly.

4   *Thesis Statement*

It may help scientists find ways to cure diseases, but it is painful for the animals and it is not the only way to test drugs.

Topic Sentences

A   There are other equally effective ways to do experiments.
B   Scientists seeking to cure diseases often use animals as part of their research.
C   Some people will not buy products from companies that use animal testing.
D   These sorts of experiments are often painful for the animals.
E   Animal testing is done with beauty products as well as with drugs.

5   *Thesis Statement*

Tourism can change the character of a place in undesirable ways, but it gives residents economic opportunities that they wouldn't have otherwise.

Topic Sentences

A   Tourism means traveling for recreational purposes.
B   Tourism is a growing industry in many parts of the world.
C   Tourism can change quiet towns into busy, crowded, expensive places.
D   Tourism creates new possibilities for businesses and jobs.
E   Tourism offices provide information for visitors new to an area.

Introduce Details

STRATEGY	Use transition words and phrases to introduce and prioritize the details that support your topic sentence.
TIP	Don't repeat the same transition words or phrases in your essay. Use a variety of transition words in each paragraph.

Common Transition Words and Phrases

first	second	so	additionally
in the first place	in the second place	therefore	furthermore
the main advantage is	then	however	moreover
another advantage	also	on the other hand	finally
another reason	and	but	the main reason is
another	or	in addition	primarily

PRACTICE 5 (answers on page 235)

Read each paragraph below. Underline the topic sentence. Complete each blank with a transition word or phrase from the above list. The first exercise has been done for you.

1 <u>Everyone knows that childhood is the best time to learn foreign languages.</u> **A** <u>In the first place,</u> it is the best time to learn anything because it is the time of life when the brain is developing. **B** ...., children are still developing skills in their native language when they are young, so their minds are open to learning language. **C** ...., children can learn to speak several languages fluently but it is more difficult for adults to do this.

2 People who have jobs and children don't have much time to care for elderly relatives. **A** ...., they spend most of the day at work. **B** ...., in their free time they have to take care of their children. **C** ...., they have to shop, clean, and do other housework. After taking care of these responsibilities, there is not a lot of time and energy left over.

3 There are other equally effective ways to do experiments. Drugs can be tested on humans, as they often already are. **A** ...., scientists use computer models as part of their research, and they often get more reliable results this way. **B** ...., scientists can use blood and cell samples from humans for their experiments. These methods are all more humane than using live animals.

4 Tourism can change quiet towns into busy, crowded, expensive places. **A** ...., hotels, restaurants, and roads have to be built to accommodate tourists. **B** ...., when the tourists arrive, they crowd the streets and public places. **C** ...., tourism usually means that prices in stores and restaurants go up. All these things change the quality of life for local residents.

5 Even if people had cigarettes, it would be hard to find a place to smoke. **A** ...., they wouldn't be able to smoke in any public place without getting arrested. **B** ...., they couldn't smoke in their own homes without leaving an odor. **C** ...., they wouldn't be able to smoke at their friends' houses without putting their friends in danger of arrest. A lot of people would quit smoking just because they couldn't find a place to do it.

Conclusion

Summarize Your Opinion

STRATEGY   In the conclusion, you should remind the reader what your opinion was and the main ideas that you discussed to support your opinion.

TIP   Remember to paraphrase yourself. Do not repeat the same words. You must show you can use a variety of words and syntax.

PRACTICE 6 (answers on page 235)

Read each introduction and the conclusions that follow. Which conclusion rephrases the ideas presented in the introduction? Circle the correct letter. The first exercise has been done for you.

1   Introduction

Tourism brings both advantages and disadvantages to local residents. From my point of view, the benefits it can bring are greater than the drawbacks. Tourism can change the character of a place in undesirable ways, but it gives residents economic opportunities that they wouldn't have otherwise.

Conclusions

A   Many towns invest a lot of money in tourism. They build hotels, widen roads, and make other improvements in order to make the area more attractive to tourists.

B   Tourism is a major industry in many towns and cities around the world. I think people in these places can make a lot of money from tourism.

C   Tourism has both positive and negative effects. It can make life more difficult for local residents in some ways; however, the economic benefits it brings are worth the cost.

2   Introduction

It is important for children to study foreign languages in school. It is my belief that they should begin this at a very early age. Children enjoy language, they learn it best when they are young, and language instruction fits in well with the rest of the primary school curriculum.

Conclusions

A   Some children are better at learning foreign languages than others. However, they all should spend some school time learning at least one foreign language.

B   Most young children enjoy school. They like learning whatever their teachers teach them, including foreign languages.

C   All children should learn foreign languages and they should begin when they first start school. This is the best time of life to learn languages.

3   Introduction

Some people feel that experimenting with drugs on animals is unkind, while others believe that it is crucial for making people's lives better. I believe this sort of testing is cruel and unnecessary. It may help scientists find ways to cure diseases, but it is painful for the animals and it is not the only way to test drugs.

Conclusions

A   Cures and treatments for many diseases have been developed with animal testing. In most cases, animals used in these experiments don't feel any pain.

B   I am opposed to using animals for drug testing. While I know that it is important to find cures for diseases, testing drugs on animals is not the only way to do this. There is no reason to cause pain to animals when there are other ways we can test new drugs.

C   Scientists use animal testing as well as other methods to develop new drugs. These days, there are many more drugs available than there were in the past. This has helped people live longer, better lives.

4   Introduction

I agree that the best way to protect people from the dangers of smoking is to make it against the law. In my opinion, this is the only way to get people to stop smoking. It would make it extremely difficult to obtain and use tobacco, and it would get people's attention.

Conclusions

A   These days fewer people smoke because they are aware of the dangers. However, smoking has recently become more popular among teenagers. Young people need to learn about the harmful effects of tobacco.

B   People will only stop smoking if it is made illegal. It will make it too difficult for them to continue the habit, and it will make them think about the harmful effects. It is the only way to protect people from tobacco.

C   Many people want to quit smoking, but it is a difficult thing to do. It is important to provide support and help them find ways to quit.

5   Introduction

There are several reasons why families opt to have their older family members live in special homes. I think, however, elderly relatives should stay living with their family whenever possible. It may be difficult for families to find time and energy to care for their elderly relatives, but it is the kinder thing to do, and it is also more economical.

Conclusions

A   Families may have good reasons for choosing to have their elderly relatives live in special homes. Despite this, I feel that it is kinder, as well as cheaper, for families to care for their elderly relatives themselves.

B   Families should research homes for the elderly carefully before choosing one. It costs a lot of money to live in one of these special homes so you want to make sure your relative gets good services.

C   Families are not always able to care for their elderly relatives at home. People have jobs and children to take care of. In addition, there may not be extra room in the house.

WRITING MODULE

Grammar

Gerunds and Infinitives

Gerunds and infinitives are verb forms. A gerund is verb + *ing*. An infinitive is *to* + verb. These verb forms are used in certain situations.

After the Main Verb

If the main verb of a sentence or clause is followed by a second verb, the second verb is usually a gerund or an infinitive.

> *Many people <u>enjoy</u> <u>smoking</u>.*
>   main verb   gerund

> *They <u>agreed</u> <u>to smoke</u> outside.*
>   main verb   infinitive

Some verbs are followed by gerunds and some are followed by infinitives. Here is a short list:

Verbs Followed by Gerunds		Verbs Followed by Infinitives	
enjoy	discuss	want	hope
quit	prohibit	need	prepare
continue	suggest	allow	offer
consider	avoid	agree	plan
prevent	dislike	attempt	learn

As Subject

A gerund can be used as the subject of a sentence or a clause.
> *<u>Smoking</u> is bad for your health.*
> *I believe that <u>raising</u> cigarette prices is a good idea.*

After Prepositions

Gerunds usually follow prepositions.

> *Some smokers are worried about <u>getting</u> cancer.*

After Adjectives

Infinitives usually follow adjectives.

> *It's important <u>to learn</u> about the dangers of tobacco.*

PRACTICE 1 (answers on page 235)

Read this paragraph from a student essay. Complete each blank with the correct form of the verb in parentheses.

In my opinion, **1** .... (smoke) should be illegal. These days there are many places where people aren't allowed **2** .... (smoke), but it is still legal. It is still easy **3** .... (buy) cigarettes. It is still possible **4** .... (smoke) in many places, and many people still enjoy **5** .... (smoke). If we are really interested in **6** .... (protect) people's health, we should pass laws against **7** .... (smoke).

Modals

Modals are words such as *can, may, might, should,* and *must.* A modal is always followed by a base form verb. Modals have different uses and meanings. Here are some common ones.

Ability—can

> Younger family members <u>can</u> help their elderly relatives with household tasks.

Possibility—could, might, may

> An elderly relative <u>could</u> feel more comfortable living in a special home for the elderly.
> Your relative <u>might</u> be happier living with family members.
> An older person <u>may</u> want to live in a quiet place.

Advice—should

> They <u>should</u> ask for help when they need it.

Obligation—must

> We <u>must</u> help our relatives when they need help.

PRACTICE 2 (answers on page 235)

Read the paragraph from a student essay. Complete each blank with a modal that has the meaning indicated in parentheses.

Often elderly people **1** .... (ability, negative) take care of themselves at home. They need help with the tasks of daily living. Some **2** .... (possibility) choose to live in a special home for the elderly, but this isn't an option for everyone. These homes are very expensive and many people **3** .... (ability, negative) pay the cost. Then the family **4** .... (obligation) find another way to care for their elderly relative. A younger family member **5** .... (possibility) invite the elderly relative to live in his home. Or the family **6** .... (possibility) decide to hire someone to help the elderly person in his own home. In all cases, the family **7** .... (advice) talk about the different options and make a decision together.

Active and Passive Voice

A sentence can be in either active or passive voice. Most sentences use active voice, but passive voice is used in certain situations.

ACTIVE

In an active voice sentence, the subject performs the action expressed by the main verb.

> *People visit zoos all the time.*
> subject   verb

The sentence above is in active voice. The subject, *people*, performs the action, *visit*.

PASSIVE

In a passive voice sentence, the subject receives the action.

> *Zoo animals are studied by scientists.*
> subject   verb

The sentence above is in passive voice. The subject, *zoo animals*, does not perform the action, *study*. The zoo animals don't study. Scientists study the animals.

We use passive voice when the agent (the one that performs the action) is unknown or unimportant. We don't have to mention the agent in a passive voice sentence, but we can. If we mention the agent, we use the preposition *by*, as in the example above.

Passive voice is formed with the verb *be* and the past participle form of the main verb. Passive voice can be used in any verb tense. The verb *be* carries the tense and the negative.

Simple Present

> The animals <u>are fed</u> every day at 5:00.
> The animals <u>aren't fed</u> in the morning.

Present Continuous

> The animals <u>are being fed</u> right now.
> The animals <u>aren't being fed</u> extra food.

Present Perfect

> The animals <u>have already been fed</u>.
> The animals <u>haven't been fed</u> yet.

Simple Past

> The animals <u>were fed</u> an hour ago.
> The animals <u>weren't fed</u> this morning.

Future

The animals <u>will be fed</u> in an hour.
The animals <u>are going to be fed</u> in an hour.
The animals <u>won't be fed</u> tonight.

Modals

The animals <u>must be fed</u> right away.
The animals <u>shouldn't be fed</u> more than twice a day.

PRACTICE 3 (answers on page 235)

Read this paragraph from a student essay. Complete each blank with the passive form of the verb in parentheses. Be sure to use the correct verb tense.

I believe that zoos aren't cruel places. In most zoos, the animals **1** .... (look) after carefully. Their cages **2** .... (keep) clean. They **3** .... (feed) healthful diets. When they are sick, they **4** .... (treat) by veterinarians who specialize in zoo animals. In many cases, zoo animals live longer than their wild cousins because they are safer and healthier in zoos. It is true that in the past, zoo animals **5** .... (treat) poorly very often. They **6** .... (give, negative) the care they needed. Their needs **7** .... (neglect) However, this is no longer the case. Now we understand a lot more about the kind of care that animals need, and every day we continue to learn even more. In the zoos of the future, the animals **8** .... (give) even better care than they are now.

Relative Pronouns—Subject

A relative pronoun introduces an adjective clause. An adjective clause describes or identifies a noun in the main clause.

> *Students <u>who wear uniforms</u> get better grades.*
>   adjective clause

The sentence above is made up of a main clause: *Students get better grades*, and an adjective clause: *who wear uniforms*. The adjective clause identifies the noun *students*. It tells us which students we are talking about.

An adjective clause begins with a relative pronoun such as *who, whom, whose, that,* or *which*. In order to choose the correct relative pronoun to use, you must identify the antecedent. The antecedent is the noun that the clause describes.

An adjective clause immediately follows the antecedent.

> <u>*Uniforms*</u> <u>*that have dark colors*</u> *are easy to wash.*
>   antecedent   adjective clause

In the sentence above, the noun *uniforms* is the antecedent for the relative pronoun *that*. The adjective clause *that have dark colors* identifies the noun. It tells us which uniforms the sentence is about.

The relative pronoun can be the subject or object of the clause. In all the previous examples, the relative pronoun is the subject of the adjective clause.

The correct relative pronoun to use depends on whether the antecedent is a person, a thing, or something that possesses, and whether the clause is restrictive or nonrestrictive. In some cases, you have more than one choice.

Relative Pronouns—Subject

	Restrictive	**Nonrestrictive**
People	*who* *that*	*who*
Things	*which* *that*	*which*
Possessives	*whose*	*whose*

An adjective clause can be restrictive or nonrestrictive. A restrictive clause provides information that is necessary to identify the noun. All of the previous examples are restrictive clauses.

A nonrestrictive adjective clause provides extra information that is not necessary to identify the noun. For example:

> <u>Mr. Jones</u>, <u>*who is the director of our school*</u>, *requires all students to wear uniforms.*
> antecedent   adjective clause

You could remove a nonrestrictive clause from a sentence and the identity of the noun would still be clear. Nonrestrictive clauses are set off with commas.

PRACTICE 4 (answers on page 235)

Read this paragraph from a student essay. Choose the correct relative pronoun to complete each blank.

Many schools require their students to wear uniforms. Students **1** .... (who/which) wear uniforms don't have to worry about following fashions. Therefore, it is easier for them to focus on their studies. Some students complain that uniforms are ugly, but I believe that uniforms can look nice. Uniforms **2** .... (who/which) are simple in design can look very attractive. Colors **3** .... (whose/that) are plain and not too bright always look nice. Skirts **4** .... (whose/which) are too long or too short can look strange and out of fashion, but uniforms don't have to have skirts **5** .... (that/who) are the wrong length. Students **6** .... (whose/who) uniforms look unattractive can talk to their school directors about changing the uniform style. School directors **7** .... (whose/who) require uniforms in their schools usually find that their students are better able to concentrate on academics.

Relative Pronouns—Object

As we saw in the previous section, Relative Pronouns—Subject, a relative pronoun introduces an adjective clause and the pronoun can be the subject or the object of the clause. Here are some examples where the relative pronoun is the object of the clause:

*The uniforms **that students buy** should not be expensive.*
    antecedent   adjective clause

In the sentence above, *students* is the subject of the clause and *buy* is the verb. The relative pronoun *that*, with the antecedent *uniforms*, is the object of the verb.

*The fashion magazines **that students read** influence their taste in clothes.*
    antecedent   adjective clause

In the sentence above, *students* is the subject of the clause and *read* is the verb. The relative pronoun *that*, with the antecedent *fashion magazines*, is the object of the verb.

The adjective clauses in both the sentences above are restrictive. They are necessary to identify the antecedent. In restrictive clauses, it is possible to omit the relative pronoun (except *whose*) when it is the object of the clause.

*The uniforms **students buy** should not be expensive.*
    antecedent   adjective clause

*The fashion magazines **students read** influence their taste in clothes.*
    antecedent   adjective clause

Remember that nonrestrictive clauses provide extra information that is not necessary to identify the antecedent. Here are some examples of nonrestrictive clauses where the relative pronoun is the object of the clause.

*Our director, **who many people admire,** agrees that uniforms are a good idea.*
    antecedent   adjective clause

*My school uniform, **which I bought last year,** still fits me.*
    antecedent   adjective clause

Whom rather than *who* is considered the correct form for an object pronoun in formal, written English. In spoken English, however, and often in written English as well, *who* is often used as an object pronoun.

Relative Pronouns—Object

	Restrictive	**Nonrestrictive**
People	*who* *whom* *that* nothing	*who* *whom*
Things	*which* *that* nothing	*which*
Possessives	*whose*	*whose*

PRACTICE 5 (answers on page 235)

Read this paragraph from a student essay. Choose the correct relative pronoun to complete each blank.

School uniforms don't have to be unattractive. The colors **1** .... (that/who) schools choose for their uniforms should be colors that look good on everyone. Plain, dark colors usually work best. It is also important to have skirt and pants styles **2** .... (whom/that) students feel comfortable with. Plain, classic styles look good on everyone and are always comfortable. If schools choose uniforms **3** .... (that/whose) the students like, then there will be no complaints. Of course, students should keep their uniforms clean and neat. Teachers, **4** .... (that/whom) the students look up to as role models, should also be careful about their appearance. They need to set good examples **5** .... (which/whose) the students can follow.

Real Future Conditionals

A conditional sentence is made up of an *if* clause, or condition, and a main clause, or result.

> *If a child studies a foreign language in primary school, she will speak it fluently.*
> condition   result

The order of the clauses can be reversed without changing the meaning of the sentence. When the main clause is first, no comma is used between the clauses.

> *A child will speak a foreign language fluently if she studies it in primary school.*
> result   condition

Real conditionals are called "real" because they are about things that are really true or that can really happen. Real future conditionals are about things that can really happen in the future. Because they are about the future, the verb in the main clause is in future tense. However, the verb in the *if* clause is in present tense, even though the sentence is about the future.

> Children <u>will learn</u> foreign languages easily if the classes <u>are</u> interesting and lively.
> future verb   present verb

> If schools <u>don't teach</u> foreign languages, children <u>won't learn</u> to speak them.
> present verb   future verb

PRACTICE 6 (answers on page 235)

Read this paragraph from a student essay. Complete each blank with the correct form of the verb in parentheses.

I think that children should learn foreign languages in primary school. It is easier to learn languages at that time of life. If children **1** .... (study) foreign languages when they are young, they **2** .... (learn) them very well. They will learn to speak them almost as well as they speak their native language. If they **3** .... (wait) until secondary school, it **4** .... (be) harder for them. Anybody can learn foreign languages at any age, but it is much easier for younger children. Primary schools **5** .... (have) to make foreign language classes a priority if they really **6** .... (want) their students to learn them well.

Unreal Conditionals

Like a real conditional, an unreal conditional is made up of an *if* clause, or condition, and a main clause, or result. The difference is that the unreal conditional is about something that isn't real or can't really happen.

If Mary spoke foreign languages, she would travel to foreign countries.
        condition   result

The example above is an unreal conditional. The truth is that Mary doesn't speak foreign languages and she doesn't travel to foreign countries.

The example above is present unreal conditional. It is about something that is not true in the present. It uses a past tense verb in the *if* clause, but it is about the present. A present unreal conditional has a past tense verb in the *if* clause and *would* + base form verb in the main clause.

If Mary <u>traveled</u> to foreign countries, she <u>would learn</u> about foreign cultures.
        past tense verb   would + base form

A past unreal conditional is about something that wasn't true in the past. It uses a past perfect verb in the *if* clause and *would* + *have* + past participle in the main clause.

If Mary <u>had studied</u> a foreign language in school, she <u>would have learned</u> it well.
        past perfect verb   would + have + past participle

The sentence above is unreal. The truth is that Mary didn't study a foreign language in school and she didn't learn it well.

PRACTICE 7 (answers on page 235)

Read this paragraph from a student essay. Complete each blank with the correct form of the verb in parentheses.

I didn't study a foreign language in primary school, and I am sorry about that. If I **1** .... (have) the opportunity to study a language then, I **2** .... (study) French. It is a beautiful language, and it is spoken in many countries. If I **3** .... (study) French in primary school, I **4** .... (learn) it well. Unfortunately, that didn't happen. I studied French at the university and I don't speak it very well. If I **5** .... (know) French well now, I **6** .... (read) French newspapers and magazines. If I **7** .... (speak) French with confidence, I **8** .... (travel) to French-speaking countries frequently.

Punctuation

Apostrophes

Apostrophes are used with contractions and with possessive nouns.

Contractions

An apostrophe takes the place of the omitted letter in a contraction.

> do not = don't
> we are = we're
> I am = I'm
> he is = he's
> John is = John's
> they have = they've

Possessives

An apostrophe is used to show possession. Add an 's to the end of singular nouns and irregular plural nouns.

> Mary's job
> The president's speech
> My boss's office
> The people's choice

Add an apostrophe only to the end of regular plural nouns.

> The students' grades
> The workers' demands

Common Problems

it's is the contraction for *it is* *its* is a possessive pronoun	*It's raining today.* *The cat hurt its paw.*
you're is the contraction for *you are* *your* is a possessive adjective	*You're a good student.* *Your grades are very good.*
they're is the contraction for *they are* *their* is a possessive adjective *there* is an adverb	*They're working today.* *Their house is on the next street.* *Put the package there, please.*
let's is the contraction for *let us* *lets* is the third person form of *let*	*Let's go to the movies.* *My boss lets me leave early on Fridays.*
who's is the contraction for *who is* *whose* is a possessive word	*Who's at the office today?* *Whose desk is this?* *John is the person whose house we visited last year.*

PRACTICE (answers on page 236)

Read this paragraph from a student essay. Find and correct ten errors about apostrophes.

Tourism brings many opportunities to the local residents. Lets say, for example, that your a young person living in a small town near the beach. There aren't many jobs in the town. You're opportunities are very few. You probably think about moving to the city, where you have more chance's of getting a good job. Now lets say that your town decides to develop the area for tourism. Hotels, restaurants, and stores are built. The roads are improved. Now you and all you're relatives and friends have many job opportunities in your own town. You can stay they're and earn a good living. You can raise your family they're knowing that your childrens opportunities for a good future are better now. I understand why some people think that tourism causes many problems, but I think its a good thing. It makes life better for local residents.

Check and Revise

As you write your response, ask yourself these questions:

INTRODUCTION

❑ Did I paraphrase the task?

❑ Did I give an opinion?

❑ Did I write a thesis statement with two or three main ideas?

BODY

❑ Did I write a paragraph for each of the main ideas?

❑ Did write a topic sentence for each paragraph?

❑ Did I include two or three supporting details in each paragraph?

CONCLUSION

❑ Did I paraphrase the task?

❑ Did I restate my opinion?

LENGTH

❑ Did I write at least 250 words?

PRACTICE 1 (answers on page 236)

Read the following tasks and responses. Use the checklist above to determine if the writer completed the task. Write comments where your answer is "NO." The first exercise is done for you.

1

> In some places, workers are required to retire at a specific age. In other places, workers can retire when they choose.
>
> In your opinion, should there be a mandatory retirement age for all workers?

Give reasons for your answer and include any relevant examples from your own knowledge or experience.

Response

In some places, workers are required to retire at a specific age. I think this is a good idea. Older people need to make room for younger people in the workplace, they slow down as they age, and companies can't always afford to pay their salaries.

Older people need to make room for younger people in the workplace. If they stay at their jobs, there will be fewer openings for younger people. Younger people have children to support, whereas older people usually don't. And, younger people need the opportunity to move up in their careers. Older people had that chance and now they need to make room for their younger colleagues.

Older people slow down as they ag_____ to work extra hours when this is required. Additionally, they may ac_____ en they were younger. Also, older people tend to have more health pr_____

Retirement at age 65 is required i_____ more opportunity for younger workers and ensures that older peo_____ down and rest.

Introduction	Is the t_____
	Comme_____
	Is an opi_____
	Comme_____
	Is there a_____ s)/ no
	Comment_____
Body	Is there a p_____
	Comments_____
	Does each pa_____
	Comments:_____
	Does each par_____)/ no
	Comments:_____
Conclusion	Is the task para_____
	Comments:_____
	Is the opinion re_____
	Comments:_____
Length	Is the response at_____

2

Some people believe that it is cruel to test_____ _____elieve that
this sort of testing is important and necessa_____

Discuss both of these views and give your ov_____

Give reasons for your answer and include any_____ experience.

Response

In my opinion animal testing is not cruel but is an esse_____ _____ of developing drugs that will help treat and cure diseases in humans. It is not painful for the animals, it is the best way to test drugs, and the results are important because they save human lives.

For the most part, animals in laboratories are treated well. Their cages are kept clean and they are well fed. They have everything they need to be healthy. The experiments that they are part of are not painful. If they were, scientists wouldn't do them.

In many cases, testing drugs on animals is an important stage in the process of developing a drug. It is the only way to find out if the drug is effective and if it has serious side effects. It is the only way to find out if the drug is safe to take. If there is a serious problem with a drug, it is better to find this out by testing on animals rather than by testing on humans. I don't think anyone can disagree with this.

Through testing drugs on animals, scientists have developed many different drugs that have saved human lives. This is an important result.

I think testing drugs on animals is very important. It doesn't cause the animals any pain and without it, many human lives would be lost.

Introduction	Is the task paraphrased? yes / no
	Comments: ....
	Is an opinion given? yes / no
	Comments: ....
	Is there a thesis statement with two or three main ideas? yes / no
	Comments: ....
Body	Is there a paragraph for each of the main ideas? yes / no
	Comments: ....
	Does each paragraph have a topic sentence? yes / no
	Comments: ....
	Does each paragraph have two or three supporting details? yes / no
	Comments: ....
Conclusion	Is the task paraphrased? yes / no
	Comments: ....
	Is the opinion restated? yes / no ....
	Comments: ....
Length	Is the response at least 250 words? yes / no

3

In some school systems, children start learning at least one foreign language in primary school. In other school systems, foreign language education begins in secondary school.

In your opinion, should children learn foreign languages in schools, and if so, at what age should they begin?

Give reasons for your answer and include any relevant examples from your own knowledge or experience.

Response

Some schools make foreign languages part of the primary school curriculum, while others don't include this until secondary school. From my point of view, primary school is not the right place to begin foreign language study.

Children of primary school age are still in the process of learning their own language. They still have a lot of vocabulary to learn. They are just beginning to read and write. It would confuse them to have to learn vocabulary and reading and writing in another language at the same time.

Children in primary school are too young to understand the reasons for studying other languages. Children of that age haven't had a lot of experiences. It is hard for them to imagine other countries if they haven't traveled. It is hard for them to imagine the need for other languages if they haven't met people who speak them. So, to them a foreign language can seem like just a game without a real purpose.

Secondary school students, on the other hand, are at a good age to study foreign languages. By this age they have developed a large vocabulary in their own language and they can read and write with confidence, so they are ready to add another language or languages to their knowledge. Also, at this age students are ready to broaden their world. They are ready to start thinking about other places and other people beyond their own experience. Learning a foreign language at this stage of life can be very enriching.

Some schools choose to teach languages in primary school while others choose to teach them in secondary school. It depends on where you are.

Introduction	Is the task paraphrased? yes / no
	Comments: ....
	Is an opinion given? yes / no
	Comments: ....
	Is there a thesis statement with two or three main ideas? yes / no
	Comments: ....
Body	Is there a paragraph for each of the main ideas? yes / no
	Comments: ....
	Does each paragraph have a topic sentence? yes / no
	Comments: ....
	Does each paragraph have two or three supporting details? yes / no
	Comments: ....
Conclusion	Is the task paraphrased? yes / no
	Comments: ....
	Is the opinion restated? yes / no
	Comments: ....
Length	Is the response at least 250 words? yes / no

4

> Developing an area for tourism changes life in that area in many ways.
>
> What are some of the advantages and disadvantages that tourism can bring to the lives of people who live in the area?

Give reasons for your answer and include any relevant examples from your own knowledge or experience.

Response

Developing an area for tourism changes life in that area in many ways. Tourism can bring both advantages and disadvantages to the lives of people who live in the area.

Tourism has many advantages for local residents. In the first place, it brings in a lot of money. This means there are more jobs for local residents and more customers for local businesses. In the second place, improvements are often made to accommodate tourists. Many of these improvements, such as better roads and parks and even better electric and water systems, also benefit the local residents. Additionally, tourist towns often have a lot of cultural entertainment such as concerts and theaters, and local residents can enjoy these things, too.

New roads and buildings that are constructed to accommodate tourists can change the character of a town. They can turn a pretty, quiet village into a noisy, crowded place. Businesses such as restaurants and stores that are set up to attract tourists might be too expensive for local residents. And even though tourism creates jobs, these jobs might not be available to all local residents. Local residents might not have skills, such as speaking foreign languages, that are required for jobs in tourism.

I believe that in most cases the advantages of tourism outweigh the disadvantages. Tourism usually brings great benefits to the residents of an area.

Introduction	Is the task paraphrased? yes / no
	Comments: ....
	Is an opinion given? yes / no
	Comments: ....
	Is there a thesis statement with two or three main ideas? yes / no
	Comments: ....
Body	Is there a paragraph for each of the main ideas? yes / no
	Comments: ....
	Does each paragraph have a topic sentence? yes / no
	Comments: ....
	Does each paragraph have two or three supporting details? yes / no
	Comments: ....

Conclusion	Is the task paraphrased? yes / no
	Comments: ....
	Is the opinion restated? yes / no
	Comments: ....
Length	Is the response at least 250 words? yes / no

5

> Making smoking illegal is the best way to protect people from the harmful effects of tobacco.
>
> To what extent do you agree or disagree?
>
> What other measures do you think might be effective?

Give reasons for your answer and include any relevant examples from your own knowledge or experience.

Response

Some people believe that making a law against smoking is the best way to get people to stop this harmful habit. I don't agree with this. Laws don't always get people to change their behavior.

People don't always obey the law, especially when the laws are about addictive substances. There are laws against using and selling harmful drugs such as heroin and cocaine, but people still use them. If people really want to do something, they will find a way to do it, whether or not it is against the law. Desire, especially when it is for something addictive, is often stronger than the law.

Education, on the other hand, can be very effective. It gives people reasons to want to quit smoking. People need to understand all the harmful effects this bad habit can have on their health. They need to know all the different ways that smoking can affect them. Then they will want to quit smoking because they won't want to suffer in all these horrible ways.

Besides education, people also need support to quit smoking. It is very hard to quit, even when you really want to, so support is important. There are many health centers that offer programs to help people quit smoking. There are also different methods that people can follow. In addition, there are drugs available that make the physical effects of quitting easier to manage. All of these things help support people who are going through the difficult process of quitting smoking.

Introduction	Is the task paraphrased? yes / no
	Comments: ....
	Is an opinion given? yes / no
	Comments: ....
	Is there a thesis statement with two or three main ideas? yes / no
	Comments: ....
Body	Is there a paragraph for each of the main ideas? yes / no
	Comments: ....
	Does each paragraph have a topic sentence? yes / no
	Comments: ....
	Does each paragraph have two or three supporting details? yes / no
	Comments: ....
Conclusion	Is the task paraphrased? yes / no
	Comments: ....
	Is the opinion restated? yes / no
	Comments: ....
Length	Is the response at least 250 words? yes / no

PRACTICE 2 (answers on page 239)

Read the task and response below. Correct any grammar, spelling, and punctuation errors that you find in the response. The first correction is done for you.

> These days, more and more people eat prepared meals from restaurants and grocery stores instead of cooking for themselves.
>
> What do you think are the reasons for this trend?
>
> To what extent do you think this is a positive trend?

Give reasons for your answer and include any relevant examples from your own knowledge or experience.

Response

People these days often buy meals instead of prepare them at home. I think this is an unfortunate trend. Modern people are often too busy to cook their own meals, but buying prepared meals is a more expensive way to eat and it doesn't encourage families to spend time together.

Modern families are very busy. The parents work hard at their jobs. The chilren are in school all day and often participate in sports or other activitys when the school day is over. Most people don't have the time and energy to cook. When they get home from work and school, they just want relax. That's why they buy prepared meals.

Buying prepared meals is not an economical way to eat. Prepared meals are expensive. This is because the cost includes the work of the cook as well as the price of the ingredients. Food who you cook at home is cheaper. It costs less to buy the food at the grocery store and cook it yourself. It's true that this takes time. On the other hand, it also takes time to earn money to pay for prepared meals.

When families buy prepared meals, they spend less time together. This may sound funny, but it's true. Mealtime is often the only time families are together. Its an important time. Chilren, who eat most of their meals with their parents feel happier and more secure. Their healthier emotionally. But when families don't cook together, they usually don't eat together either.

Eat prepared meals is popular for busy people these days, but I don't think it's a good idea. If more families cooked at home they would have saved money and they would enjoy a better family life.

CORRECTIONS
Paragraph 1

1 Change prepare to preparing..

Paragraph 2

2 ....

3 ....

4 ....

Paragraph 3

5 ....

Paragraph 4

6 ....

7 ....

8 ....

9 ....

Paragraph 5

10 ....

11 ....

12 ....

STRATEGY REVIEW

Plan Your Essay

(answers on page 239)

Read the tasks below and make an outline to respond to the task. The first exercise is done for you.

1

> In some places, workers are required to retire at a specific age. In other places, workers can retire when they choose.
>
> In your opinion, should there be a mandatory retirement age for all workers?

Give reasons for your answer and include any relevant examples from your own knowledge or experience.

INTRODUCTION

Task Paraphrase   People should not have to stop working at any specific age.

My Opinion   This is unfair and unnecessary.

My Thesis Statement

    Main Idea 1   Some people enjoy working.

    Main Idea 2   Some people need to keep earning money.

    Main Idea 3   Everybody needs to feel a purpose in life.

BODY 1

Main Idea 1   Some people enjoy working.

    Supporting Detail 1   They may like the kind of work they do.

    Supporting Detail 2   They may enjoy interacting with their colleagues.

    Supporting Detail 3   They may like to feel they are part of something.

BODY 2

Main Idea 2   Some people need to keep earning money.

    Supporting Detail 1   They don't have savings or a pension.

    Supporting Detail 2   Their savings or pension doesn't cover expenses.

    Supporting Detail 3   They need money for medical expenses.

BODY 3

Main Idea 3   Everybody needs to feel a purpose in life.

    Supporting Detail 1   A job gives a person a sense of purpose.

    Supporting Detail 2   A job makes a person feel useful.

    Supporting Detail 3   A job makes a person feel like she is contributing.

CONCLUSION

Task Paraphrase   Some people want to stop working at a certain time while others want to work longer.

My Opinion   It is not right to make everyone retire at the same age.

2

> Many students choose to complete at least some part of their university studies in a foreign country.
>
> What are some of the advantages and disadvantages of studying abroad?

Give reasons for your answer and include any relevant examples from your own knowledge or experience.

INTRODUCTION

Task Paraphrase ....

My Opinion ....

My Thesis Statement **Main Idea 1** ....

Main Idea 2 ....

Main Idea 3 ....

BODY 1

Main Idea 1 ....

Supporting Detail 1 ....

Supporting Detail 2 ....

Supporting Detail 3 ....

BODY 2

Main Idea 2 ....

Supporting Detail 1 ....

Supporting Detail 2 ....

Supporting Detail 3 ....

BODY 3

Main Idea 3 ....

Supporting Detail 1 ....

Supporting Detail 2 ....

Supporting Detail 3 ....

CONCLUSION

Task Paraphrase ....

My Opinion ....

WRITING MODULE

3

> Some schools require their students to wear uniforms because they believe it helps the students focus on their schoolwork rather than on their clothes.
>
> Discuss this view and give your own opinion.

Give reasons for your answer and include any relevant examples from your own knowledge or experience.

INTRODUCTION

Task Paraphrase ....

My Opinion ....

My Thesis Statement   **Main Idea 1** ....

        Main Idea 2 ....

        Main Idea 3 ....

BODY 1

Main Idea 1 ....

   Supporting Detail 1 ....

   Supporting Detail 2 ....

   Supporting Detail 3 ....

BODY 2

Main Idea 2 ....

   Supporting Detail 1 ....

   Supporting Detail 2 ....

   Supporting Detail 3 ....

BODY 3

Main Idea 3 ....

   Supporting Detail 1 ....

   Supporting Detail 2 ....

   Supporting Detail 3 ....

CONCLUSION

Task Paraphrase ....

My Opinion ....

4

Zoos should be banned because it is cruel to keep wild animals in captivity.

To what extent do you agree or disagree with this statement?

Give reasons for your answer and include any relevant examples from your own knowledge or experience.

INTRODUCTION

Task Paraphrase ....

My Opinion ....

My Thesis Statement **Main Idea 1** ....

Main Idea 2 ....

Main Idea 3 ....

BODY 1

Main Idea 1 ....

Supporting Detail 1 ....

Supporting Detail 2 ....

Supporting Detail 3 ....

BODY 2

Main Idea 2 ....

Supporting Detail 1 ....

Supporting Detail 2 ....

Supporting Detail 3 ....

BODY 3

Main Idea 3 ....

Supporting Detail 1 ....

Supporting Detail 2 ....

Supporting Detail 3 ....

CONCLUSION

Task Paraphrase ....

My Opinion ....

5

> These days, more and more people eat prepared meals from restaurants and grocery stores instead of cooking for themselves.
>
> What do you think are the reasons for this trend?
>
> To what extent do you think this is a positive trend?

Give reasons for your answer and include any relevant examples from your own knowledge or experience.

INTRODUCTION

Task Paraphrase ....

My Opinion ....

My Thesis Statement | **Main Idea 1** ....

Main Idea 2 ....

Main Idea 3 ....

BODY 1

Main Idea 1 ....

   Supporting Detail 1 ....

   Supporting Detail 2 ....

   Supporting Detail 3 ....

BODY 2

Main Idea 2 ....

   Supporting Detail 1 ....

   Supporting Detail 2 ....

   Supporting Detail 3 ....

BODY 3

Main Idea 3 ....

   Supporting Detail 1 ....

   Supporting Detail 2 ....

   Supporting Detail 3 ....

CONCLUSION

Task Paraphrase ....

My Opinion ....

Write Your Essay

(answers on page 242)

Take the outlines you wrote for the five topics above and create an essay for each one. Model essays are in the answer key, but remember your answers will vary. Use your own paper.

WRITING MODULE

....
....
....
....
....
....
....
....
....
....
....
....
....
....
....
....
....
....
....
....
....
....
....
....
....
....

Revise Your Essay

After you write, take a few minutes to reread your essay to check the organization and correct grammar and spelling if necessary.

Do not make major changes. You don't have time. Make small corrections as necessary.

IELTS SPEAKING MODULE

OVERVIEW

In this chapter, you will learn and practice specific strategies based on the different tasks in the three parts of the Speaking Module. You also will review the importance of key words that you learned in the first chapter of this book. You will learn how these key words will help you answer the questions in the Speaking Module.

At the end of this chapter, you will find a Strategy Review that is similar to the actual IELTS Speaking test.

SPECIFIC STRATEGIES

PART 1—GENERAL QUESTIONS ABOUT YOURSELF AND EVERYDAY SITUATIONS

    Everyday Vocabulary
    Verb Tense

PART 2—SPEAK ON A TOPIC GIVEN BY THE EXAMINER

    Introduce Your Talk
    Pay Attention to Question Words
    Personal Feelings

PART 3—CONVERSATION ON ABSTRACT TOPICS

    Introduction
    Supporting Details
    Clarification

STRATEGY REVIEW

Speaking Tips

There are some general tips that will help you during the Speaking Module.

1. Keep talking. The examiner needs to hear you use English. Don't be shy.
2. Don't worry about small mistakes. You will make mistakes, but don't worry about them. Even native speakers make mistakes. Correct your mistakes if you can and keep talking.
3. Don't try to memorize responses. Just speak spontaneously and naturally.
4. Don't worry about a particular Part. Your score is a composite of all three Parts, not just one.
5. Take advantage of your preparation time in Part 2.
6. Don't worry if the examiner stops you. Each part has a time limit.

Part	Total Time	Preparation Time
	11–14 minutes	
1	4–5 minutes	none
2	3–4 minutes	1 minute
3	4–5 minutes	none

Part 1—General Questions About Yourself and Everyday Situations

The examiner will ask you a few questions on two or three topics. You may be asked to talk about your family, food, school, work, neighborhood, your home town, or other similar topics.

Everyday Vocabulary

STRATEGY 1	Know the vocabulary to talk about yourself and everyday situations.
TIP	Don't give short answers. Give one or two sentence answers. Don't memorize answers. Knowing nouns and adjectives for each of the topics will be very helpful.

Track 26

PRACTICE 1 (answers on page 244)

Listen to these IELTS test takers answer the examiner's questions. Write the missing words in the blanks. Then write your own answer to the examiner's question.

Family

Question 1: Tell me something about your family.

1   I have a .... family. There is my mother and father. Plus I have two .... brothers and a .... sister.

2   I have a .... family, just me and my mother and father. But my .... and aunts and .... live very nearby, so we seem like a .... family.

3   I recently got married, and my .... and I live alone in a small apartment. But her .... live nearby, and she has lots of .... She is very .... to her family.

4   I have a .... brother. He is my only sibling, so ours is a .... family. Most of our relatives live in another city, so we don't see them often. We have some .... cousins who live near us, but I don't know them well.

5   YOU: ....
....
....

Question 2: What do you enjoy doing with your family?

1   My brothers and sisters and I all enjoy ...., so we spend a lot of time playing soccer and tennis together. Also, we usually .... our cousins every weekend and have a big .... with them.

2   We all like to .... in our family, and we really enjoy .... books together. We don't always have the same .... about books, so we argue a lot. It may sound ...., but we think that's really fun.

3   We usually take a big family .... every summer. We .... a big house at the beach and .... all our cousins to stay with us.

4   Unfortunately, I am usually too .... to spend much time with my family because of my job. But I visit my parents when I can. My mother .... a nice dinner for me, and we sit around and .... about things. It's quiet and ....

5   **YOU:** ....
    ....
    ....

Question 3: Do you prefer spending time with your family or with friends?

1   I like spending time with both family and friends. But to tell the truth, I have more .... with my friends. My friends and I .... a lot of .... That's why they're my friends.

2   I have a new ...., so I don't have much time for friends. He takes most of my .... For now, my friends are my .... and my son. That's .... with me.

3   I really enjoy spending time with my family. My brothers and sisters and I enjoy many of the same .... We have a lot ....

4   I have a lot of friends, and I enjoy spending time with them. We go out together in large .... My friends are .... a large family to me. I .... better with my friends than I do with my family.

5   **YOU:** ....
    ....
    ....

Food

Question 1: What kinds of food do you prefer to eat?

1   I like .... all kinds of food. I especially like .... from .... countries. I always enjoy trying food that is new and ....

2   I like the .... my mother cooks. She cooks food that is .... in our country. It's really .... Nobody cooks as .... as my mother does.

3   I am a ...., so I never eat meat. I prefer food that's .... with .... vegetables. I eat a lot of ...., too.

4   I generally prefer to eat beef or .... with .... And I love .... I like anything that's .... I almost never eat ....

5   **YOU:** ....

....

....

Question 2: Do you usually eat at home or at restaurants?

1   I almost always eat at restaurants because I am .... all day. I always have .... at a .... When I have to work late, which is often, I usually buy a .... to eat in the office. That's my dinner.

2   I always eat .... and .... at home, and I eat lunch at home, too, when I can. But on ...., I often go to restaurants with my friends.

3   I usually eat at home because it's too .... to eat at restaurants. I only .... a meal at a restaurant when it's a .... , for example, someone's birthday.

4   I eat at home because it's more .... I have three children, so it's easier for us to eat at home. Also, there aren't many good restaurants in my .... I think the food we eat at home .... better.

5   **YOU:** ....

....

....

Question 3: What is your favorite restaurant?

1   My favorite restaurant is a small place near my house. It .... the most delicious .... It's a great place to go for an afternoon .... I .... meet my friends there.

2   There is a very .... restaurant downtown that has French food. I had my .... dinner there last year. The .... are high, so I can't go there very often, but I really like it.

3   I like to go to a .... restaurant near my school. I don't usually have a lot of time for lunch so it's a good place for me. I can get a .... or a sandwich there and eat it .... It's ...., too.

4   My favorite restaurant is a .... restaurant near my house. I like it because I like .... It has lots of other kinds of food on the ...., too.

5   **YOU:** ....

....

....

Hometown

Question 1: Tell me something about your hometown.

1 My hometown is very .... and .... We only have a few stores and one movie theater. It's a .... place to live, but it isn't very .... The .... is small, so everyone knows everyone else.

2 I come from a .... city. It's a very .... place. The streets are always .... A lot of .... people live and work there.

3 My hometown is in the .... There is a lot of beautiful .... around it, so .... like to visit. It's a ....-sized city, but during the summer it .... up with visitors.

4 I come from a .... outside a large city. It's a .... place, but there isn't much to do there. Everybody goes to the city to .... or look for ....

5 **YOU:** ....
....
....

Question 2: What do you like about your hometown?

1 People come from all over the .... to work and .... in my city. You can always .... interesting people there. I really like that.

2 My town is a very .... place. There are lots of gardens and .... In the spring, it's very .... when all the flowers bloom. In fact, my town is .... for its flowers.

3 There are a lot of .... for both work and study in my hometown. We have several .... Also, since it's a big city, there are a lot of ...., and it's .... to find a job.

4 My town is a very quiet and .... place. That's why it's a good place to .... a family. There is very little .... in my town.

5 **YOU:** ....
....
....

Question 3: What is something you don't like about your hometown?

1 My town can be a very .... place to be. There aren't many things to do there. Everything is always the .... Nothing ever ....

2   I come from a big city, and there is a lot of .... on the streets. Because of that, the streets are always ...., and the air is .... I don't really like that, but I guess it's the same in every big city in the world.

3   My hometown is in a very cold .... We have long, dark .... It can get very .... I think I would .... to live in a .... place.

4   Everything in my hometown is very .... It costs a lot to rent an .... It costs a lot to buy food or to ride the .... If you don't have a good job, you can't .... to live there.

5   **YOU:** ....
....
....

School

Question 1: What was your high school like?

1   I went to a very small high school. When I ...., there were only forty students in my class. Because the school was so small, we didn't study a large .... of subjects. However, I had some very .... teachers, and I learned a lot from them.

2   My high school was .... The classrooms were always .... We had a good .... program, and I played on several ....

3   I went to an .... high school. I'm sure it was like most other high schools. We studied the .... subjects and did the same kinds of .... that high school students do everywhere. I was on the .... team, and I was a member of the computer ....

4   My high school was in a .... building. Everything in the school was new. We had a beautiful .... and a large .... We had all new .... for our science classes. It was a great place to go to school.

5   **YOU:** ....
....
....

Question 2: What was your favorite subject in high school?

1   I really enjoyed my .... class. I've always liked ...., and I think biology is .... interesting. I liked learning about .... and ....

2   I always liked .... classes best. I took an art class every year I was in high school. Maybe I'm not a very .... artist, but I enjoy painting and .... and things like that.

3 .... was .... my favorite subject in high school. I wasn't the .... student in this subject. In fact, it has always been .... for me, but I like it anyhow.

4 I liked studying .... a lot. I think it's the most .... subject. I still read about it often. I like .... about how things were in the ....

5 **YOU:** ....
....
....

Question 3: What advice do you have for high school students today?

1 They should .... hard, of course, and .... to their teachers. What students learn in high school is very important for the ...., so they should take it ....

2 I think high school students should remember to enjoy their .... When they ...., they will have a lot of .... , so they should .... during their high school years.

3 High school students .... to start thinking about their future .... They should study subjects that will help them later on at the .... and in their jobs. High school is a time to .... for the future.

4 I think high school students should study a lot of different .... They need to .... what things interest them. The only way to know is to .... different things.

5 **YOU:** ....
....
....

Transportation

Question 1: What is transportation like in your city or town?

1 I live in a big city, so we have a lot of .... and .... People also .... their cars, but the traffic .... slowly because the streets are so crowded.

2 I live in a small town, and we don't have any .... transportation. People usually drive their own .... We have a ...., but that's for .... travel.

3 In my city, people usually .... the bus or use their cars. Also, a lot of people ride .... We have special bicycle .... on some of the bigger streets.

4   We have a lot of transportation .... in my city. We have subways and buses and .... If you live and work downtown, you can .... everywhere you need to go. Our downtown .... are always busy.

5   **YOU:** ....

....

....

Question 2: How do you usually get to school or work?

1   I usually drive to school because my school is .... from my house. It .... me about an hour to get there. I usually .... to some of my classmates, so the trip isn't boring.

2   I take the subway to work. The .... is about a ten-............................. walk from my apartment. It's very ....

3   I always walk to school. It takes .... an hour. It's a good way to get ...., but I have to leave my house early in order to get to school ....

4   I ride the bus to work. The .... is very close to my house. I have to .... to another bus downtown.

5   **YOU:** ....

....

....

Question 3: Are there any problems with your transportation to school or work?

1   My biggest problem is that I have to .... a lot of money to put .... in my car. Also, it takes a long time to get to school from my house. But the only .... to those problems would be to find an apartment .... to my school.

2   I don't really have any problems with taking the subway. It's very .... The only thing is that the subway .... is high, and it costs more during ....

3   I don't have any problems with .... to school. I really enjoy it. It takes a long time, but I don't .... For me, it's ....

4   The biggest problems with transportation in my city is the .... It takes a long time to .... anywhere because of that. It doesn't matter if you .... the bus or .... a car. Traffic is always a problem.

5   **YOU:** ....

....

....

Weather

Question 1: What is the weather like in your city or town?

1 In my town we have four ...., so the weather .... on the time of year. It .... a lot, from very .... to very ...., and everything in between.

2 I live in a .... part of the world, so the weather is always .... in my city. We have two seasons—............................ and .... During the rainy season, it rains in the afternoons, but the mornings are usually ....

3 My city is in the far north, so we have .... weather. The .... aren't cold, but they are very short. The .... are long, and we get a lot of ....

4 We have a very .... climate in my town. The weather is usually .... The .... never gets too high or too low.

5 **YOU:** ....
....
....

Question 2: What do you like to do when the weather is rainy?

1 I love rainy weather. I like to make a hot cup of .... and get a good book and sit by the .... listening to the .... on the glass.

2 I feel .... when the weather is rainy. Everything seems gray and .... and .... I don't like to do anything when it rains. I just .... that the weather will .... soon.

3 This may sound funny, but I like to go .... when it rains. I like to feel the rain .... on me, and I like to walk through the .... But, if it's raining ...., I stay ....

4 I don't do anything .... in rainy weather. I don't .... about it, except if there's a big .... If there's .... and lightning, I feel .... I don't like that at all.

5 **YOU:** ....
....
....

Question 3: What kind of climate would you prefer to live in?

1 I would love to live where the .... is always .... because I don't like to feel .... I like to go outside every day and enjoy the ....

2   I would like to live in a place that has a .... winter with .... of snow. That's because I love to .... I enjoy all winter ...., so I'd like to live where I could do them easily.

3   I like living in a place that has four seasons. Each one .... something different. .... and .... are very pretty times of year. Summer always has .... weather. I even like the .... and snow in the winter.

4   I don't like .... days, so I would like to live in a dry climate, maybe even near a .... I'd like to live in a place where the sun always .... and there are never any .... in the sky.

5   **YOU:** ....
....
....

Exercise

Question 1: What kinds of physical exercise do you like to do?

1   I play soccer, so that's the main way I .... exercise. I also try to .... at least a few times a week to .... for soccer.

2   I like to ride my ...., but I don't do it very often. I also play .... sometimes when I can find someone to play with. I guess I'm not a very .... person.

3   I like to .... at the gym. That's my .... way to exercise. Sometimes I ...., also, but the .... at the gym is often crowded and I don't like that.

4   I enjoy .... I take classes, and I also .... at home. It's a good way to .... up your ....

5   **YOU:** ....
....
....

Question 2: What kind of exercise did you do when you were younger?

1   When I was in school, I .... on several different sports .... I really enjoyed .... sports then. I .... a lot more exercise then than I do now.

2   I .... walk to school every day when I was younger. In addition, I .... tennis ...., and I also played volleyball. I had a lot of .... then.

3   I played .... a lot when I was younger. I wasn't very .... it, but I really liked it. I always .... a good time, even if my team lost.

4 When I was a child, I spent a lot of time outside with my friends. We didn't do any .... kinds of exercise. We just played a lot of different games. We .... and .... a lot as part of our games.

5 **YOU:** ....
....
....

Question 3: Is exercise important to you? Why or why not?

1 I think it's important to exercise .... Unfortunately, I don't exercise often .... I always feel better after exercise, but I get .... about it sometimes.

2 I try to exercise every day. It's really important for my .... I try to eat a good ...., too. I think that's the reason why I am almost never ....

3 I think exercise is good, but I am usually .... for it. I don't have a lot of ...., and when I do have time, I prefer to ....

4 I don't like exercise at all. I just think it's really .... I can think of lots of better ways to .... time. I would .... go to the movies or be with my friends, for example.

5 **YOU:** ....
....
....

Verb Tense

Many of the questions in Part 1 are about the present, but the examiner may also ask you about the past and the future. Be sure to give the information that the examiner asks for.

STRATEGY	Pay close attention to the verb tense that the examiner uses.
TIP	Listen for tense markers in the examiner's question.

Common Tense Markers

Present	now, at this moment, presently, do/does, these days, usually
Past	in the past, when you were younger, when you were a child, before, did
Future	in the future, in a few years, later, will

(Track 27) **PRACTICE 2** (answers on page 245)

Listen to these IELTS examiner's questions. Underline the tense markers in the examiner's question. Then choose the answer that matches the tense of the question.

Family

Question 1: When you were younger, did you spend more time with family or with friends?

A   I spent most of my free time with my friends.
B   I spend more time with my family these days.

Question 2: In the past, did you spend more or less time with your family than you do now?

A   I spend almost every weekend with my parents.
B   I spent a lot more time with my family.

Question 3: Do you ask your family for help when you have a problem?

A   Yes, I always talked to my family when I had a problem.
B   Yes, my parents are always the first people I talk to when I have a problem.

Food

Question 1: What did you like to eat when you were younger?

A   I will probably eat more vegetables and fewer sweets.
B   I loved to eat sweet things like ice cream and cookies.

Question 2: Who usually does the cooking in your house?

A   My mother cooks most of our meals.
B   My mother cooked for us every day.

Question 3: Did you eat at restaurants often when you were a child?

A   No, we almost always ate at home.
B   No, I rarely eat at restaurants.

Hometown

Question 1: Do you think you will live in your hometown later on?

A   I lived in my hometown with my family until I got married.
B   I won't live in my hometown after I finish school because there are few job opportunities there.

Question 2: What did you like about your hometown when you were a child?

A   I like the variety of stores and restaurants that we have.
B   I liked playing in the park with my friends.

Question 3: How do you think life in your hometown will be different in the future?

A   I think my hometown will be busier and more crowded because the population is growing rapidly.
B   I think my hometown is a very pleasant place to live.

Work

Question 1: Why did you choose your profession?

A   I chose to be a doctor because my father was also a doctor.
B   I enjoy my work as a doctor very much.

Question 2: What do you like most about the job you have now?

A   I will help people who need it.
B   I like having the chance to help other people.

Question 3: Do you think you will have a different kind of job in the future?

A   I think I will always be a doctor.
B   I worked as an office assistant right after I finished high school.

Transportation

Question 1: How did you get to school when you were a child?

A   I prefer to walk to school.
B   I always took the bus to school.

Question 2: Will you buy a car when you start working?

A   No, I will probably continue traveling by bus and subway.
B   No, I didn't, because it was too expensive.

Question 3: Do many people in your city ride the buses?

A   Yes, they rode the buses a lot.
B   Yes, most people ride the buses to work.

Weather

Question 1: What kind of weather do you dislike?

A   I really dislike very hot days because they make me feel so tired.
B   I used to dislike snowy weather, but now I like it.

Question 2: How does the weather affect your mood?

A   I always feel very happy when the sun is shining.
B   I will be very happy if it snows soon.

Question 3: What was your favorite season when you were a child?

A   Summer is my favorite season because I like to be outdoors.
B   I always loved the winter because I enjoyed playing in the snow.

Exercise

Question 1: Do you think your exercise habits will change in the future?

A   I have very good exercise habits.
B   I will probably have less time to exercise when I start working.

Question 2: How often do you exercise?

A   I swim or play tennis at least twice a week.
B   I will probably ride my bike every weekend.

Question 3: Did you exercise differently in the past?

A   I usually take a walk in the morning.
B   I used to run every day, but I don't anymore.

Part 2—Speak on a Topic Given by the Examiner

You will be given a topic. There will be three questions on the topic and one question about your opinion on the topic.

Introduce Your Talk

STRATEGY Introduce the main idea to your talk using key words from the first sentence of the topic. Introducing the main idea will help you organize your thoughts and will help the examiner follow your ideas.

Topic

> Describe a trip you have taken recently.
>   You should say:
>   where you went
>   who went with you
>   why you went there
> and explain what you enjoyed most about this trip.

TIP Talk a lot and talk spontaneously.

PRACTICE 1 (answers on page 246)

Look at the following topics. Circle the key words; then write an introduction for each topic. The first exercise has been done for you.

1   **Topic:** Describe a (trip) you have taken (recently).

     Introduction: I recently took a trip to my father's hometown, Bourmedes.

2   **Topic:** Talk about a holiday you enjoy celebrating.

     Introduction: ....

3   **Topic:** Describe something expensive that you recently bought for yourself.

     Introduction: ....

4   **Topic:** Describe a book you enjoyed reading.

     Introduction: ....

5   **Topic:** Talk about someone who influenced you when you were a child.

     Introduction: ....

SPEAKING MODULE

...rds

...e the phrase *You should say:* followed by a list of three questions that
...need to answer these questions in depth, but you do need to give the

...the question words (*who, what, when, where, why, how*) to help you
...e of information you need to provide.

...the questions in any order.

...*ne question words and make notes about what you will say about each*
...*uring the IELTS Speaking test, you will not be allowed to write in the*
...*done for you.*

...en recently.

...you
...here

Where	about 40 kilometers from home
Who	my entire family
Why	visit to our grandparents

2

Talk about a holiday you enjoy celebrating.
You should say:
what the name of the holiday is and why people celebrate it
who you usually celebrate it with
what you usually do on this holiday

Notes

....

....

....

....

....

3

Describe something that you recently bought for yourself.
You should say:
what it is and what it looks like
when you bought it
what you use it for

Notes

....

....

....

....

....

4

> Describe a book you enjoyed reading.
>   You should say:
>   what the title is and who wrote it
>   what type of book it is
>   what the book is about

Notes

....

....

....

....

....

5

> Talk about someone who influenced you when you were a child.
>   You should say:
>   who the person was
>   how you met this person
>   what things you did together

Notes

....

....

....

....

....

Personal Feelings

The last part of the Part 2 topic will ask you to explain something about your personal feelings about the topic, for example, why it is important to you or why you like it.

STRATEGY	Think of three logical responses to the question; then say a couple of sentences about each one.
TIP	Don't memorize your response. Talk naturally, and try not to be nervous.

PRACTICE 3 (answers on page 247)

Read these topics. Think of three logical responses to the last line of each one, and make notes about what you will say. Then practice speaking for two minutes in response to the entire card. Use your notes from Practices 1 and 2. The first exercise has been done for you.

1

> Describe a trip you have taken recently.
>   You should say:
>   where you went
>   who went with you
>   why you went there
> and explain what you enjoyed most about this trip.

Notes

What I enjoyed: grandparents
                   cousins
                   ice cream

Talk

I recently took a trip to my father's hometown, Bourmedes. Bourmedes is about forty kilometers from our present home. I went with my family—my parents, of course, and my two sisters. We went to visit my grandparents. I enjoyed spending time with my grandparents. My grandfather always tells funny stories, and my grandmother is a great cook. I had a good time with my cousins, too. We played games in the park and talked about school, friends, and other things going on in our lives. Also, my father took all of us out to get ice cream in the afternoon. That's something we always do when we go to Bourmedes, so it's something I always look forward to. It's really fun to get together with the whole family and enjoy games and ice cream and just sitting around and talking.

2

> Talk about a holiday you enjoy celebrating.
>   You should say:
>   what the name of the holiday is and why people celebrate it
>   who you usually celebrate it with
>   what you usually do on this holiday
> and explain what you enjoy most about it

Notes

....

....

....

....

....

3

> Describe something that you recently bought for yourself.
>   You should say:
>   what it is and what it looks like
>   when you bought it
>   what you use it for
> and explain why it is important to you to own it

Notes

....

....

....

....

....

4

> Describe a book you enjoyed reading.
>   You should say:
>   what the title is and who wrote it
>   what type of book it is
>   what the book is about
> and explain why you enjoyed it.

Notes

....

....

....

....

....

5

> Talk about someone who influenced you when you were a child.
>   You should say:
>   who the person was
>   how you met this person
>   what things you did together
> and explain how this person influenced you.

Notes

....

....

....

....

....

Part 3—Conversation on Abstract Topics

The examiner may ask you a few questions on a topic from Part 2, if there is time left. Then she or he will make a transition to Part 3. The purpose of Part 3 is to get your opinion on abstract topics related to the Part 2 topic.

Part 2	Personal question	Describe your favorite holiday.
	Transition	You've just talked about holidays. Now I'd like to discuss this topic more generally. First, let's talk about the importance of observing holidays.
Part 3	Abstract question	Do you think that it is important to observe holidays?

Introduction

STRATEGY	Introduce your response by stating your opinion. Mention examples or reasons for your opinion, which you will expand on as you talk. You can use some of the expressions below to introduce your opinion:
TIP	You do not have to believe in your opinion. When you practice, give reasons for both sides of an argument.

Common words and phrases to express a personal opinion

In my opinion	Speaking for myself
I believe that	I'd like to point out that
I'd say that	There's no doubt in my mind that
To be honest	It seems to me that
Personally, I think	As I see it
In my experience	

Common words and phrases to express a general opinion

Some people think that	It is generally believed that
Some people say that	It is often said that
It is often thought that	

PRACTICE 1 (answers on page 249)

Read these questions for Part 3. Make notes about your opinion and your reasons or examples. Then write an opinion statement for each question. This is for practice only. When you take Part 3 of the IELTS, you will not be given time to prepare notes. The first exercise has been done for you.

1   Do you think it is important to observe holidays?

Opinion   *yes*

Reasons/Examples   *connect with family*
                                     connect with traditions

Opinion Statement   *Personally, I think it is important to observe holidays because they keep us connected with our families and our traditions.*

2   Do you believe that reading books is important? Why or why not?

Opinion   ....

Reasons/Examples   ....

                                     ....

Opinion Statement   ....

3   Is it better to use a vacation as a time to relax or as an opportunity to learn about new places?

Opinion   ....

Reasons/Examples   ....

....

Opinion Statement   ....

4   What are the characteristics of someone who is a good role model for children?

Opinion   ....

Reasons/Examples   ....

....

Opinion Statement   ....

5   Do you think people who have a lot of money are happier than others?

Opinion   ....

Reasons/Examples   ....

....

Opinion Statement   ....

SPEAKING MODULE

Supporting Details

STRATEGY	Expand your answer by providing details about the examples or reasons that you mentioned in your opinion statement.
TIP	Follow an example with at least two supporting details. Three details are even better.

PRACTICE 2 (answers on page 250)

Look at your notes in Practice 1. Provide supporting details for your examples and reasons. Then use your notes to practice speaking your answer to the question. The first exercise has been done for you.

1 reasons/examples

connect with family

connect with traditions

supporting details

time with family, especially cousins, etc.
share special activities
have fun together

history
culture
food

Model Talk

Personally, I think it is important to observe holidays because they keep us connected with our families and our traditions. Holidays are a chance to spend time with our family, especially with cousins and other relatives that we might not see often. On holidays, we share special activities with our relatives, such as singing traditional songs and playing traditional games. We have a lot of fun together, and this brings us closer as a family. Holidays are also a chance to learn about and practice our traditions. Some holidays remind us of the history of our country. They remind us of things that are important to our culture. And, my favorite part, holidays are an opportunity to cook and enjoy traditional food. That always makes me happy!

2 reasons/examples   supporting details

3 reasons/examples   supporting details

4 reasons/examples   supporting details

5 reasons/examples   supporting details

Clarification

STRATEGY	You should always directly answer a question. If you are not sure you understand the question, ask for clarification. Don't give an answer that is not relevant to the question.
TIP	Asking for clarification gives you some extra time to think of a good answer.

Common phrases to ask for clarification

Do you mean …
Do you want me to say …
If I understand you correctly, you want to know …
You're asking me if …
You'd like me to give you …

PRACTICE 3 (answers on page 251)

Rephrase these questions to ask for clarification. The first exercise has been done for you.

1   **Question:** Why do people observe holidays?

   Clarification: *Do you want me to explain the reasons people observe holidays?*

2   **Question:** Do you think that it's important to travel to foreign countries?
   Clarification: ....

3   **Question:** Do you think that reading books will be less common in the future?
   Clarification: ....

4   **Question:** Why do people buy expensive things?
   Clarification: ....

5   **Question:** How important is it for children to have good role models?
   Clarification: ....

STRATEGY REVIEW

(answers on page 252)

Read the transcript of a Speaking Module, Parts 1, 2, and 3 below. Match the underlined numbers with the strategies they represent.

STRATEGIES

PART 1—GENERAL QUESTIONS ABOUT YOURSELF AND EVERYDAY SITUATIONS

Everyday Vocabulary
Verb Tense

PART 2—SPEAK ON A TOPIC GIVEN BY THE EXAMINER

Introduce Your Talk
Pay Attention to Question Words
Personal Feelings

PART 3—CONVERSATION ON ABSTRACT TOPICS

Introduction
Supporting Details
Clarification

PART 1

Examiner: What kind of job do you have?

Test Taker: I **1** <u>work</u> as a **2** <u>paralegal</u> in a small **3** <u>law firm</u> in my city.

Examiner: What are your responsibilities at your job?

Test Taker: My **1** <u>duties</u> **2** <u>include</u> **3** <u>legal research</u>, **4** <u>preparing documents</u>, and talking with **5** <u>clients</u>.

Examiner: What did you study in order to qualify for this job?

Test Taker: I **1** <u>took</u> a course at a local college, and I **2** <u>got</u> **3** a <u>certificate</u> as a paralegal. I **4** <u>learned</u> about law and about how to do legal research.

Examiner: Do you think you will have a different kind of job in the future?

Test Taker: I **1** <u>will definitely have</u> a different job in the future. I **2** <u>will go</u> to law school soon and then I **3** <u>will become</u> a **4** <u>lawyer</u>.

PART 2

Test Taker

> Describe a place you like to go to on weekends.
> You should say:
>   where it is
>   who you go there with
>   what you do there
>   and explain why you like to go there.

Test Taker: **1** <u>A place like to go on weekends is my friend Mary's house.</u> **2** <u>Mary has a really nice house near the beach, about a one-hour bus ride from my house.</u> **3** <u>Sometimes I go there alone, and sometimes I invite a few friends to go with me.</u> **4** <u>We spend most of our time on the beach, swimming, playing volleyball, or just lying in the sun.</u> I really love visiting Mary's house. Part of the reason is that **5** <u>Mary is a good friend of mine, and I like to spend time with her.</u> **6** <u>I also love swimming in the ocean.</u> It feels so good to be in the water. **7** <u>And I enjoy being outdoors in the sunshine.</u> It's great to have a friend who lives near the beach.

PART 3

Examiner: Do you prefer to spend your free time alone or with other people?

Test Taker: **1** <u>To be honest, I prefer to spend my free time alone because I'm with people all week and I rarely get time to myself.</u> **2** <u>During the week while I'm at school, I see my classmates and teachers all day.</u> **3** <u>Most of my friends go to my school, so I have a lot of opportunities to see them there, too.</u> Every moment of my week is filled with people and activities. **4** <u>Weekends are the only opportunity I have to relax quietly.</u> **5** <u>I need quiet time so I can rest and be ready to start the new week.</u>

Examiner: Do you think people need more free time than they generally have? Why or why not?

Test Taker: **1** <u>In my opinion, most people need more free time than they have, whether they are in school or working.</u> High school and university **2** <u>students have busy schedules.</u> They **3** <u>spend all week in classes</u>; then they often have to **4** <u>do homework on weekends,</u> as well. So **5** <u>they don't have enough time to relax</u> and get their energy back. Many **6** <u>people who have jobs</u> have to **7** <u>work extra time on weekends,</u> or they have to **8** <u>spend a lot of their free time taking care of their families.</u> So **9** <u>they don't get enough time to relax,</u> either.

Examiner: How are free-time activities now different from the way they were in the past?

Test Taker: **1** <u>I think the differences between free-time activities now and in the past come from technology.</u> Now **2** <u>people use electronic devices like computers and phones for entertainment.</u> They use them to **3** <u>play games</u> and **4** <u>watch movies</u> and **5** <u>read books.</u> In the past, **6** <u>people didn't have these devices.</u> So, they did **7** <u>more things in the company of their friends.</u> They got together with their friends to **8** <u>go to movies</u> or to **9** <u>play games.</u>

APPENDIX

ANSWER KEYS

KEY WORD STRATEGIES
Reading
PRACTICE 1
Passage 1

Oceans make up over seventy percent of the Earth's surface. But an ocean is more than just a large area of water. Oceans consist of several zones with different conditions, providing habitat for a variety of plant and animal species. The <u>littoral</u> zone is the area where the ocean meets the <u>land</u>. This zone consists of several subzones: land that is only underwater when there are super high tides such as during a storm (the supralittoral zone), the area that is submerged when the tide is high and exposed when the tide is low (the intertidal zone), and the area below the low tide line that is always underwater (the sublittoral zone). <u>Snails, crabs</u>, and small fish as well as various types of seaweed are all inhabitants of this part of the ocean.

The <u>pelagic</u> zone is the area farther out from the <u>shore</u>. This zone covers most of the ocean, excepting the areas close to <u>shore</u> and near the ocean <u>floor</u>. The top 200 meters of this zone is where sunlight is most abundant and is home to the <u>highest diversity</u> of plant and animal <u>species</u> in the ocean. In addition to various seaweeds and fishes, <u>marine mammals</u> such as whales and dolphins also inhabit this area and feed on the abundant plankton.

As you move into the deeper waters, less and less sunlight is able to penetrate the water. In the <u>benthic</u> zone, near the ocean <u>floor</u>, there is no light at all and photosynthesis cannot take place. <u>Animals that live here</u> are scavengers, getting their <u>nutrition</u> from dead and dying <u>organisms</u> that float down from the upper regions of the water.

A   the <u>littoral</u> zone
B   the <u>pelagic</u> zone
C   the <u>benthic</u> zone

1   the area along the <u>shore</u>
2   the area at the <u>bottom</u> of the ocean
3   home to <u>crabs</u> and <u>snails</u>
4   home to <u>sea mammals</u>
5   has the <u>greatest variety</u> of plant and animal <u>types</u>
6   <u>inhabitants eat</u> dead <u>animals</u>

Explanation

1. **A Paragraph 1:** *The <u>littoral</u> zone is the area where the ocean meets the <u>land</u>.* This sentence contains two key words. *Land* can mean the same as *shore*. The word shore is also used later in the passage, but this sentence gives the definition of *littoral zone*.

2. **C Paragraph 3:** *In the <u>benthic</u> zone, near the ocean <u>floor</u>....* This sentence tells us where the benthic zone is. *Floor* and *bottom* have the same meaning.

3. **A Paragraph 1:** *<u>Snails,</u> <u>crabs,</u> and small fish as well as various types of seaweed are all inhabitants of this part of the ocean.* This sentence contains two key words, and it is part of the description of the littoral zone.

4. **B Paragraph 2:** *...<u>marine mammals</u> such as whales and dolphins also inhabit this area....Sea* and *marine* have the same meaning. This sentence is part of the description of the pelagic zone.

5. **B Paragraph 2:** *...home to the <u>highest diversity</u> of plant and animal <u>species</u> in the ocean. Highest diversity of species* means the same as *greatest variety of types*. This sentence is part of the description of the pelagic zone.

6. **C Paragraph 3:** *<u>Animals that live here</u> are scavengers, getting their <u>nutrition</u> from dead and dying organisms.... Animals that live here* means the same as *<u>inhabitants</u>*. *Nutrition* is related to *eat* and the word *organisms* is similar in meaning to *animals* in this sentence. This is part of the description of the benthic zone.

Passage 2

The use of <u>wheeled carts</u> in the ancient world was limited by the fact that to be truly useful they needed smooth roads. The <u>ancient Romans</u> are renowned for the <u>stone roads</u> they constructed all over Europe, beginning in 312 BC with the <u>Appian Way</u>. This 260-kilometer road <u>connected Rome with</u> the city of <u>Taranto</u>. As more and more territory came under Roman control, roads were built throughout the empire, extending from Rome to what is today <u>Great Britain</u>, Romania, North Africa, and Iraq. These roads facilitated <u>all types of travel</u>, <u>wheeled</u> or not.

Wooden work carts were common throughout Europe for centuries. In fact, they were the major mode of transportation until the 1500s, when <u>Hungarians</u> began to build <u>coaches</u>. With smooth, finished wood and soft, cushioned seats, coaches provided a much more comfortable ride than rough wooden carts. Their popularity spread across the continent. In the following centuries, various styles of coaches, carriages, and wagons were developed to provide transportation for all types of situations.

1   The <u>Appian Way</u> was the first <u>stone road</u> built by the ancient <u>Romans</u>.
2   The <u>Appian Way</u> led from Rome to <u>Great Britain</u>.
3   The <u>Appian Way</u> was the most <u>heavily used</u> Roman road.
4   Ancient Roman <u>roads</u> were used only by <u>travelers</u> in <u>wheeled carts</u>.
5   The first European <u>coaches</u> were made in <u>Hungary</u>.

Explanation

1. **TRUE. Paragraph 1:** *The <u>ancient Romans</u> are renowned for the <u>stone roads</u> they constructed all over Europe, beginning in 312 BC with the <u>Appian Way</u>.* This sentence contains all the key words of the question and tells us that the first stone road was built by the ancient Romans.

2. **FALSE. Paragraph 1:** *…beginning in 312 BC with the Appian Way. This 260-kilometer road connected Rome with the city of Taranto.* This sentence tells us that the Appian Way led to Taranto, not Great Britain. Great Britain is mentioned later in the paragraph as the destination of other Roman roads.

3. **NOT GIVEN.** The sentence quoted in the answer above is the only information the passage gives about the Appian Way. There is no mention of how heavily it was used. The key words *Appian Way* do not appear anywhere else in the passage.

4. **FALSE. Paragraph 1:** *These roads facilitated all types of travel, wheeled or not.* This sentence explains that wheeled vehicles were not the only way people traveled on these roads.

5. **TRUE. Paragraph 2:** *…until the 1500s, when Hungarians began to build coaches.* This sentence contains the two key words related to the question.

Passage 3

List of Headings

i   Reasons to Use Wind Power
ii   Wind Power in the Twentieth Century
iii Arguments Against Wind Power
iv   Wind Power in Early History

A

People have been harnessing the power of the wind for centuries. The first documented use of wind power was in Persia about 1500 years ago, where windmills were used to pump water and grind grain. Windmills may actually have been in use in China earlier than this; however, the first documented use of wind power there was in the thirteenth century, again for pumping water and grinding grain. Windmills were also being used in Europe at the same time and were an important source of power for several centuries. Their use eventually declined in the nineteenth century with the introduction of the steam engine.

B

Throughout the 1900s, the development and use of windmills was focused on the generation of electricity. In the early part of the century, wind-generated electricity was widely used in the Midwestern United States. As the demand for electricity grew and the electrical grid was extended through that part of the country, wind power fell out of use. In the latter part of the century, there was a renewed interest in wind power as an alternative to the use of fossil fuels to generate electricity.

C

In the twenty-first century, the use of wind-generated electricity is growing as many see the benefits of this source of power. In addition to reducing dependency on fossil fuels, wind power is also clean and inexpensive to use. The wind, after all, is free. Wind turbines can be built on open farmland, thus providing the farmer with another source of income. Wind turbines don't occupy a large amount of space and the land around them can be cultivated.

D

As with anything, however, there are also drawbacks. Although using wind turbines is inexpensive, the initial investment required to construct them is quite high. Wind turbines have to be located where they can capture the wind, often on high mountain ridges or in open areas free of obstacles, such as tall buildings. This means they are usually located away from population centers where the most electricity is needed. So there is the additional cost of installing lines to transmit the electricity to cities. Some people are concerned about the high level of noise spinning wind turbines create. Others are concerned about the effect on wildlife, especially birds, which have been killed by flying into the turbines.

Explanation

1. **iv.** The underlined key words in paragraph A, especially *1500 years ago* and *thirteenth century* tell us that this paragraph contains information about early history.
2. **ii.** The topic sentence of paragraph B contains the key word *1900s*, which means the same as *twentieth century*.
3. **i.** The topic sentence of paragraph C contains the key word *benefits,* which can be similar in meaning to *reasons to use something*.
4. **iii.** The topic sentence of paragraph D contains the key word *drawbacks,* which can be similar in meaning to *arguments against*.

Passage 4

As with anything, however, there are also drawbacks. Although using wind turbines is inexpensive, the initial investment required to construct them is quite high. Wind turbines have to be located where they can capture the wind, often on high mountain ridges or in open areas free of obstacles, such as tall buildings. This means they are usually located away from population centers where the most electricity is needed. So there is the additional cost of installing lines to transmit the electricity to cities. Some people are concerned about the high level of noise spinning wind turbines create. Others are concerned about the effect on wildlife, especially birds, which have been killed by flying into the turbines.

A   Wind turbines can cause harm to animals.
B   Wind turbines in a rural landscape can spoil the scenery.
C   The best wind turbine sites are usually far from cities.
D   It costs a lot to build wind turbines.
E   Wind speed is not reliable.
F   Wind turbines are very noisy.
G   Wind turbines don't generate as much electricity as fossil fuel power stations do.

Explanation

Disadvantages mentioned:

A   The last sentence contains several key words related to the key words in this question and explains a specific way that wind turbines can harm animals: birds have been killed by them.
C   The key words *away from population centers* in the fourth sentence mean the same as the words in the question *far from cities*.
D   The first sentence mentions the *high initial investment*.
F   The second to the last sentence contains the key word *noise* and explains that some consider this a problem with wind turbines.

Passage 5

Psychologist Jean Piaget identified four stages in the intellectual development of children, from birth to about twelve years of age. He identified the ages at which most children pass through each stage and the concepts and abilities they develop. While he acknowledged that children may go through each stage at different rates or at somewhat different ages, he was firm in his belief that the cognitive development of all children always follows the same sequence.

According to Piaget, children from birth to around two years of age are in the sensorimotor stage of development. During this stage, children learn that objects can be manipulated. They learn that their actions can have an effect on objects. They experiment by touching, holding, or throwing things or by putting them in their mouths and seeing what results. Initially, infants are concerned only with things that are directly <u>before their eyes</u>. During this stage, they develop the concept of object permanence. They learn that things continue to exist even when out of sight.

The <u>preoperational</u> stage is the period from around two to seven years of age. Children in this stage are able to think symbolically. They develop their <u>use of language</u>. They are also very egocentric, assuming that everyone else shares their same <u>point of view</u>. Another characteristic of this stage is animism—the belief that inanimate <u>objects</u> can <u>think</u> and <u>feel</u> in the same way the child does. Thus, a child might feel sorry for a broken toy, for example.

*Choose the correct letter, **A, B,** or **C.***

1   Piaget <u>believed</u> that <u>all children</u>
   A   <u>learn</u> at the same <u>pace</u>.
   B   develop <u>cognitive abilities</u> in the same <u>order</u>.
   C   pass through <u>twelve stages</u> of development.

2   During the <u>sensorimotor</u> stage, infants learn by
   A   <u>manipulating objects.</u>
   B   <u>focusing only</u> on what they can <u>see</u>.
   C   being <u>touched</u> and <u>held</u> by their <u>parents</u>.

3   Children in the <u>preoperational stage</u>
   A   have very <u>limited</u> use of <u>language</u>.
   B   are interested in other people's <u>viewpoints</u>.
   C   believe that <u>things</u> have <u>thoughts</u> and <u>feelings</u>.

Explanation

1.   **B. First paragraph:** *…he was firm in his <u>belief</u> that the <u>cognitive</u> development of all children always follows the same <u>sequence</u>.* This clause contains several key words related to question 1. *Sequence* means the same as *order*, and a reading of the complete clause shows that choice B is the correct answer. The first part of the same sentence, *While he acknowledged that children may go through each stage at different <u>rates</u>…* contains the key word *rates*, a synonym for *pace* in choice A. However a reading of the complete clause shows a contradiction to choice A, since it talks about *different* rates. Choice C contains the key word *twelve*. A reading of the sentence in the passage which contains this key word shows that it refers to *age*, not *stages* and that Piaget identified *four*, not *twelve*, stages.
2.   **A.** The key word *sensorimotor* appears in the second paragraph and is the topic of that paragraph. The key words in choice A appear in this sentence: *During this stage, children learn that <u>objects</u> can be <u>manipulated</u>.* The key words for choice C appear in the fourth sentence. However, they are used in a different context. It is about children holding and touching objects, rather than parents holding and touching children. In the next sentence, *before their eyes* is similar in meaning to *see*, a key word in choice B. Here again, the words are used in a different way in the passage. The sentence describes a characteristic of children at this stage of development, not a way in which they learn.
3.   **C.** The key word *preoperational* appears in the third paragraph and is the topic of that paragraph. In the second to the last sentence, the key words *think* and *feel* are related to the words in choice C, *thoughts* and *feelings*, and *objects* means the same as *things*. This sentence describes the same situation that choice C does. The second sentence contains the same key word as choice A, *language*; however, it says something completely different about language. The third sentence contains key words *points of view*, related to the key word in choice B, *viewpoints*. However, it says the opposite of choice B: Children are not even aware of other people's viewpoints.

Listening

PRACTICE 2

Passage 1

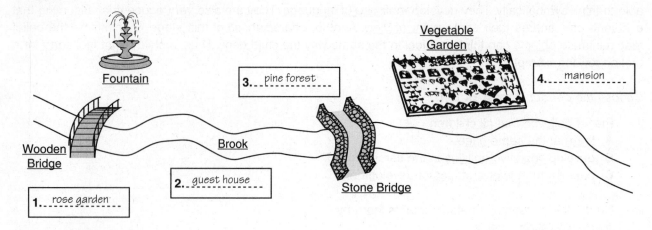

Audioscript

Welcome to Richland Mansion. We'll begin our tour of the grounds in just a minute. Afterwards you are free to tour the inside of the mansion on your own or join a guided tour. There is one every hour. OK, here we are at the <u>fountain</u>, which Mr. Richland imported from Italy in 1885. If you'll take a look at this map here, I'll show you where the tour will continue. The rose garden is right <u>across</u> the <u>brook</u> from here, and we'll cross this <u>wooden bridge</u> to get to it. <u>Then</u> we'll stroll <u>along</u> the banks of the <u>brook</u> to the guest house, which we will view from the outside, but the inside is not open to visitors. <u>After</u> that, we'll continue <u>along</u> the <u>brook</u> until we come to the <u>stone bridge</u>, here, where we'll cross back <u>over</u> the <u>brook</u> to get to the pine forest, here. It's really just a small forested area. We'll follow a trail that will bring us out on the other side of the forest and then take us up to the mansion. On the way, we can stop and look at the <u>vegetable garden</u>, here, and you'll see that the mansion is just <u>beyond</u> that.

Explanation

1. **rose garden.** In a map labeling exercise, the key words are the labels provided. In addition, you can listen for prepositions that describe the relative positions of the labeled parts of the map to the unlabeled parts. Also listen for sequencing words such as *next, after, then*. The speaker says that the tour begins at the *fountain* and that the rose garden is *across* the *brook* from it. A further clue is that they will cross the *wooden bridge* to get there.
2. **guest house.** The tour will visit the rose garden. *Then* they will go *along* the *brook* to get to the guest house. Follow the map from the rose garden along the brook to blank #2, the guest house.
3. **pine forest.** *After* the guest house, the tour will go *along* the *brook* to the *stone bridge* and go *over* the *brook* to the pine forest. Follow the map from the guest house over the stone bridge to blank #3, the pine forest.
4. **mansion.** The tour will walk through the pine forest, *then* continue to the mansion, which is just *beyond* the *vegetable garden*. Follow along on the map.

Passage 2

1 a <u>guest speaker</u>
2 <u>charts and graphs</u>
3 <u>photographs</u>
4 <u>interview transcripts</u>
5 their <u>questionnaire</u>

Audioscript

Man:	So, we've got all the research done. We sure did a lot of interviews! Now we've got to get to work on the report and the class presentation.
Woman:	Let's plan the presentation first. We've got to give it next week.

Man:	Right. OK, so I thought we could invite one of the people we interviewed to be a guest speaker.
Woman:	I don't think the professor would like that at all. The presentation is supposed to be completely by us.

Man:	Well, maybe you're right. OK, so we won't do that, but we should show some charts and graphs.
Woman:	Agreed. That's the best way to explain the data we gathered. I can prepare those. What about photographs? You took a lot when we were going around interviewing people.

Man:	Yes, but I want to look through them to see if there are any good ones.
Woman:	OK, so if there are some good ones, maybe we'll show them. I was thinking maybe we should pass out transcripts of some of the interviews we did.

Man:	I don't think so. That's way too much. I think we should just summarize that information orally. But we definitely should pass out copies of the questionnaire.
Woman:	Definitely. They'll want to see exactly what questions we asked in the interviews.

Explanation

1. **C.** The man mentions a *guest speaker*. The woman replies *I don't think the professor would like that at all.* The man agrees that it isn't a good idea.
2. **A.** The man suggests showing *charts and graphs* and the woman agrees.
3. **B.** The woman suggests showing *photographs*. The man says he is not sure, and the woman agrees that maybe they will show them.
4. **C.** The woman suggests passing out *transcripts* of *interviews*, but the man says this is not a good idea.
5. **A.** The man suggests passing out copies of the *questionnaire*, and the woman agrees.

Passage 3

Advantages	Disadvantages
People will more probably recycle because the system is so 1 *simple*	Some residents are angry because they 2 *don't understand* the system.
It costs little to 3 *pick up* recyclables from residences.	The cost of building the 4 *processing plant* is high.

Audioscript

Single stream recycling is a system of collecting recyclables from residences that is gaining increased attention from around the country. Traditionally, households have had to sort their recyclables into different bins according to material—paper, glass, plastic—for pick up by city trucks. In single stream recycling, all the materials go into one bin. They are later sorted at a recycling facility. One of the major benefits of this system is that, because it is so simple, more people are likely to recycle their waste instead of putting it in the trash. On the other hand, some cities that have implemented this system have been receiving phone calls from furious residents who don't understand how the system works. They continue to sort their recyclables and can't see why everything is thrown together into one truck. So clearly, some education is needed. Another attraction for cities using this system is the low cost of pickup. Since all recyclables can be mixed together in one truck, multiple trips to each neighborhood are not necessary. On the downside, there are high start-up costs, not only for initial purchase of the trucks but also for the <u>construction</u> of the processing plant where the recyclables are sorted. In addition, processing recyclables under this system can be more expensive than under older systems.

Explanation

1. **simple.** When completing the *advantages* column of the chart, listen for related key words. The sentence where the speaker mentions *benefits* (synonym for *advantages*), also contains key words *so* and *likely* (synonym for *probably*).
2. **don't understand.** *On the other hand* signals a change to the opposite. Since the discussion before was about advantages, we can guess that what follows this phrase will be about the opposite, disadvantages, and we should start listening for an answer for the second column. *Furious* (synonym for *angry*) residents call the city because they don't understand how the system works.
3. **pick up.** Key word *attraction* (synonym for *advantage* in this context) signals that we should start listening for an answer for the first column. *Low cost* is similar in meaning to *costs little*, and the answer, *pick up*, comes almost immediately after this phrase in the talk.
4. **processing plant.** *Downside* is similar in meaning to *disadvantage*, so this phrase in the talk signals that we should start listening for an answer for the second column. *Construction* is a synonym for *building*, and the answer, *processing plant*, comes almost immediately after this word.

Passage 4

Piano Rentals Unlimited
Client Information Form

Name: Patricia **1** *Gable*
Address: **2** *13 Main Street*

Instrument requested: *upright piano*
Delivery date: **3** *June 1*
Length of rental: **4** *six months*

Payment method: **5** *credit card*

Man: Good afternoon. Piano Rentals Unlimited. How may I help you?
Woman: Yes. Thank you. I'd like to rent a piano for my daughter. She's interested in learning to play.

Man: All right. We certainly can help you with that. I'll just need to take some information first. Your <u>name</u>?
Woman: <u>Patricia </u>Gable.

Man: Gable? Could you spell that please?
Woman: G-A-B-L-E.

Man: B-L-E. Thanks. And what's your <u>address</u>?
Woman: 13 Main Street.

Man: 13 Main Street. Got it. What type of piano were you looking to rent?
Woman: Oh, just an upright piano, one that would fit in our living room. We don't have a whole lot of space.

Man: I think we can find something to suit you. Now, did you want it right away?
Woman: No, my daughter won't be starting lessons until the beginning of next month, so we won't need it until then.

Man:	I can have it <u>delivered</u> to you on <u>June first</u>. Will that do?
Woman:	Perfect. I don't know how <u>long</u> your rentals usually are, but I was hoping we could have it for six months.
Man:	Six months will be fine. I'll make a note of that. Now, did you want to <u>pay</u> today with a credit card, or will you send us a check?
Woman:	I'll <u>pay</u> now. Just let me find my credit card so I can give you the number.

Explanation

1. **Gable.** Listen for the key words *name* and *Patricia* (the woman's first name). She says her first and last names together. The man repeats it and asks for the spelling, and the woman spells it out.
2. **13 Main Street.** Listen for the key word *address*. The man asks for the address and the woman gives it, then the man repeats it.
3. **June 1.** The key word *delivered* in the talk is related to the key word *delivery* on the form. Listen for a date following soon after that key word.
4. **six months.** The key word *long* in the talk is related to the key word *length* on the form. Listen for an amount of time following soon after that key word.
5. **credit card.** The key word *pay* in the talk is related to the key word *payment* on the form. The man asks how the woman will pay. She replies that she will give him her credit card number.

Passage 5

Ⓐ   <u>bicycles</u>
B̶   <u>water bottles</u>
C̶   <u>maps</u>
Ⓓ   <u>food</u>
Ⓔ   <u>hats</u>
F̶   <u>tents</u>
Ⓖ   <u>cameras</u>

Audio

Good evening. Welcome to the Riverdale Cyclists Club meeting. Before we show the slides from last month's trip, I'm going to go over a few things you should know for next month's upcoming trip to the White River Valley. I believe most of you in the audience are planning to participate in that trip. So, the first question I'm always asked is: What should I bring from home? The number one item you should bring on this trip is your own <u>bike</u>. Don't laugh. On many of our trips it's possible to rent <u>bikes</u> but unfortunately there will be no rentals available on the White River Valley trip. However, the tour company will be providing each one of you with your own personalized <u>water bottle</u>, so that's one thing you won't have to pack. And <u>maps</u>, of course. We'll have several experienced guides who know the area well, so <u>maps</u> and guide books won't be needed. While all <u>meals</u> will be provided, you'll probably want to bring along some <u>snacks</u> to help keep your energy up on the road, so don't forget that. And it's quite sunny in that part of the country, so a protective sun <u>hat</u> is also a good idea. We'll be spending nights at different hotels along the way, so no <u>camping equipment</u> will be necessary. The area we'll be biking through is very scenic and I'm sure most of you will want to take <u>photographs</u>, so bring along any <u>photographic equipment</u> you want.

Explanation

In this type of question, all the answer choices are key words.

Correct answers

A   The first choice is *bicycles* and the speaker uses the related word, *bikes*. The speaker says: *The number one item you should bring on this trip is your own bike*.

D   The speaker uses words related to the key word *food*: *meals* and *snacks*. Meals will be provided but participants should bring snacks.

E   The speaker says that it's a good idea to bring a hat.

G   The speaker uses words related to the key word *camera*: *photographs* and *photographic equipment*. The speaker says: *…bring along any photographic equipment you want*.

Incorrect answers

B   The speaker uses the key words *water bottle*, then says: *…that's one thing you won't have to pack*.

C   Key word *maps*. The speaker says: *…maps and guide books won't be needed*.

F   Key word *tents*. The speaker uses the related words *camping equipment* and says it won't be necessary.

Listening Module

GENERAL STRATEGIES

Listening for Words

PRACTICE 1

Audio 1

Key words: breakfast, exercise room, pool, afternoon tea, movies

Gap Completion:
1. complimentary breakfast
2. exercise room
3. small fee
4. pool
5. free of charge
6. afternoon tea
7. price list
8. extra fee
9. movies

Answers

A, C

Audio 2

Key words:
1. have lunch, park, river, museum
2. after lunch, walk, museum, shopping

Gap Completion:
1. City Park
2. White River Bridge
3. history museum
4. lunch
5. one block away
6. brief walk
7. guided tour
8. shopping district
9. purchases

Answers

1. C
2. B

Audio 3

Key words: favorite, interesting, difficult, big

Gap Completion:
1. difficult
2. chemistry class
3. too many students
4. math class
5. math
6. so boring
7. psychology class
8. the best

Answers

1. D
2. B
3. A

Audio 4

Key words: babies, blind, groups, above ground, diet, woody plants, diet, soft vegetation

Gap Completion:
1. Baby hares
2. can see
3. rabbits are born
4. cannot see
5. underground burrows
6. above the ground
7. eating habits
8. woody plants
9. softer grasses

Answers

1. A
2. A
3. B
4. B
5. A

Listening for Numbers

PRACTICE 2

1. April 1, 2016
2. $15.50
3. $10.75
4. 6:30
5. 555 637-1204
6. 20843799
7. June 7, 2010
8. 231
9. 9:15
10. $3.45
11. 301 234-1325
12. 6573381
13. $680
14. 10:45
15. 1706

SECTION 1

Complete a Form

PRACTICE 1

Conversation 1

Key words: Name, License #, Insurance company, Type of car, Pick up date

Answers

1. Harville
2. 5036731
3. Green Brothers
4. van
5. December 12

Conversation 2

Key words: Date, Time, Number of tickets, Location, Discount

Answers

1. Sunday
2. 3:00
3. 2
4. balcony
5. senior citizen

Conversation 3

Key words: Name, Length of stay, Room type, View, Credit card number

Answers

1. Cathy
2. three nights
3. single
4. ocean
5. 4792854

Conversation 4

Key words: Address, Phone, Course title, Days, Payment

Answers

1. 351 Bond Street
2. 436-5801
3. Beginning French
4. Monday and Wednesday
5. check

Conversation 5

Key words: Address, Date available, Job type, Experience, Skills

Answers

1. 275
2. September 1
3. part-time
4. none
5. computer

Complete a Table

PRACTICE 2

Conversation 1

1. Intermediate Spanish
2. $450
3. Saturday
4. 10–14
5. Wednesday and Friday

Conversation 2

1. Film Festival
2. Main Lobby
3. $42
4. 3
5. Concert

Conversation 3

1. Manager
2. October 22
3. Hotel
4. $15
5. Law office

Conversation 4

1. $35
2. five
3. Sun roof
4. Van
5. Bed

Conversation 5

1. subway
2. hike
3. Downtown
4. three
5. taxi

Choose Answers from a List

PRACTICE 3

(Related Words answers are suggestions. There may be other possible answers)

Conversation 1

Related Words
A. prepare meals, food
B. parties, clubs, games
C. films, theater
D. sports, hikes, walks
E. novels, stories, read, discussion

Answers

B, C

Conversation 2

Related Words
A. traveled
B. practiced a language
C. made friends
D. ate, dishes, meals
E. New Year, Independence Day, Christmas

Answers

B, D

Conversation 3

Related Words

A. family, parents, cousins
B. learn, class, school, university
C. rest
D. hike, camp, climb
E. books, stories, magazines, newspapers

Answers

A, D

Conversation 4

Related Words

A. cut grass, gardens, bushes
B. car
C. repairs, fix
D. gym, equipment, work out
E. garbage pick up, waste

Answers

A, E

Conversation 5

Related Words

A. staff, employees
B. boss, director
C. pay, wages
D. place
E. calendar, hours, days

Answers

A, C

SECTION 2

Complete Sentences

PRACTICE 1

Talk 1

Key words:
1. 1999
2. underground stories
3. elevators

Grammatical forms:
1. noun
2. number
3. adjective

Answers

1. Construction
2. five
3. fastest

Talk 2

Key words:
1. tourists, visit
2. Stone House
3. Office workers, river

Grammatical forms:
1. noun
2. adjective
3. verb/ verb + object

Answers

1. monuments
2. oldest
3. enjoy/eat (their) lunch

Talk 3

Key words:
1. skating rink, summertime
2. path, reservoir
3. closed, automobiles

Grammatical forms:
1. singular noun
2. plural noun, or noun + modal
3. time expression

Answers

1. swimming pool
2. Runners
3. weekends

Talk 4

Key words:
1. construction
2. near, shopping complex
3. children, Community Center

Grammatical forms:
1. date
2. plural noun
3. verb

Answers

1. (early) 2010
2. apartments/ apartment buildings
3. play soccer

Talk 5

Key words:
1. first used
2. basement
3. summer, porch

Grammatical forms:
1. singular noun
2. singular noun
3. verb

Answers

1. (small clothing) factory
2. kitchen
3. slept

Label a Diagram, Plan, or Map

PRACTICE 2

Talk 1

1. Local History
2. Photograph
3. Garden

Talk 2

1. C
2. A
3. B
4. D

Talk 3

1. (the) park; recreation area
2. (the) school
3. (the) bank

Talk 4

1. D
2. B
3. C
4. A

Talk 5

1. tents
2. showers
3. pond
4. drinking water

Give a Short Answer

PRACTICE 3

Talk 1

Key words:
1. When, first film
2. How much, one film

Answers

1. next Tuesday
2. seven dollars

Talk 2

Key words:
1. What, in front
2. What time, bus, leave

Answers

1. a (marble) statue
2. 10:15/quarter past ten; in 20 minutes

Talk 3

Key words:
1. When, snack bar, selling
2. Where, buy, meal

Answers

1. February 1
2. the club house

Talk 4

Key words:
1. How often, leave, mall, downtown
2. Where, catch, downtown bus

Answers

1. every 15 minutes
2. the east entrance

Talk 5

Key words:
1. How long, hike
2. What, pond

Answers

1. (about) two hours
2. swim/go swimming

SECTION 3

Choose an Answer from Multiple Choices

PRACTICE 1

Conversation 1

Key words:
1. What, Introductory Spanish, took it, easy, schedule, room
2. Intermediate Spanish, foreign language, required, convenient, preparation, Mexico
3. Monday and Wednesday afternoons, Intermediate Spanish, European History, Latin American History

Answers

1. B
2. A
3. C

Conversation 2

Key words:
1. not done, research topic, made, list, spoken, professor
2. What, include, interviews, photographs, charts and graphs
3. When, due, two weeks, next month, end, semester

Answers

1. C
2. A
3. A

Conversation 3

Key words:
1. grew, knotweed, hiding structures, attractive flowers, repel bees
2. get rid, cover, ground plastic, herbicides, roots
3. used, food, medicine, rat poison

Answers

1. B
2. C
3. A

Conversation 4

Key words:
1. Why, meeting, discuss, classwork, grade, assignment
2. improve attendance, assignments, on time, participate
3. recent paper, organization, clarity, conclusion

Answers

1. A
2. B
3. C

Conversation 5

Key words:
1. What kind, school, elementary, middle, high
2. enjoy, small groups, planning lessons, field trips
3. What, say, staff, supportive, building, modern, textbooks, outdated

Answers

1. B
2. A
3. A

Label a Diagram

PRACTICE 2

Conversation 1

1. layer
2. growth
3. pith

Conversation 2

1. Grand Gallery
2. Queen's
3. Underground

Conversation 3

1. heater
2. plant material
3. oil

Conversation 4

1. grassland
2. pine; forest; pine forest
3. mixed

Match Words and Phrases

PRACTICE 3

Conversation 1

Paraphrases:
A. You have to work on Saturday and Sunday.
B. The pay isn't good.
C. It isn't close to his house/apartment.
D. They hired someone./It's been taken.

Answers

1. C
2. B
3. D

Conversation 2

Paraphrases:
A. Write articles.
B. Prepare a presentation.
C. Take excursions.
D. Read books/articles.

Answers

1. D
2. A
3. C

Conversation 3

Paraphrases:
A. meant anger
B. used for things in a row
C. used in paintings/drawings/art of the gods
D. symbolized rocks

Answers

1. C
2. A
3. B

Conversation 4

Paraphrases:
A. It has the most cities./It is the least rural.
B. It has the largest number of volcanoes.
C. It was the first island formed.
D. It is still expanding.

Answers

1. D
2. A
3. C

Conversation 5

Paraphrases:
A. It isn't mandatory./It isn't necessary./Students don't have to do it.
B. It is the most significant/essential task.
C. It should be handed in at the end of next month.
D. It should be done with a classmate/friend.

Answers

1. A
2. C
3. D

SECTION 4

Classify Words or Statements

PRACTICE 1

Talk 1

1. C
2. A
3. B
4. C
5. B

Talk 2

1. A
2. C
3. C
4. B
5. A

Talk 3

1. A
2. B
3. C
4. C
5. B

Complete Notes

PRACTICE 2

Talk 1

Key words:
1. colorblindness, inability
2. most common form
3. causes, genes, chemicals

Answers

1. distinguish (certain) colors
2. red/green
3. injury

Talk 2

Key words:
1. 4000 BC
2. wool, worn
3. AD 562, die

Answers

1. (first) domesticated
2. (the) common people
3. drought

Talk 3

Key words:
1. start
2. your own
3. hire, people

Answers

1. business plan
2. money
3. qualified

Complete a Flowchart

PRACTICE 3

Talk 1

Grammatical forms:
1. preposition/prepositional phrase
2. noun
3. noun

Answers

1. on a plant
2. water
3. its skin

Talk 2

Grammatical forms:
1. passive verb/adjective
2. noun
3. noun

Answers

1. heated
2. heat exchanger
3. storage tank

Talk 3

Grammatical forms:
1. adverb
2. noun
3. adverb

Answers

1. consistently
2. emotions
3. positively

STRATEGY REVIEW

SECTION 1

1. Hartford
2. 4
3. July 10
4. 2 weeks
5. Pine
6. $850
7. kitchen
8. 4
9. B
10. E

SECTION 2

11. C
12. A
13. F
14. A
15. B
16. D
17. C
18. B
19. A
20. C

SECTION 3

21. C
22. B
23. B
24. C
25. A
26. B
27. A
28. B
29. A
30. C

SECTION 4

31. teeth
32. dolphin
33. seven feet
34. pointed
35. blunt
36. cones
37. spades
38. curved
39. species
40. whistling sounds

Reading Module

Matching

PRACTICE

1. D
2. A
3. E
4. B
5. D
6. E
7. D
8. A
9. C

Short Answer

PRACTICE

1. 26.2 miles
2. Marathon and Athens
3. London
4. Thomas Malory
5. It is allegorical.
6. *Pamela*
7. seventeen; 17
8. the southern hemisphere
9. seafood/fish/shrimp, krill, squid

True, False, Not Given and Yes, No, Not Given

PRACTICE 1

True/False/Not Given

1. **FALSE.** *However, many structures are still covered under a thick layer of jungle growth and have yet to be excavated.*
2. **NOT GIVEN.**
3. **TRUE.** *Archeologists have excavated the remains of cotton, tobacco, beans, pumpkins, and peppers, as well as tools used to grow these crops, showing that this was an agricultural society.*
4. **NOT GIVEN.**
5. **FALSE.** *The chain consists of eight major islands, the largest being the island of Hawaii, as well as some 124 smaller islands and islets.*
6. **TRUE.** *He called them this in honor of the fourth Earl of Sandwich, who had provided the financial backing for Cook's expeditions.*

PRACTICE 2

Yes/No/Not Given

1. **YES.** *Note that these numbers show only reported information. The number of traffic deaths caused by distracted drivers with cell phones is likely a good deal higher.*
2. **YES.** *Statistics also show that it is the 30- to 39-year-old age group has the highest number of cell phone-related traffic deaths, rather than the under 20 age group, as would be expected.*
3. **NOT GIVEN.**
4. **NO.** *Both these approaches recognize that children learn differently, and they can be used effectively together in the classroom.*
5. **YES.** *The environment, for example, can affect learning in terms of sound (some children learn better in a quiet environment while others prefer noise), light (some children prefer a brightly lit environment while others feel better in softer light), and other factors.*
6. **NOT GIVEN.**

Labeling a Diagram

PRACTICE

1. all-over
2. medallion
3. one-sided
4. inner core
5. outer core
6. mantle
7. crust
8. anchor pier
9. anchor arm
10. cantilever arm
11. suspended span

Completing Sentences

PRACTICE

1. Acute
2. Constant
3. health (or, medical)
4. day
5. wings
6. moths
7. thirty; 30
8. weight-bearing
9. mood

Matching Sentence Endings

PRACTICE

1. F
2. C
3. B
4. E
5. C
6. A

Choosing Headings

PRACTICE

1. v
2. vii
3. iv
4. ii
5. v
6. ii
7. vii
8. iii

Matching Information

PRACTICE

1. C
2. B
3. A
4. B
5. D
6. C

Choosing Answers from a List

PRACTICE

Passage 1

B. *… Mexican jays which, in turn, prey on hummingbird eggs.*
C. *… hummingbird nests located near hawk nests had a survival rate as high as thirty percent*
F. *Hawks are predators, but not of hummingbirds.*

Passage 2

B. *The outstanding talents seen in savants usually occur within a limited range of categories…*
D. *Savant syndrome is a condition in which a mentally disabled individual exhibits exceptional skills in a particular area.*
E. *Savant syndrome is generally congenital but may also occur following an injury or disease.*

Classifying Information

PRACTICE

Paragraph 1

Mallard: green head, brown breast, bright yellow bill, bright orange, brown plumage, whitish tail
Black Duck: secluded areas, drab greenish yellow or olive, brown plumage, darker in color

1. A
2. B
3. A
4. B
5. B

Paragraph 2

Vermont: continental shelf, limey soil, sheep, rich agriculture land, twenty percent more wool
New Hampshire: deeper ocean, bedrock of granite, gravelly, acidic soil, oak and pine trees, lumber for oceangoing boats, major product

6. A
7. B
8. B
9. A
10. B

Paragraph 3

Classic period: for personal use, wool of churro sheep, vegetable dyes
Transitional period: synthetic dyes, varied and brighter colors, machine spun cotton, merino sheep wool, thicker yarn
Rug period: 1900 to 1930, tourist trade, similar to oriental carpet designs, thicker

11. A
12. A
13. B
14. C
15. B
16. C

Completing Notes and Summaries

PRACTICE

1. H
2. C
3. F
4. D
5. crossed the Pacific Ocean
6. material and technology
7. an Incan god
8. six men
9. D
10. A
11. E

Completing Tables and Flowcharts

PRACTICE

1. physical
2. Blocked; Blocked coronary
3. blood clots
4. diabetes; type 2 diabetes
5. Operation
6. Construction
7. pollution
8. underground conditions
9. bridge
10. V
11. spiral

Multiple Choice

PRACTICE

1. C
2. A
3. B
4. D
5. C

STRATEGY REVIEW

Passage 1

1. B
2. C
3. E
4. H
5. framework; poles
6. smoke; smoke hole
7. seam
8. door flaps
9. replaceable; easily replaceable
10. six feet long
11. longer/fifteen feet tall
12. possessions; more possessions
13. kill

Passage 2

14. ix
15. xi
16. v
17. viii
18. vii

19. xii
20. i
21. iii
22. True
23. True
24. Not Given
25. False
26. True
27. False

Passage 3

28. H
29. F
30. D
31. C
32. A
33. B
34. D
35. A
36. C
37. C
38. B
39. D
40. C

Writing Module

TASK 1

General Strategies

Recognize the Parts of a Graphic

PRACTICE 1

2. **Units:** years—2012, 2013, 2014, 2015, 2016
   Categories: bushels
   Key: solid line—wheat
   broken line—corn
3. **Units:** percentages—25%, 10%, 30%, 35%
   Categories: fields of study—botany, biology, chemistry, physics

4. **Units:** temperatures (degrees)—73, 89, 60, 82, 62, 60, 67, 45, 66, 42
   Categories: cities—London, Rome, Sydney, Tokyo, Bogota

Use the Title

PRACTICE 2

1. E
2. F
3. C
4. B

Opening Statement

Summarize the Information

PRACTICE 3

2. B
3. B
4. A

Describe the Graphic Using Time

PRACTICE 4

2. The graph shows how many students enrolled in Brownsville College in each of five years, from 2012 to 2016.

3. The graph shows the literacy rates in two different countries at the beginning of each of the past four centuries.
4. The table shows what the temperature was in Oslo, Norway every hour from 1 to 6 PM on August 10.

Describe the Graphic Using Location

PRACTICE 5

2. The graph shows the average prices of housing in four different neighborhoods in the city of Plimsburgh during 2005 and 2015.
3. The table shows how many different bird species were found in four different areas of Plimsburgh Park.
4. The graph shows the size of the population in five different countries.

Describe a Process Diagram

PRACTICE 6

2. steps
3. removing
4. vehicles
5. vegetables
6. making

Describing Data

Ask *Wh-* Questions

PRACTICE 7

Graphic A
2. 200,000
3. Bingham
4. spring

Graphic B
5. ten percent
6. 2015

7. rural
8. rural

Graphic C
9. 21°
10. 4:00 PM
11. 6:00 PM

PRACTICE 8

Graphic A
2. In the spring, 200,000 people attended museums in Bingham.
3. Summer museum attendance was over 400,000 in Bingham.
4. Morrisville had its lowest museum attendance in the spring.

Graphic B
5. Ten percent of the population lived in suburban areas in 1915.
6. In 2015, half the population lived in urban areas.
7. Only ten percent of the population lived in rural areas in 2015.
8. Over half the population lived in rural areas 1915.

Graphic C
9. The temperature was 21° at 1:00 PM.
10. The temperature first started to drop at 4:00 PM.
11. The temperature was 18° at 6:00 PM.

Show the Steps in a Process

PRACTICE 9

1. 2, 3, 1, 5, 4
2. 2, 1, 4, 5, 3
3. 1, 5, 3, 4, 2

Analyzing Data

Compare and Contrast Data

PRACTICE 10

3. Although sales of wheat went up in 2016, sales of corn went down.
4. Tokyo's average rainfall is 60 inches while Cairo's is only one inch.
5. The average rainfall in Caracas is 33 inches, and the average rainfall in Buenos Aires is the same.
6. The average rainfall in Paris is 25 inches; however, the average rainfall in New York is 48 inches.
7. In both Sydney and Washington, DC, the average rainfall is 40 inches.
8. A gallon of milk cost almost $3.00 in April 2015, and it cost almost the same in April 2016. OR A gallon of milk cost almost $3.00 in both April 2015 and April 2016.
9. A gallon of milk cost almost $4.00 in January 2015; however [*or* but], it cost just $3.00 in January 2016. OR While a gallon of milk cost almost $4.00 in January 2015, it cost just $3.00 in January 2016.
10. A gallon of milk cost almost $4.00 in January 2015; however [*or* but], it cost a little more than $2.00 in June of the same year. OR While a gallon of milk cost almost $4.00 in January 2015, it cost a little more than $2.00 in June of the same year.

Summarize Similarities and Differences

PRACTICE 11

2. highest
3. most

4. least
5. largest
6. smallest
7. least
8. most
9. oldest
10. youngest
11. most
12. fewest

Describe Changes and Trends

PRACTICE 12

1. B, C
2. A, C
3. B, D

PRACTICE 13

2. sudden jump
3. increased marginally
4. dropped significantly
5. sharp fall

State Facts

PRACTICE 14

2. O
3. F
4. O
5. F
6. F
7. O
8. F
9. F
10. O
11. F
12. F

Conclusion

State the Purpose

PRACTICE 15

2. C
3. A
4. C

Grammar

Prepositions of Time

PRACTICE 1

1. from
2. In
3. until
4. In
5. Between
6. in

Prepositions of Amount

PRACTICE 2

1. by
2. by
3. to
4. from
5. to
6. from
7. to
8. by

Comparisons

PRACTICE 3

1. busier
2. higher
3. lower
4. more
5. more
6. fewer
7. more; higher
8. higher

Plurals

PRACTICE 4

1. salaries
2. doctors
3. years
4. salary
5. woman
6. doctor
7. man
8. years
9. rate
10. salaries
11. women
12. men

13. rate
14. men
15. women

Articles

PRACTICE 5

1. ∅
2. ∅
3. a
4. a
5. the
6. ∅
7. ∅
8. ∅
9. the
10. a
11. The
12. the

Subject–Verb Agreement

PRACTICE 6

1. shows
2. spend
3. spend
4. take
5. spends
6. is
7. takes
8. take
9. account
10. shows
11. spend
12. is

Verb Tenses

PRACTICE 7

1. spent
2. went
3. took
4. went
5. has increased
6. has remained
7. has decreased
8. will spend
9. will rise
10. will stay
11. will drop
12. spends

Spelling

The graph gives information about ~~litracy~~ literacy rates in two ~~countrys~~ countries over a period of ~~sevral~~ several centuries, from 1700 until 2000. While the literacy rates in both ~~countrys~~ countries ~~incresed~~ increased in each century, the rates in Country X remained higher than in Country Y in every year shown.

In 1700, more than 40 percent of the ~~popalation~~ population in Country X was literate. In Country Y, however, a much smaller ~~percenage~~ percentage of the people could read. In fact, the ~~litracy~~ literacy rate was ~~amost~~ almost zero. ~~Allthough~~ Although the number of people who could read grew in both ~~contrys~~ countries over the next centuries, the ~~litrey~~ literacy rate in Country Y remained low. By 1900 only about 30 percent of the people in that country could read, while the ~~litrey~~ literacy rate in Country X in the same year was well over 80 percent.

By 2000, the last year shown on the graph, 100 percent of the people in Country X could read. The ~~litrey~~ literacy rate in Country Y had ~~reeched~~ reached 80 percent, but this was still low as ~~compard~~ compared with Country X.

CHECK AND REVISE

PRACTICE

2. The opening statement is complete. It paraphrases the task and makes it more specific with information about both time and location. Important data are included and one trend is described—the difference between sales in 2015 and 2016. The other trend—the months when sales were highest and lowest—is not described but only given a brief mention in the concluding paragraph. More details and analysis of this trend should be included earlier in the response. The final sentence is an opinion, not a fact, so shouldn't be included. At 150 words, this response is a good length.

3. The opening statement is incomplete. It is missing information about location (Wardsville). The important trends—the different proportions of time teachers spend in different activities—are described and compared. The second sentence of the last paragraph is an opinion, not a fact, so shouldn't be included. At 158 words, this response is a good length.

4. The opening statement is complete. It paraphrases the task and mentions both the diagrams. All the important steps of the process diagram and all the important features of the structure diagram are mentioned. Two important pieces of information are missing—the temperature of the ocean required for a hurricane to form, and the minimum wind speed of a hurricane. At 121 words, this response is too short.

STRATEGY REVIEW

Model answers

1. The charts show the percentage of Roslindale High School students who spoke different native languages in 2005 and 2015.

   In 2005, the largest group of students—sixty-five percent—spoke English as their native language. Spanish speakers made up the next largest group. Twenty percent of students spoke that language. Ten percent spoke Chinese and five percent spoke other languages.

   The sizes of the different language groups changed in 2015. Native English speakers still made up the largest group, but the percentage of these students shrank from sixty-five percent to forty-five percent. In the meantime, the number of Spanish speakers grew to thirty-five percent and the number of Chinese speakers grew to fifteen percent. Speakers of other languages made up five percent of the population, the same as in 2005.

   Overall, the charts show that at Roslindale High School, the percentage of students who speak English is decreasing while the percentage who speak Spanish and Chinese is increasing.

2. The graph shows the average prices of single family homes in four different neighborhoods in the city of Plimsburgh during 2005 and 2015. In all but one neighborhood, prices were lower in 2015 than they had been in 2005.

In 2005, the most expensive place to live in Plimsburgh was the Uptown neighborhood, where the average price of a single family home was $275,000. The least expensive neighborhood was Waterfront. The average price of a single family home there was $140,000.

By 2015, prices had fallen in all neighborhoods except University Park. There, the price of a single family home had increased from $200,000 to $225,000, and this neighborhood became the most expensive one in Plimsburgh. The downtown neighborhood became the least expensive one in 2015. Prices there plummeted to $100,000 for a single family home in that year. The neighborhood with the least change in price was Waterfront. The average housing price dropped by only $5,000 between 2005 and 2015. Overall, the graph shows that in the fifteen-year time period, housing prices fell in most parts of the city.

3. The diagram shows the process of recycling paper and the equipment used to do this. Recycling paper involves the use of several vats as well as different kinds of chemicals, including bleach. The process begins when bales of paper are carried by a conveyer belt to a vat. In the vat, the paper is mixed together with water and chemicals to form pulp. After this, the pulp is pushed through a screen in order to remove any debris. Now the pulp is clean. It then moves into a flotation cell where it gets de-inked. Next, the de-inked pulp moves into a refiner. Here, it is beaten until it is smooth and refined. The refined pulp is transferred to a vat filled with bleach. Finally, after the pulp has been bleached, it is transferred to a new vat. Now the clean and bleached pulp is ready for use.

TASK 2
Introduction
Restate the Task
PRACTICE 1

Possible answers
2. Some people feel that experimenting with drugs on animals is unkind, while others believe that it is crucial for making people's lives better.
3. There are several reasons why families opt to have their older family members live in special homes.
4. Tourism brings both advantages and disadvantages to local residents.
5. I agree that the best way to protect people from the dangers of smoking is to make it against the law.

Give Your Opinion
PRACTICE 2

Possible answers
2. I believe this sort of testing is cruel and unnecessary.
3. I think, however, elderly relatives should stay living with their family whenever possible.
4. From my point of view, the benefits it can bring are greater than any drawbacks.
5. In my opinion, this is the only way to get people to stop smoking.

Write a Thesis Statement

PRACTICE 3

B. 5
C. 1
D. 3
E. 4

Body

Expand Your Thesis Statement

PRACTICE 4

2. A, B, E
3. B, D, E
4. A, B, D
5. C, D

Introduce Details

PRACTICE 5

Possible answers

1. B. In the second place
    C. Finally
2. **Topic sentence:** People who
    have jobs and children don't
    have much time to care for
    elderly relatives.
    A. First
    B. Then
    C. Additionally
3. **Topic sentence:** There are
    other equally effective ways to
    do experiments.
    A. In addition
    B. Moreover
4. **Topic sentence:** Tourism can
    change quiet towns into busy,
    crowded, expensive places.
    A. In the first place
    B. Then
    C. In addition
5. **Topic sentence:** Even if peo-
    ple had cigarettes, it would be
    hard to find a place to smoke.
    A. First
    B. Also
    C. Furthermore

Conclusion

Summarize Your Opinion

PRACTICE 6

2. C
3. B
4. B
5. A

GRAMMAR

Gerunds and Infinitives

PRACTICE 1

1. smoking
2. to smoke
3. to buy
4. to smoke
5. smoking
6. protecting
7. smoking

Modals

PRACTICE 2

1. can't
2. may/might/could
3. can't
4. must
5. may/might/could
6. may/might/could
7. should

Active and Passive Voice

PRACTICE 3

1. are looked
2. are kept
3. are fed
4. are treated
5. were treated
6. weren't given
7. were neglected
8. will be given

Relative Pronouns— Subject

PRACTICE 4

1. who
2. which
3. that
4. which
5. that
6. whose
7. who

Relative Pronouns— Object

PRACTICE 5

1. that
2. that
3. that
4. whom
5. which

Real Future Conditionals

PRACTICE 6

1. study
2. will learn
3. wait
4. will be
5. will have
6. want

Unreal Conditionals

PRACTICE 7

1. had had
2. would have studied
3. had studied
4. would have learned
5. knew
6. would read
7. spoke
8. would travel

PUNCTUATION

Apostrophes

PRACTICE

Tourism brings many opportunities to the local residents. ~~Lets~~ Let's say, for example, that ~~your~~ you're a young person living in a small town near the beach. There aren't many jobs in the town. ~~You're~~ Your opportunities are very few. You probably think about moving to the city, where you have more ~~chance's~~ chances of getting a good job. Now ~~lets~~ let's say that your town decides to develop the area for tourism. Hotels, restaurants, and stores are built. The roads are improved. Now you and all ~~you're~~ your relatives and friends have many job opportunities in your own town. You can stay ~~they're~~ there and earn a good living. You can raise your family ~~they're~~ there knowing that your ~~childrens~~ children's opportunities for a good future are better now. I understand why some people think that tourism causes many problems, but I think ~~its~~ it's a good thing. It makes life better for local residents.

CHECK AND REVISE

PRACTICE 1

2

Introduction	Is the task paraphrased? yes/(no)	
	Comments: The introduction begins with the writer's opinion. Also, the task asks the writer to discuss both views, but only one point of view is mentioned.	
	Is an opinion given?(yes)/ no	
	Comments:	
	Is there a thesis statement with two or three main ideas?(yes)/ no	
	Comments:	
Body	Is there a paragraph for each of the main ideas?(yes) / no	
	Comments:	
	Does each paragraph have a topic sentence?(yes)/ no	
	Comments:	
	Does each paragraph have two or three supporting details? yes/(no)	
	Comments: The fourth paragraph doesn't have any supporting ideas.	
Conclusion	Is the task paraphrased? yes/(no)	
	Comments: Add a paraphrase of the task similar to: Whether drugs should be tested on animals or not is a major issue.	
	Is the opinion restated?(yes)/ no	
	Comments:	
Length	Is the response at least 250 words? yes/(no)	

3

Introduction	Is the task paraphrased? (yes) / no
	Comments: ....
	Is an opinion given? (yes) / no
	Comments: ....
	Is there a thesis statement with two or three main ideas? yes/(no)
	Comments: Since there is no thesis statement, the main ideas aren't presented in the introduction, but there are three paragraphs and each has a main idea. The thesis statement should be something like this: Children are still learning their own language and are too young to recognize the need for being bilingual.
Body	Is there a paragraph for each of the main ideas? (yes) / no
	Comments: ....
	Does each paragraph have a topic sentence? (yes) / no
	Comments: ....
	Does each paragraph have two or three supporting details? (yes) / no
	Comments: ....
Conclusion	Is the task paraphrased? (yes) / no
	Comments: ....
	Is the opinion restated? yes/(no)
	Comments: Although I think that secondary language instruction should begin in secondary school, local schools can make the decision themselves.
Length	Is the response at least 250 words? (yes) / no

4

Introduction	Is the task paraphrased? yes/(no)
	Comments: The task is copied almost exactly.
	Is an opinion given? yes/(no)
	Comments: No opinion is stated. Suggestion: I believe the advantages outweigh the disadvantages.
	Is there a thesis statement with two or three main ideas? yes/(no)
	Comments: You could add more information to your opinion. I believe the advantages such as increased revenue and improved infrastructure outweigh the disadvantages.

Body	Is there a paragraph for each of the main ideas? (yes) / no
	Comments: ....
	Does each paragraph have a topic sentence? yes/(no)
	Comments: The paragraph about disadvantages does not have a topic sentence.
	Does each paragraph have two or three supporting details? (yes) / no
	Comments: ....
Conclusion	Is the task paraphrased? yes/(no)
	Comments: ....
	Is the opinion restated? yes/(no)
	Comments: It is stated for the first time.
Length	Is the response at least 250 words? yes/(no)

5

Introduction	Is the task paraphrased? (yes) / no
	Comments: ....
	Is an opinion given? (yes) / no
	Comments: ....
	Is there a thesis statement with two or three main ideas? yes/(no)
	Comments: The thesis statement only presents one main idea.
Body	Is there a paragraph for each of the main ideas? (yes) / no
	Comments: ....
	Does each paragraph have a topic sentence? (yes) / no
	Comments: ....
	Does each paragraph have two or three supporting details? (yes) / no
	Comments: ....
Conclusion	Is the task paraphrased? yes/(no)
	Comments: There is no conclusion.
	Is the opinion restated? yes/(no)
	Comments: A possible conclusion: Even though there are laws to regulate behavior, I believe that people will not change unless they change their habits, become educated about the problems, and get support from those around them.
Length	Is the response at least 250 words? (yes) / no

PRACTICE 2

2. Change *chilren* to *children*.
3. Change *activitys* to *activities*.
4. Change *want relax* to *want to relax*.
5. Change *food who you cook* to *food that you cook*.
6. Change *Its an important time* to *It's an important time*.
7. Change *chilren* to *children*.
8. Omit the comma after *children*.
9. Change *Their healthier* to *They're healthier*.
10. Change *Eat* to *Eating*.
11. Add a comma after *If more families cooked at home*.
12. Change *would have saved* to *would save*.

STRATEGY REVIEW

Plan Your Essay

Model answers

2   INTRODUCTION

Task Paraphrase	There are both benefits and drawbacks to studying abroad.
My Opinion	I feel that going to a university in a foreign country can be a valuable experience.

My Thesis Statement	**Main Idea 1**	Starting a career at home may be difficult.
	Main Idea 2	It allows students to learn about another language and culture.
	Main Idea 3	It provides educational opportunities.

BODY 1

Main Idea 1   Starting a career at home may be difficult.

Supporting Detail 1   The student may not have had the right training.

Supporting Detail 2   She hasn't made professional connections.

Supporting Detail 3   These problems are easy to overcome.

BODY 2

Main Idea 2   It allows students to learn about another language and culture.

Supporting Detail 1   Foreign language skills are important.

Supporting Detail 2   Understanding cultures is important.

Supporting Detail 3   These are advantages when looking for a job.

BODY 3

Main Idea 3   It provides educational opportunities.

Supporting Detail 1   Their own country doesn't have good universities.

Supporting Detail 2   Another country has the best training for a certain profession.

Supporting Detail 3   The training they want is not available at home.

CONCLUSION

Task Paraphrase	There are both advantages and disadvantages to studying at a foreign university.
My Opinion	I think everyone should do it.

3   INTRODUCTION

Task Paraphrase	In many schools, uniforms are mandatory for the students in order to help them concentrate on their schoolwork better.
My Opinion	This is an ineffective practice.

My Thesis Statement

Main Idea 1   Schools believe that if students don't have a choice about their clothes, they will think more about their studies.

Main Idea 2   Students will always use their clothes for self expression.

Main Idea 3   Students will always find a way to compete with each other socially.

BODY 1

Main Idea 1   If students don't have a choice about their clothes, they will think more about their studies.

Supporting Detail 1   They will be more interested in their class work.

Supporting Detail 2   They won't worry about dressing fashionably.

Supporting Detail 3   I disagree with this.

BODY 2

Main Idea 2   Students will always use their clothes for self expression.

Supporting Detail 1   They can wear their skirts longer or shorter.

Supporting Detail 2   They can tie their ties in different ways.

Supporting Detail 3   They can roll their socks up or down.

BODY 3

Main Idea 3   Students will always find a way to compete with each other socially.

Supporting Detail 1   Making fashions out of uniforms is a way to do this.

Supporting Detail 2   Showing interest in certain types of music or movies is another way.

Supporting Detail 3   Choosing certain types of friends is another way.

CONCLUSION

Task Paraphrase	Schools often try to help students focus on academics by requiring uniforms.
My Opinion	However, in most cases this won't work. Uniforms won't change natural behavior.

4   INTRODUCTION

Task Paraphrase	Some people believe it is cruel to keep wild animals in zoos and therefore zoos should be prohibited.
My Opinion	I feel that zoos actually benefit wild animals.

My Thesis Statement

Main Idea 1   Zoos help scientists do better research.

Main Idea 2   With better research we can do more to help wild animals.

Main Idea 3   Zoos are a great way to educate the public.

BODY 1

Main Idea 1   Zoos help scientists do better research.

Supporting Detail 1   They can observe animals more closely.

Supporting Detail 2   They can set up experiments.

Supporting Detail 3   They can control the research environment.

BODY 2

Main Idea 2   With better research we can do more to help wild animals.

   Supporting Detail 1   We learn about how animals live and survive.

   Supporting Detail 2   Then we can do more to protect their habitat.

   Supporting Detail 3   We can do more to stop harmful human activity.

BODY 3

Main Idea 3   Zoos are a great way to educate the public.

   Supporting Detail 1   People become interested in wild animals.

   Supporting Detail 2   They learn about wild animals and environmental issues.

   Supporting Detail 3   They learn about the effects of human activity.

CONCLUSION

Task Paraphrase   Zoos are not cruel places.

My Opinion   Zoos help us gain knowledge that benefits wild animals.

5   INTRODUCTION

Task Paraphrase   Many people nowadays buy food that has been prepared at restaurants and grocery stores rather than cooking at home.

My Opinion   I believe this is a result of the busy lives people lead. I think it is a good thing.

My Thesis Statement   **Main Idea 1**   People lead busy lives.

   Main Idea 2   People have more time to spend on important activities.

   Main Idea 3   People can still eat good food.

BODY 1

Main Idea 1   People lead busy lives.

   Supporting Detail 1   They work hard at their jobs.

   Supporting Detail 2   Then they want to relax with family and friends.

   Supporting Detail 3   They spend time on sports, hobbies, and classes.

BODY 2

Main Idea 2   People have more time to spend on important activities.

   Supporting Detail 1   They don't have to plan meals, shop, and cook.

   Supporting Detail 2   They can just buy a meal and eat it.

   Supporting Detail 3   They can spend their time as they like.

BODY 3

Main Idea 3   People can still eat good food.

   Supporting Detail 1   People often eat snack food when they are in a hurry.

   Supporting Detail 2   Snack food is not nutritious and doesn't satisfy.

   Supporting Detail 3   A prepared meal is delicious and nutritious.

CONCLUSION

Task Paraphrase   Buying prepared meals has become common in the modern world.

My Opinion   Prepared meals give people time to pursue activities of interest to them.

Write Your Essay

Possible answers

1 People should not have to stop working at any specific age. In my opinion this is unfair and unnecessary. Some people enjoy working, some people need to keep earning money, and everybody needs to feel a purpose in life.

Some people look forward to the day they can quit working, but others enjoy their jobs. They may like the kind of work they do. They may also enjoy interacting with their colleagues. And they may like to feel that they are part of something, such as their company or their profession. It isn't fair to take these things away from them just because they reach a certain age.

Some people need to keep earning money no matter how old they are. If they don't have savings or a pension, then they depend on their salaries to pay their bills. Or, they may have these things but they don't provide enough money to cover all their expenses. Furthermore, people often have more medical needs as they grow older and they need money for these expenses.

Everybody, no matter what age, needs to feel a purpose in life. A job can give this sense of purpose. It can make a person feel useful. It can make a person feel like she is contributing something to the world.

Everybody is different and has different needs. Some people want to stop working at a certain time while others want to work longer. For these reasons, I don't think it is right to make everyone retire at the same age.

2 There are both benefits and drawbacks to studying abroad. I feel that going to a university in a foreign country can be a valuable experience. Although it may make starting a career at home a little difficult, it allows students to learn about another language and culture and also provides educational opportunities they may not have at home.

After returning from studying abroad, a student may have a hard time starting a career at first. This is the main disadvantage of studying abroad. The student may not have had the same kind of training that is required in her country for her career. Also she probably hasn't had the opportunity to make professional connections in her own country. However, with a little time and patience, these disadvantages are easy to overcome.

A big advantage of studying abroad is the opportunity to learn about another language and culture. Foreign language skills are very important for anybody to have, and studying abroad is the best way to develop these skills. Understanding another culture is also very important in today's global economy. This type of knowledge is a big advantage to have when looking for a job.

Sometimes people study abroad because they are looking for a better education. Their own country might not have good universities. Or another may have the best training available in a certain profession. Or the type of training they want may not be available at all where they live.

While there are some disadvantages to studying at a foreign university, the advantages are greater. I think everyone should do it.

3 In many schools, uniforms are mandatory for the students in order to help them concentrate on their schoolwork better. I think this is an ineffective practice. Schools believe that if students don't have a choice about their clothes, they will think more about their studies, but students will always find a way to express themselves through their clothing and they will always find a way to compete with each other socially.

According to some schools, if students all wear the same uniform, they will think about their schoolwork and not about their clothes. They will be more interested in doing well in class. They won't spend time worrying about dressing fashionably. I disagree with this point of view.

I believe that students will always use their clothes for self expression, even if those clothes are a uniform. Students can wear their skirts longer or shorter. They can tie their ties in different ways. They can roll their socks up or down. There are many ways to create fashions with uniforms by making small changes.

It is natural for students, especially high school students, to find ways to compete with each other socially. Making fashions out of uniforms is one way to do this. Showing interest in certain types of music or movies is another way. Choosing certain types of friends is yet another. Wearing uniforms will not stop students from being concerned about their social lives.

Schools often try to help students focus on academics by requiring uniforms. However, in most cases this won't work. Uniforms won't change natural behavior.

4   Some people believe it is cruel to keep wild animals in zoos and therefore zoos should be prohibited. I completely disagree with this opinion because I feel that zoos actually benefit wild animals. Zoos help scientists do better research, and with better research we can do more to help wild animals. Additionally, zoos are a great way to educate the public.

In zoos, scientists can do research that they can't do in the wild. They can observe animals more closely in order to better understand their habits. They can set up experiments to see how animals respond to different situations. They can control the research environment in ways they can't do in the wild.

Better research helps us understand and help wild animals more. It helps us learn more about how animals live and what they need to survive. With this knowledge, we can do more to protect the habitat of wild animals. We can do more to stop human activity that harms them.

Zoos are important because they educate the pubic about animals. By going to zoos, people can develop an interest in wild animals. They can learn about wild animals and environmental issues. They can learn about the effects of human activity on the natural environment.

Zoos are not cruel places. In most zoos, animals are well cared for. The knowledge that we gain by studying animals in zoos can be a big benefit for wild animals. It helps us learn to take better care of them and the natural environment that they live in.

5   Many people nowadays buy food that has been prepared at restaurants and grocery stores rather than cooking at home. I believe this is a result of the busy lives people lead. I think it is a good thing because it means people have more time for activities that are important to them, but they still can eat good food.

Modern people lead busy lives. They work hard at their jobs all day long. In their free time, they want to relax with their family and friends. They also want to pursue activities such as sports or hobbies. Many people also like to take classes to improve their professional knowledge or just to learn something new.

By buying prepared meals, people have more time to spend on the activities that are important to them. They don't have to plan and shop and cook. They can just pick up a meal at a store or restaurant and eat it. Then the rest of their time is free to spend as they like: relaxing, playing with their children, learning something new, or anything else they enjoy.

When people buy prepared meals, they eat good food and get the nutrition they need. People often eat things like potato chips or other snack food when they are in a hurry. This type of food has no nutrition and doesn't really satisfy hunger. A prepared meal, on the other hand, usually includes a variety of delicious and nutritious food. It is a much more healthful way to eat.

Buying prepared meals has become common in the modern world. These days people just don't have time to cook. Eating prepared meals means they can pursue all their activities and eat well at the same time.

Speaking Module

PART 1

PRACTICE 1

Family

Question 1
1. large, older, younger
2. small, uncles, cousins, large
3. wife, parents, relatives, close
4. twin, quiet, distant

Question 2
1. sports, visit, meal
2. read, discussing, opinions, strange
3. vacation, rent, invite
4. busy, cooks, talk, relaxing

Question 3
1. fun, share, interests
2. baby, attention, husband, fine
3. activities, in common
4. groups, like, get along

Food

Question 1
1. trying, dishes, foreign, different
2. meals, traditional, delicious, well
3. vegetarian, prepared, fresh, fruit
4. chicken, rice, desserts, sweet, vegetables

Question 2
1. out, lunch, cafeteria, sandwich
2. breakfast, dinner, weekends
3. expensive, have, special occasion
4. convenient, neighborhood, tastes

Question 3
1. serves, cakes, snack, frequently
2. elegant, birthday, prices

3. fast food, hamburger, quickly, cheap
4. seafood, fish, menu

Hometown

Question 1
1. small, quiet, peaceful, exciting, population
2. large, busy, crowded, interesting
3. mountains, scenery, tourists, medium, fills
4. suburb, pretty, work, entertainment

Question 2
1. world, live, meet
2. attractive, parks, beautiful, famous
3. opportunities, universities, businesses, easy
4. safe, raise, crime

Question 3
1. boring, same, changes
2. traffic, noisy, polluted
3. climate, winters, depressing, prefer, warmer
4. expensive, apartment, bus, afford

School

Question 1
1. graduated, variety, excellent
2. huge, crowded, sports, teams
3. ordinary, usual, activities, basketball, club
4. modern, gym, library, equipment

Question 2
1. biology, science, especially, plants, animals
2. art, talented, drawing

3. Math, definitely, best, challenging
4. history, fascinating, learning, past

Question 3
1. study, pay attention, future, seriously
2. youth, graduate, responsibilities, have fun
3. need, careers, university, prepare
4. subjects, figure out, try out

Transportation

Question 1
1. subways, buses, drive, moves
2. public, cars, train station, long distance
3. take, bicycles, lanes
4. options, taxis, walk, sidewalks

Question 2
1. far, takes, give a ride
2. station, minute, convenient
3. almost, exercise, on time
4. bus stop, transfer

Question 3
1. spend, gasoline, solution, closer
2. fast, fare, rush hour
3. walking, mind, relaxing
4. traffic jams, get, take, drive

Weather

Question 1
1. seasons, depends, varies, warm, cold
2. tropical, hot, rainy, dry, sunny
3. cold, summers, winters, snow
4. pleasant, mild, temperature

Question 2
1. coffee, window, raindrops
2. depressed, dark, cold, hope, change
3. outside, falling, puddles, hard, inside
4. special, care, storm, thunder, scared

Question 3
1. weather, warm, cold, sunshine
2. long, lots, ski, sports
3. offers, Spring, fall, nice, ice
4. rainy, desert, shines, clouds

Exercise

Question 1
1. get, run, keep fit
2. bike, tennis, active
3. work out, favorite, swim, pool
4. yoga, practice, build, strength

Question 2
1. played, teams, competitive, got
2. used to, took, lessons, energy
3. baseball, good at, had
4. particular, ran, jumped

Question 3
1. regularly, enough, lazy
2. health, diet, sick
3. too busy, free time, relax
4. uninteresting, spend, rather

Verb Tense

PRACTICE 2

Family

Question 1
Tense markers: When you were younger, did
Answer: (A)

Question 2
Tense markers: In the past, did
Answer: (B)

Question 3
Tense markers: Do
Answer: (B)

Food

Question 1
Tense markers: did, when you were younger
Answer: (B)

Question 2
Tense markers: usually, does
Answer: (A)

Question 3
Tense markers: Did, when you were a child
Answer: (A)

Hometown

Question 1
Tense markers: will, later on
Answer: (B)

Question 2
Tense markers: did, when you were a child
Answer: (B)

Question 3
Tense markers: will, in the future
Answer: (A)

Work

Question 1
Tense markers: did
Answer: (A)

Question 2
Tense markers: do, now
Answer: (B)

Question 3
Tense markers: will, in the future
Answer: (A)

Transportation

Question 1
Tense markers: did, when you were a child
Answer: (B)

Question 2
Tense markers: Will
Answer: (A)

Question 3
Tense markers: Do
Answer: (B)

Weather

Question 1
Tense markers: do
Answer: (A)

Question 2
Tense markers: does
Answer: (A)

Question 3
Tense markers: when you were a child
Answer: (B)

Exercise

Question 1
Tense markers: will, in the future
Answer: (B)

Question 2
Tense markers: do
Answer: (A)

Question 3
Tense markers: did, in the past
Answer: (B)

PART 2

Introduce Your Talk

PRACTICE 1

(The Introduction answers are samples only. Many answers are possible.)

2. **Topic:** Talk about a (holiday) you (enjoy celebrating.)
   Introduction: The holiday that I most enjoy celebrating is my country's Independence Day.
3. **Topic:** Describe something (expensive) that you (recently bought) for yourself.
   Introduction: An expensive thing that I bought recently was a bicycle.
4. **Topic:** Describe a (book) you (enjoyed reading.)
   Introduction: A book I enjoyed reading was *Oliver Twist*.
5. **Topic:** Talk about (someone) who (influenced) you when you were a (child.)
   Introduction: My uncle was someone who influenced me when I was a child.

Pay Attention to Question Words

PRACTICE 2

(The notes are samples only. Many answers are possible.)

2

> Talk about a holiday you enjoy celebrating.
> You should say:
> > (what) the name of the holiday is and (why) people celebrate it
> > (who) you usually celebrate it with
> > (what) you usually do on this holiday

Notes

what/why:	Independence Day; to celebrate the independence of our country
who:	my family and neighbors
what:	picnic and games in our neighborhood

3

> Describe something that you recently bought for yourself.
> You should say:
> > (what) it is and (what) it looks like
> > (when) you bought it
> > (what) you use it for

Notes

what:	a racing bicycle; blue, black seat, 12 speeds
when:	six months ago
what:	ride to school and work

4

> Describe a book you enjoyed reading.
> You should say:
> > (what) the title is and (who) wrote it
> > (what kind) of book it is
> > (what) the book is about

Notes

what/who: *Oliver Twist/Charles Dickens*
what kind: *novel*
what: *a poor, innocent orphan boy who gets into a lots of trouble*

5

> Talk about someone who influenced you when you were a child.
> You should say:
> > (who) the person was
> > (how) you met this person
> > (what) things you did together

Notes

who: *my Uncle Tom*
how: *he's part of my family*
what: *hiking and camping*

Personal Feelings

PRACTICE 3

(These are samples only. Many answers are possible.)

2

> Talk about a holiday you enjoy celebrating.
> You should say:
> > what the name of the holiday is and why people celebrate it
> > who you usually celebrate it with
> > what you usually do on this holiday
> and explain what you enjoy most about it

Notes

spend the day outside
play soccer
eat good food

Talk

The holiday that I most enjoy celebrating is my country's Independence Day. This is the day when we celebrate the independence of our country, of course. I celebrate it with my family, including my cousins and aunts and uncles, and my neighbors. We have a big celebration in my neighborhood. Everybody contributes some food, and we all go to the neighborhood park. We spend the day there cooking and eating and playing all kinds of games. I really like this holiday because it's so much fun to spend the day outside having a good time with my family and neighbors. We always have a big soccer game, and I like that because I love playing soccer. I like picnics, too, because I really love to eat, and the food at our Independence Day celebrations is always so good. I always look forward to this holiday.

3

> Describe something that you recently bought for yourself.
>   You should say:
>   what it is and what it looks like
>   when you bought it
>   what you use it for
> and explain why it is important to you to own it

Notes

convenient
no more waiting for the bus
fast

Talk

Something that I bought recently was a bicycle. It's a racing bicycle, even though I don't use it for racing. It's blue with a black seat, and it has twelve speeds. I bought it about six months ago, so I haven't had it for very long. I use it to ride to school and to work. This bike is really important to me because it makes transportation much more convenient. Most days, I have to go to school and then to my job. Before I bought my bicycle, I had to ride the bus at least three times a day. I used to spend a lot of time waiting for buses. Now I don't waste time waiting anymore. I just get on my bicycle and go whenever I'm ready. I can get everywhere much faster than I did before. It makes my life a lot easier.

4

> Describe a book you enjoyed reading.
>   You should say:
>   what the title is and who wrote it
>   what type of book it is
>   what the book is about
> and explain why you enjoyed it.

Notes

I like Dickens.
I like the characters.
I like the setting.

Talk

A book I enjoyed reading was *Oliver Twist*. It was written by Charles Dickens, and it's a novel. It's about a poor orphan boy named Oliver Twist. He is an innocent boy, but he always gets into trouble. A rich man finds him and tries to take care of him, but then he ends up living with some thieves. Then the rich man finds him again, so the story has a happy ending. I enjoyed this book because Dickens is one of my favorite authors. I've read several of his books and they are all very interesting. I like the characters in *Oliver Twist*. Some of them are funny and some are sad, but each one has something real. I also like the setting. The story took place in the past, and I like to read about the past. I like to get an idea of what life was like in a different time and place.

5

> Talk about someone who influenced you when you were a child.
>   You should say:
>   who the person was
>   how you met this person
>   what things you did together
> and explain how this person influenced you.

Notes

I learned to enjoy the outdoors.
I learned about nature.
He influenced my career choice.

Talk

My Uncle Tom was someone who influenced me when I was a child. I've always known him since he's part of my family. I spent a lot of time with him when I was young. He often took me hiking in the mountains, and sometimes we went camping, too. Uncle Tom taught me to love the outdoors. I still like to go hiking and to spend time outdoors. It's still one of my favorite things to do. My uncle also taught me to love nature. He taught me a lot about plants and animals while we were hiking. Because of that, I've decided to study biology. So I can say he really influenced my career choice.

PART 3
Introduction
PRACTICE 1

Sample answers. (Many answers are possible; these are just samples.)

2 **opinion:** yes, but not just books
reasons/examples: books provide facts and information
there are other sources of information
opinion statement: Most people believe that reading is important because it is how we learn facts and ideas, and I agree. However, I think there are other sources of information besides books.

3   **opinion:**   learning about new places is better

reasons/examples: we have other opportunities to relax

vacations are the only opportunity to travel to other places

opinion statement: In my opinion, it's better to use vacation time to visit new places because we have plenty of other opportunities to relax but no other time to travel.

4   **opinion:**   two important characteristics

reasons/examples: honesty

kindness

opinion statement: As I see it, the two most important characteristics of a good role model are honesty and kindness.

5   **opinion:**   yes

reasons/examples: fewer things to worry about

more opportunities for fun

opinion statement: In my opinion, people who have a lot of money are happier because they have fewer things to worry about and more opportunities to have fun.

Supporting Details

PRACTICE 2

Sample answers. (Many answers are possible; these are just samples.)

2   **reasons/examples**   **supporting details**

books   books have limits

other sources   magazines

Internet

Talk

Most people believe that reading is important because it is how we learn facts and ideas, and I agree. However, I think there are other sources of information besides books. Books are an important source of information, but they have limits. It takes a long time to write and publish a book, so the information might be out of date. Magazines are another important source of information. Since they are published weekly or monthly, the information in them is newer than the information in books. The Internet has the newest information since things can be published there instantly. I think it is important to read a lot of different things and get information from different kinds of sources.

3   **reasons/examples**   **supporting details**

other opportunities to relax   evenings

weekends

vacations are the only opportunity to   need time

travel   it's important to see other places

Talk

In my opinion, it's better to use vacation time to visit new places because we have plenty of other opportunities to relax but no other time to travel. Every evening you can go home after work and relax with your friends and family. On weekends you have two entire days to relax. There's no reason to travel far away just to take a rest. However, evenings and weekends don't give us enough time to travel to other places. We only have enough time for this during vacations. I think everyone should travel to other places when they can. It's important to see what life is like in other countries or even in other parts of your own country. It's important to understand other people. Travel is the best way to do this.

4	reasons/examples	supporting details
	honesty	don't tell lies
		show your true self
	kindness	help others
		be nice to others

Talk

As I see it, the two most important characteristics of a good role model are honesty and kindness. A good role model demonstrates honesty. Children need to learn the importance of being truthful and not telling lies. A good role model is also honest about who she is. She isn't afraid to show her true self to others. A good role model is also kind. She helps others who need help. In general, she is nice to other people. Her actions show children how to treat other people with kindness.

5	reasons/examples	supporting details
	fewer things to worry about	enough money for food, housing, clothes, other needs
	more opportunities for fun	pay for entertainment, vacations
		can pay for friends, too

Talk

In my opinion, people who have a lot of money are happier because they have fewer things to worry about and more opportunities to have fun. People with money are happy because they don't have to worry about paying the rent. They always have enough money for food and to buy clothes for their growing children. They never have to think about how they will pay for the things they need. They also have more opportunities to have fun. They can easily pay for any entertainment they like, such as movies, concerts, or theater tickets. They can go on any kind of vacation they like without wondering if it's too expensive. In addition, they can invite anyone they like to accompany them because they have enough money to pay for their friends, too. So they never have to do anything alone.

Clarification

PRACTICE 3

Sample answers
2. You're asking me if I think foreign travel is important.
3. If I understand you correctly, you want to know whether people will read less in the future.
4. You'd like me to give some reasons for spending money on certain things.
5. Do you want me to explain why role models are important?

Strategy Review

PART 1

What kind of job do you have?
1. Pay attention to verb tense.
2. Know vocabulary to talk about yourself.
3. Know vocabulary to talk about yourself.

What are your responsibilities at your job?
1. Know vocabulary to talk about yourself.
2. Pay attention to verb tense.
3. Know vocabulary to talk about yourself.
4. Know vocabulary to talk about yourself.
5. Know vocabulary to talk about yourself.

What did you study in order to qualify for this job?
1. Pay attention to verb tense.
2. Pay attention to verb tense.
3. Know vocabulary to talk about yourself.
4. Pay attention to verb tense.

Do you think you will have a different kind of job in the future?
1. Pay attention to verb tense.
2. Pay attention to verb tense.
3. Pay attention to verb tense.
4. Know vocabulary to talk about yourself.

PART 2

1. Introduce your talk.
2. Pay attention to question words.
3. Pay attention to question words.
4. Pay attention to question words.
5. Think of three reasons.
6. Think of three reasons.
7. Think of three reasons.

PART 3

Do you prefer to spend your free time alone or with other people?
1. Introduce your response by stating your opinion.
2. Expand your answer with supporting details.
3. Expand your answer with supporting details.
4. Expand your answer with supporting details.
5. Expand your answer with supporting details.

Do you think people need more free time than they generally have? Why or why not?
1. Introduce your response by stating your opinion.
2. Expand your answer with supporting details.

3. Expand your answer with supporting details.
4. Expand your answer with supporting details.
5. Expand your answer with supporting details.
6. Expand your answer with supporting details.
7. Expand your answer with supporting details.
8. Expand your answer with supporting details.
9. Expand your answer with supporting details.

How are free-time activities now different from the way they were in the past?
1. Introduce your response by stating your opinion.
2. Expand your answer with supporting details.
3. Expand your answer with supporting details.
4. Expand your answer with supporting details.
5. Expand your answer with supporting details.
6. Expand your answer with supporting details.
7. Expand your answer with supporting details.
8. Expand your answer with supporting details.
9. Expand your answer with supporting details.

AUDIOSCRIPTS

Narrator: This CD includes the audio for the Listening and Speaking Modules for IELTS Strategies and TIPS by Lin Lougheed.

Narrator: Key Word Strategies

NARRATOR: EXAMPLE 1

Woman: Our agency has quite a few apartments listed in your price range. So a lot will depend on which part of the city you are interested in.
Man: I'd prefer not to be too far from downtown, or at least close to the subway.

Woman: Well, that gives us several options. You may like Luxury Towers. There are several vacant apartments there now. There is one on the top floor that has a view that's quite spectacular. You can see the harbor very clearly from there.
Man: Great. How big is the apartment?

Woman: All the apartments in the building are quite spacious, and in addition to a large living room, each also has a separate dining room as well as an eat-in kitchen.
Man: I'd definitely like to visit Luxury Towers. But I'd like to look in other buildings, too.

Woman: Parkview Apartments will have some vacancies soon. All the ground floor apartments there have a small patio, which is a very nice feature.
Man: Will any of the ground floor apartments be vacant soon?

Woman: Yes, there will be one available next month. Now, if you'd like to be right downtown, I can show you some apartments on Main Street.
Man: Yes, I'd like to see them.

Woman: They're the smallest apartments I have to show you, but despite that, they're also the most expensive, because of the location, you know.
Man: I think it's still worth looking at.

NARRATOR: EXAMPLE 2

Theory X and Theory Y are theories of motivation in the workplace developed by social psychologist Douglas McGregor in the 1960s. They describe how managers may perceive their employees rather than how employees actually act.

A Theory X manager assumes that workers are not motivated and dislike their jobs. Therefore, they have to be controlled and supervised every step of the way or they will not carry out their duties. They avoid responsibility or taking on any extra work. Workplaces that ascribe to Theory X are hierarchical with many levels of managers and supervisors to keep the workers under control.

Theory Y describes the opposite situation. This theory assumes that employees are self-motivated and enjoy their work, that they want greater responsibility and don't need a lot of supervision. Theory Y managers believe that their employees want to do well at work and that, given the right conditions, they will. In a Theory Y workplace, even lower-level employees are involved in decision making.

Narrator: Practice

Narrator: Passage 1

Welcome to Richland Mansion. We'll begin our tour of the grounds in just a minute. Afterwards you are free to tour the inside of the mansion on your own or join a guided tour. There is one every hour. OK, here we are at the fountain, which Mr. Richland imported from Italy in 1885. If you'll take a look at this map here, I'll show you where the tour will continue. The rose garden is right across the brook from here, and we'll cross this wooden bridge to get to it. Then we'll stroll along the banks of the brook to the guest house, which we will view from the outside, but the inside is not open to visitors. After that, we'll continue along the brook until we come to the stone bridge, here, where we'll cross back over the brook to get to the pine forest, here. It's really just a small forested area. We'll follow a trail that will bring us out on the other side of the forest and then take us up to the mansion. On the way, we can stop and look at the vegetable garden, here, and you'll see that the mansion is just beyond that.

Narrator: Passage 2

Man: So, we've got all the research done. We sure did a lot of interviews! Now we've got to get to work on the report and the class presentation.
Woman: Let's plan the presentation first. We've got to give it next week.

Man: Right. OK, so I thought we could invite one of the people we interviewed to be a guest speaker.
Woman: I don't think the professor would like that at all. The presentation is supposed to be completely by us.

Man: Well, maybe you're right. OK, so we won't do that, but we should show some charts and graphs.
Woman: Agreed. That's the best way to explain the data we gathered. I can prepare those. What about photographs? You took a lot when we were going around interviewing people.

Man: Yes, but I want to look through them to see if there are any good ones.
Woman: OK, so if there are some good ones, maybe we'll show them. I was thinking maybe we should pass out transcripts of some of the interviews we did.

Man: I don't think so. That's way too much. I think we should just summarize that information orally. But we definitely should pass out copies of the questionnaire.
Woman: Definitely. They'll want to see exactly what questions we asked in the interviews.

Narrator: Passage 3

Single stream recycling is a system of collecting recyclables from residences that is gaining increased attention from around the country. Traditionally, households have had to sort their recyclables into different bins according to material—paper, glass, plastic—for pickup by city trucks. In single stream recycling, all the materials go into one bin. They are later sorted at a recycling facility. One of the major benefits of this system is that, because it is so simple, more people are likely to recycle their waste instead of putting it in the trash. On the other hand, some cities that have implemented this system have been receiving phone calls from furious residents who don't understand how the system works. They continue to sort their recyclables and can't see why everything is thrown together into one truck. So clearly, some education is needed. Another attraction for cities using this system is the low cost of pickup. Since all recyclables can be mixed together in one truck, multiple trips to each neighborhood are not necessary. On the downside, there are high start-up costs, not only for initial purchase of the trucks but also for the construction of the processing plant where the recyclables are sorted. In addition, processing recyclables under this system can be more expensive than under older systems.

Narrator: Passage 4

Man: Good afternoon. Piano Rentals Unlimited. How may I help you?
Woman: Yes. Thank you. I'd like to rent a piano for my daughter. She's interested in learning to play.

Man:	All right. We certainly can help you with that. I'll just need to take some information first. Your name?
Woman:	Patricia Gable.

Man:	Gable? Could you spell that please?
Woman:	G-A-B-L-E.

Man:	B-L-E. Thanks. And what's your address?
Woman:	13 Main Street.

Man:	13 Main Street. Got it. What type of piano were you looking to rent?
Woman:	Oh, just an upright piano, one that would fit in our living room. We don't have a whole lot of space.

Man:	I think we can find something to suit you. Now, did you want it right away.
Woman:	No, my daughter won't be starting lessons until the beginning of next month, so we won't need it until then.

Man:	I can have it delivered to you on June first. Will that do?
Woman:	Perfect. I don't know how long your rentals usually are, but I was hoping we could have it for six months.

Man:	Six months will be fine. I'll make a note of that. Now, did you want to pay today with a credit card, or will you send us a check?
Woman:	I'll pay now. Just let me find my credit card so I can give you the number.

Narrator: Passage 5

Good evening. Welcome to the Riverdale Cyclists Club meeting. Before we show the slides from last month's trip, I'm going to go over a few things you should know for next month's upcoming trip to the White River Valley. I believe most of you in the audience are planning to participate in that trip. So, the first question I'm always asked is: What should I bring from home? The number one item you should bring on this trip is your own bike. Don't laugh. On many of our trips it's possible to rent bikes, but unfortunately there will be no rentals available on the White River Valley trip. However, the tour company will be providing each one of you with your own personalized water bottle, so that's one thing you won't have to pack. And maps, of course. We'll have several experienced guides who know the area well, so maps and guide books won't be needed. While all meals will be provided, you'll probably want to bring along some snacks to help keep your energy up on the road, so don't forget that. And it's quite sunny in that part of the country, so a protective sun hat is also a good idea. We'll be spending nights at different hotels along the way, so no camping equipment will be necessary. The area we'll be biking through is very scenic and I'm sure most of you will want to take photographs, so bring along any photographic equipment you want.

NARRATOR: LISTENING MODULE

General Strategies

NARRATOR: PRACTICE 1

Narrator: Audio 1

Woman:	A room for two people is two hundred fifty dollars a night.
Man:	That seems a bit high.

Woman:	The rooms are very comfortable. And we serve complimentary breakfast to all our guests every morning from seven to nine.
Man:	That sounds nice. Do you have an exercise room?

Woman:	No, but there is a club across the street you can use, for a small fee. We do have our own pool, which guests can use free of charge.
Man:	Oh, that's good. I'll certainly use that. Do you serve other meals besides breakfast?

Woman: Yes, we serve three meals a day, plus afternoon tea. The menu and price list are available on our website if you'd like to see them.

Man: Oh, OK. I'll take a look at it.

Woman: You might also like to know that each room has a large screen TV, and for an extra fee you can order movies.

Narrator: Audio 2

Welcome to Urban Tours. We'll begin our tour today with a bus ride through City Park, which is known for its landscaping and gardens. We'll spend an hour walking through the park's Central Flower garden, which is in full bloom this time of year. Then we'll get back on the bus and ride over the White River Bridge and on to the history museum. Before visiting the museum, we'll enjoy lunch at Shell's Café, located just one block away, and then take a brief walk through the neighborhood to view some historic buildings. Then we'll enjoy a special guided tour of the museum, and we'll have an hour or two after that to visit the nearby shopping district where you can make any purchases you want before returning to the hotel.

Narrator: Audio 3

Man: I have a really tough schedule this semester.

Woman: You're taking some difficult classes, aren't you?

Man: It's not that so much, but I think I chose the wrong courses. My chemistry class, for example, has way too many students in it.

Woman: Really?

Man: Yeah. It's impossible to ask a question or get any attention from the instructor because of that.

Woman: What about your math class? You were really looking forward to taking that.

Man: I was, but, like I said, I chose the wrong class. I never knew math could be so boring.

Woman: That's too bad. So I guess you feel like this semester is a complete waste.

Man: Actually, no. Believe it or not, I'm really enjoying my psychology class. I like it the best of all my classes.

Narrator: Audio 4

Although rabbits and hares are very similar in appearance, they are different animals with different characteristics. We can say that the differences start at birth. Baby hares are able to defend themselves, at least to some degree, because they can see when they are born. When rabbits are born, however, they cannot see and so are completely helpless. Unlike hares, rabbits stick together, living with other rabbits in colonies. They live in underground burrows, which provide a safe place to hide from predators. Hares, on the other hand, live most of their lives as loners. They stay above the ground and are able to avoid predators because they are such good runners. Hares and rabbits also have different eating habits. Hares tend to favor bark, twigs, and other woody plants, while rabbits prefer softer grasses, leaves, and stems.

NARRATOR: PRACTICE 2

1. The project will start on April first two thousand sixteen.
2. Each ticket costs fifteen dollars and fifty cents.
3. A meal costs ten seventy-five.
4. The program begins at half past six.
5. My phone number is five five five six three seven one two oh four.
6. My credit card number is two zero eight four three seven nine nine.
7. I started working here on June seventh, twenty-ten.
8. I live at two thirty-one Main Street.
9. The bus will depart at a quarter past nine.

10. The bus fare is three forty-five per person.
11. The phone number is three oh one two three four thirteen twenty-five.
12. My membership number is six five seven double three eight one.
13. The course fee is six hundred eighty dollars.
14. The class begins at ten forty-five.
15. My home address is seventeen oh six Maple Avenue.

Narrator: Section 1

NARRATOR: PRACTICE 1

Narrator: Conversation 1

Woman:	Good morning. Argyle Car Rentals. How may I help you?
Man:	Yes. Thank you. I'd like to find out about renting a car.
Woman:	Certainly. Just let me take some information first. May I have your name?
Man:	William Harville.
Woman:	Harville. That's h-a-r-v...?
Man:	h-a-r-v-i-double l-e
Woman:	double l-e. Got it. And may I have your address?
Man:	17 North Cameron Street, Compton.
Woman:	Thank you. Do you have a valid driver's license?
Man:	Yes, of course.
Woman:	I'll need to know the number, then.
Man:	Oh, certainly. It's five zero three six seven three one.
Woman:	... six seven three one. Right. OK. Are you insured? We require automobile insurance.
Man:	Yes. I'm insured with Green Brothers.
Woman:	Green Brothers, great. Most of our customers are with them, though some go with Sillington Insurance.
Man:	Well, I'm with Green. Um, OK, so I'm going to need a somewhat large car, so I'm hoping you've got something that's not compact.
Woman:	We have a range of choices. You might want to go with a mid-size sedan.
Man:	No, larger.
Woman:	A small truck? A van?
Man:	Not a truck. I think a van will do.
Woman:	Fine. I'll put you down for that. What date did you want to pick it up?
Man:	December twelfth. Is that possible?
Woman:	Of course. Will you be paying by credit card?
Man:	Yes.

Narrator: Conversation 2

Man:	Crystal Theater Box Office.
Woman:	Good Morning. This is Petronella Jones speaking. I'd like to order some tickets for your current show.
Man:	*Romeo and Juliet.* Yes. We still have seats available. What date were you interested in?
Woman:	I was hoping to go next Friday.

Man: I'm sorry, but Friday is sold out. We do have some seats available for Saturday evening, and for both Sunday afternoon and evening.

Woman: Hmmm. I think it'll have to be Sunday.

Man: OK, that's March tenth. Which show are you interested in? Show times are three o'clock and seven thirty.

Woman: Put me down for the earlier one.

Man: Three o'clock, then. How many tickets would you like?

Woman: It'll just be me and my husband.

Man: So, that would be two. Fine. Now what part of the theater would you like to sit in? We still have several boxes available.

Woman: I think a box would be too expensive.

Man: Well, there are orchestra seats, or the other location would be the balcony.

Woman: We'll take the balcony. What's the price?

Man: That depends. You might be eligible for a discount. Patrons over age sixty, for example, can get a senior citizen discount.

Woman: Put me down for that.

Man: Fine. I'll make a note of it. Will you be picking up the tickets, or shall I mail them to you?

Woman: Mail them, please.

Narrator: Conversation 3

Man: Sanditon Hotel. May I help you?

Woman: Yes, I'd like to reserve a room for next week. Do you have any available?

Man: We do. Just let me take your information. Name?

Woman: Cathy Wiggins.

Man: Is that Cathy with a K or a C?

Woman: With a C. C-a-t-h-y.

Man: And what date do you plan to arrive?

Woman: June twenty-third. That's a Friday. I was planning to stay the entire weekend, Friday, Saturday, Sunday.

Man: Three nights, then. Fine. We have several rooms available for those nights. What type of room did you want? I have several singles and doubles open, and I have some suites available, too.

Woman: A suite would be very nice; however, I'm traveling alone, so I think I'll just need a single room.

Man: Fine. There are several to choose from. I have one looking out over the park and another with a view of the ocean.

Woman: Oh, the ocean. I definitely want to see the ocean from my room.

Man: I'll put you in room number 34 then. Now, I'll just need your credit card number.

Woman: It's four seven nine two eight five four.

Man: Four seven nine two eight five four. Thank you.

Narrator: Conversation 4

Woman: Good afternoon. Westfield Language Academy.

Man: Good afternoon. I'm interested in signing up for some French classes.

Woman: Perfect. We have new classes beginning next week. Just let me get some information from you. I'll need your name and address.

Man: My name is Ronald McGraw and I live at three fifty-one Bond Street.

Woman:	Is that Bond with a B?
Man:	Yes. B-o-n-d.

Woman:	Perfect. If you would just give me your phone number.
Man:	Four three six five eight oh one.

Woman:	Five eight oh one. OK. You said you were interested in French classes. Have you ever studied French before?
Man:	Yes, but only a little.

Woman:	Then you probably wouldn't want to take an advanced class. What about intermediate?
Man:	I think I would be more comfortable with a beginning level class.

Woman:	Then I'll sign you up for Beginning French. We have two of those courses starting next week. One is on Monday and Wednesday evenings and the other is on Tuesday and Thursday afternoons.
Man:	It'll have to be the first one because I'm not free in the afternoons.

Woman:	Perfect. OK, the course costs five hundred dollars for four weeks. You can pay now by credit card, or would you prefer to mail us a check.
Man:	I think I'll send a check.

Woman:	All right. We'll need to receive it before Friday in order to hold your place in the class.
Man:	I'll send it this afternoon.

Narrator: Conversation 5

Woman:	Hello. I'm a student here at the university, and I'm looking for a job.
Man:	Then you've called the right place. I'd be happy to help you. First, could I have your name and address, please?

Woman:	Oh. Yes. My name is Shirley Chang. My address is PO Box two seventy-five Bradford.
Man:	Box two seventy-five Bradford. OK. Next, I'll need to know when you're available to start work.

Woman:	Well, I guess as soon as possible. How about the first of next month? That's very soon.
Man:	That sounds fine. I'll put you down for September first. Now, what type of job are you looking for? I'm guessing you're not looking for a full-time job.

Woman:	No. I'm a student, so I can only work part-time.
Man:	That's just fine. We have a lot of part-time listings. What can you tell me about your previous work experience?

Woman:	Well, I've never worked, so I guess I have none.
Man:	I'll just put down none, then. That's not a problem. Most of our jobs are entry level. What about skills? Do you speak any other languages? Spanish? Chinese?

Woman:	Unfortunately, no. But I know a lot about computers. I have good computer skills.
Man:	Excellent. I think we have several job listings that would be suitable for you.

NARRATOR: PRACTICE 2

Narrator: Conversation 1

Woman:	Could you tell me the schedule for the Spanish classes?
Man:	Yes. It depends on the level. We don't have any Beginning Spanish courses this term. We do have an Intermediate Spanish class that meets two afternoons a week, Monday and Wednesday from one to three.

Woman:	And how much does it cost?
Man:	The four-week course is just five hundred seventy-five dollars. That's a class for adults only. You must be over eighteen to take it.

Woman:	Yes, naturally. What about advanced Spanish? When does that meet?
Man:	That's just one afternoon a week, on Tuesday. It's fewer hours, so a four-week course costs only four hundred fifty dollars.
Woman:	Do you have any classes for children?
Man:	Beginning Chinese is for children ages ten to fourteen. It meets on Saturday.
Woman:	I meant for younger children.
Man:	We have a Beginning French class that meets Wednesday and Friday for children ages six to ten.
Woman:	And what's the cost?
Man:	All our children's classes cost three hundred twenty-five dollars.

Narrator: Conversation 2

Woman:	I've been looking over the August calendar for the Arts Center. There are a number of interesting events coming up.
Man:	I know. I definitely want to attend the film festival on August tenth. It's all day from ten in the morning till eight at night. I think that's a great deal for just thirty-five dollars.
Woman:	And it's taking place in the new Circle Theater. I hear it's very nice. Oh, and the next day, on the eleventh is another all-day event from nine to five. A crafts fair.
Man:	You can go if you like. I think I'll skip that one.
Woman:	I don't mind. I see it's being held in the main lobby, so I don't imagine it will be very large. That lobby doesn't have a lot of space.
Man:	Hmm, yes. I definitely don't want to miss this event on the seventeenth in the Starlight Theater—*Romeo and Juliet*.
Woman:	Oh, I want to see that, too. Although forty-two dollars for the tickets does seem a bit steep.
Man:	I'm sure it'll be worth it. What do you think about this afternoon event on August twenty-fourth? A three o'clock concert in Rigby Hall.
Woman:	I think that sounds nice. It's been a while since I've heard good music.
Man:	I'll order the tickets, then. Eighteen dollars, not bad.

Narrator: Conversation 3

Woman:	What are you looking for on the Internet?
Man:	I'm checking the online employment listings. I need a job but the problem is I can only work part time because I'm taking a full load of classes this semester.
Woman:	But it looks like a lot of these listings are for part-time jobs. Look, here's one at that restaurant on Maple Street.
Man:	I can't see working at a restaurant. I don't want to be a waiter.
Woman:	Keep reading. It's a job for a manager. It starts October 15. Hey, that's next week. And the pay's 18 dollars an hour. Not bad.
Man:	Hmm, maybe. But I can't start that soon. I'll be away visiting my family until the 19th.
Woman:	Well, here's a clothing store looking for a bookkeeper. It doesn't start until October 22.
Man:	And they pay 21 dollars an hour. I could live with that! Oh, here's a hotel that needs a receptionist to start October 23. That might be kind of fun.
Woman:	But, they're only paying 15 dollars an hour.
Man:	I need to earn more than that.
Woman:	Then I suppose you wouldn't want to apply for this job: administrative assistant at a law office. I can't believe they're only paying 13 dollars an hour.
Man:	I'm definitely not interested in that. I think I might try for that job in the clothing store, though. I know a little bit about bookkeeping.

Narrator: Conversation 4

Woman: I need to rent a car for the week I'll be in Miami, but I can't decide what to get.

Man: Let's check out Argyle's website. They've usually got good prices. [Pause, sound of computer keys] See? They charge only 35 dollars a day for a compact car. Oh, and this is cool—all their compact cars are equipped with a roof rack for carrying extra bags, just in case you've got a lot of luggage.

Woman: That sounds good, but how many passengers can one of those cars hold?

Man: Let's see. It says here that there's room for up to four passengers to ride comfortably.

Woman: I'm afraid that isn't large enough.

Man: They have mid-size cars that can carry five passengers comfortably. But they cost 50 dollars a day.

Woman: Yes, but I see you get a sunroof with that size car. Nice. The only problem is, I'll be traveling with a group of six people.

Man: Maybe you should rent a van. It looks like their vans can carry eight passengers, but you have to pay 75 dollars a day to rent one.

Woman: Well, if I want a bigger car, I guess I'll have to pay for it. I wonder if the vans have sun roofs, too.

Man: It doesn't look like they do. But they do have DVD players.

Woman: The van definitely sounds good. But maybe a small truck would be better.

Man: I don't think so, because it says here they can carry no more than four passengers at a time. You could rent two, but that would get expensive since it would cost you 85 dollars a day each. Of course, you might want the truck if you plan to go camping.

Woman: Why is that?

Man: Because, look, it says here that the seats fold down to form a large bed. It sounds more comfortable than sleeping in a tent.

Woman: I think I'll take the van.

Narrator: Conversation 5

Woman: Have you seen this brochure? There are a number of interesting tours we can take while visiting the city.

Man: I know. I really want to view the paintings in the art museum. It's only a two-hour tour, so that would leave plenty of time to do other things the rest of the day.

Woman: And I see we would take the subway to get to the museum. That's convenient. What about this tour of the National Park?

Man: I'm not sure. It's a hike and it lasts four hours. Just the thought of it makes me feel tired.

Woman: But you get to ride back to the hotel afterwards on the bus.

Man: No, I don't think I want to do that tour. But if you want to walk, what about this tour of downtown? We would get to visit all the monuments, and it's only three hours of city walking. That sounds a little easier than the four-hour hike.

Woman: OK, I'll do that one with you if you promise to go to Grover Mansion with me.

Man: Do I have to?

Woman: Oh, come on. It's just a two-hour house tour. You'll love it. And it looks like we'll be getting there by taxi, so you don't have to worry about crowded subways or walking far or anything like that.

Man: Oh, OK. Put it on our schedule.

NARRATOR: PRACTICE 3

Narrator: Conversation 1

Man: I'm looking forward to the French class I'll be taking at the language academy. I was wondering if you offer any activities outside of class. I know some language schools teach students how to prepare meals, for example, as a sort of cultural activity.

Woman: I'm afraid we don't have anything like that specifically, but we do offer a number of other activities. For example, there's usually a party every Saturday evening, and you are only allowed to speak the language you are studying at the party.

Man: That sounds challenging, but a good way to learn. What about foreign language films?
Woman: Oh, yes, we have quite a good series of both French and Spanish films, and we also hope to show some Chinese films soon. You can find the schedule on our website.

Man: I really enjoy sports. I especially like to play soccer. Does the academy have any teams? Or any organized hikes, or any other outdoor activities?
Woman: I'm afraid we're too small to put together anything like that.

Man: Too bad. I have just one more question. Where can I buy the books for my French class?
Woman: At the Academy Bookstore, just across the hall.

Narrator: Conversation 2

Man: I'd really like to hear about your homestay experience since I'd like to try a homestay, too. What was it like living with a Chinese family? I bet you got to travel a lot.
Woman: Actually, my family didn't take any trips while I was staying with them. But that's OK. I really enjoyed being at home with them and having the opportunity to practice my Chinese.

Man: Yes, that's the best way to learn to speak a foreign language, isn't it? You probably met a lot of people during your homestay, didn't you?
Woman: Well, that's the funny part of it. I actually didn't meet a lot of new people. The family I stayed with just wasn't that way. But I'll tell you something they did like to do. Eat. They ate a lot. I ate a lot of different Chinese dishes that I'd never tried before. It was great.

Man: That makes me really want to try a homestay. I'm going to sign up for one as soon as I return from my holiday.

Narrator: Conversation 3

Woman: Have you made your summer plans yet, Lee?
Man: I'm working on them. The first thing I'll do, as soon as I'm finished with my classes, is go spend some time with my family.

Woman: You haven't seen your parents in a while, have you?
Man: Not since the beginning of the semester. I'll probably see some of my cousins, too.

Woman: Will you come back here after that to take any summer classes? That's what I plan to do.
Man: Oh, no. I need a break from studying.

Woman: Then you must be planning to just relax all summer.
Man: Not exactly. I actually have a big trip planned. I'm going to take a long hike through the northern mountains. I'm really looking forward to it.

Woman: You're crazy! That sounds difficult. And dangerous. Have you ever done anything like that before?
Man: Just a little bit. But I've read quite a lot about it, so I think I'm fairly well prepared for it. And I'm going with some friends who have a lot of experience.

Woman: Well, good luck!

Narrator: Conversation 4

Man: I noticed that the monthly fee for these condominiums is quite high. What services, exactly, are covered by the fee?
Woman: Oh, the usual things. All the outside is taken care of, you know, they cut the grass, trim the bushes, keep the gardens nice, that sort of thing.

| Man: | Good, good. What about parking? The fee includes a space in the garage, doesn't it? |
| Woman: | Actually, no. You can park your car in the outdoor lot, of course, but if you want a space in the garage, you have to pay extra. |

| Man: | That's a disappointment. Hmmmm. Well, what about repairs to the individual apartments? |
| Woman: | Maintenance of the outside of the buildings is included, of course, but each owner is responsible for repairs to his or her own apartment. |

| Man: | Well, I guess that makes sense. I actually don't mind doing a little work around my own apartment. At least it gives me the chance to get some exercise. |
| Woman: | I know what you mean. |

| Man: | It sounds like there's a lot the condo fee doesn't include. Is there anything else that it does cover? |
| Woman: | There's the weekly garbage pick up. The condo fee pays for that. |

| Man: | Well, at least that's something. |

Narrator: Conversation 5

| Man: | I'm applying for a job here and I wonder if you could tell me a little bit about what the work is like. |
| Woman: | Oh, sure. It's a great place to work. |

| Man: | Really? |
| Woman: | Yes. Everyone on the staff is really nice. They're all very helpful to new employees. |

| Man: | That's good to know. |
| Woman: | It's a good place for a student like yourself to work. You probably don't have a lot of experience, right? |

| Man: | Right. |
| Woman: | But you get good training here and everyone is patient while you're learning. |

| Man: | Well, I'm glad to hear that. |
| Woman: | Yes, and the manager is talking about raising our pay next month. It's already pretty good. I mean, this job pays at least as well as other similar jobs, and now they want to give us a raise. |

| Man: | It sounds like they know how to treat their employees well. |
| Woman: | They do. Really, the only problem I have with this job is that it's so far from my house. I wish it were in another place. But it's good for you since it's so near the university. |

| Man: | Yes, that's the main reason I applied to work here. |
| Woman: | OK. Well, I guess they'll be giving you your schedule soon. I look forward to working with you. |

Track 13

Narrator: Section 2

NARRATOR: PRACTICE 1

Narrator: Talk 1

Welcome to the Tapei 101 building. At 509 meters, it is the tallest building in Taiwan and also one of the tallest in the world. Construction of this skyscraper took five years, beginning in 1999. It was completed in 2004. The structure's 101 aboveground stories are occupied by stores, offices, and restaurants, including a shopping mall that takes up six floors. In addition, there are five stories below the ground. In a minute, we will use the elevators to travel to an observation deck near the top of the building. These are the fastest in the world.

Narrator: Talk 2

Washington, DC is a city of monuments. In fact, they are among the most popular tourist attractions in the city. We will be visiting several of them on our bus tour today, and we will go inside one of the most famous of them all, the

Washington Monument. It is the tallest structure in the city, but by no means the oldest. That honor goes to the Stone House, in the Georgetown neighborhood, which we will also visit. We have lovely sunny weather for our tour today. As we ride by the river, we may see crowds of office workers as they enjoy their lunch outside. The park by the river is a popular lunchtime spot on nice days such as this.

Narrator: Talk 3

Welcome to Central Park, one of New York City's most famous landmarks. Central Park covers an area of eight hundred forty-three acres in the middle of Manhattan. Aside from being an area of natural beauty, the park offers many recreation opportunities for local residents and visitors alike. You will find several lakes and ponds in the park. Additionally, there are two skating rinks for wintertime skating. During the summer months of July and August, one of these is converted into a swimming pool.

A large reservoir covers one hundred six acres near the middle of the park. In the early mornings, especially, you will find large numbers of runners on the path that encircles the reservoir. It certainly is a scenic place to get your daily exercise! Additionally, the six miles of roads throughout the park are enjoyed by walkers, joggers, cyclists, and horseback riders. They are particularly crowded on weekends, when automobile traffic is prohibited.

Narrator: Talk 4

Good morning, and thank you for coming out today to tour Green Acres, the city's newest residential community. Green Acres includes a mix of apartments and single-family homes and was built for the families of the twenty-first century. Although quite large, the community took just over two years to complete. Work on the first building began in early 2010, and the last nail was driven well before the end of 2012. You'll see on this map here that the hub of the community is this large shopping complex, containing a variety of stores as well as banks, a post office, and other services. Just over here, almost right next to the complex, are the apartment buildings. So shopping and errands are quite convenient for the residents living there. Down here is the Community Center building, which has a variety of programs for both adults and children. There are different kinds of classes, organized trips, and even an indoor tennis court. The community center has a particularly good sports program for children, and on most days you can see a kids soccer game going on in the field just in back of the center. OK, I think that's enough of an introduction. Let's begin our tour.

Narrator: Talk 5

Welcome to Grover Mansion. Let me give you a bit of information before we begin our tour. Now, it may be hard to imagine when you look at the building today, but, in fact, its original purpose was not a residence. The building was originally constructed to house a small clothing factory, and that continued to be its purpose for about fifty years until it was bought by the Grover family in 1910 and converted into a family home. We'll begin our tour in the base-ment. Don't expect to see a furnace or storage space, such as you would find in a modern house. Instead, that part of the house contains the kitchen, which is how most houses were designed at that time. From there, we'll continue to the ground floor. Of particular interest there is the back porch, a large and spacious area which is now furnished with chairs and coffee tables but which the Grover family usually used as a sleeping place on hot summer evenings.

NARRATOR: PRACTICE 2

Narrator: Talk 1

Good afternoon and welcome to the City Museum of History. We're starting our tour right here in the lobby by the main entrance. This room itself is of historical interest as it was the first house ever built in the city. You can see that a good deal has been added to it since then, as the museum now contains several large galleries in addition to the lobby. Moving straight ahead, we're now in the Local History exhibit. Over here we have a display showing the founding of the city, and around the room you can see displays about various other historical events. After you've enjoyed the displays in here, you may follow me into the next room, where we'll find a photograph gallery filled with photos dating as far back as the nineteenth century. They'll give you a good idea of how the appearance of our city has changed over time. On the other side of the gallery is the theater. I believe a film will be starting at eleven pm. That gives you plenty of time to look around first. The price of the film, of course, is included in the price of your entrance ticket. You may also wish to visit the gift shop, which is just beyond the theater. You can buy some simple snacks there as well as souvenirs of your visit. The gift shop looks out on the garden, which is quite lovely this time of year, and you may want to enjoy your snacks out there.

Narrator: Talk 2

As you know, we have been discussing for several months the best way to make use of the open land on our club property. This evening I am happy to be able to share with you our new plan for using this land. If you'll just take a look at this map of the club. Over here is the club house. We've decided to move the parking lot away from the building for several reasons. For one thing, we think it should be more centrally located. So, we plan to make an area for parking cars over here, on the other side of Center Road, just across Main Drive from the tennis courts. You'll be happy to know that our plan includes a new swimming pool. We've decided to make use of this land right next to the club house for that purpose. It will be professionally landscaped and add to the beauty of that area of the club. This area here to the left of the lake is rather wild and neglected, but it is a lovely spot we should take advantage of. So we've decided to clear out all the brush and add some tables and fire pits so members can enjoy outdoor meals while relaxing by the lake. The snack bar will remain where it already is. Across Main Drive from there is a large open space which we plan to develop into an area where children can play soccer, and we'll probably also include a baseball diamond and some volleyball nets.

Narrator: Talk 3

The Green Acres Residential Community is known for its convenient design, as this map illustrates. Right here, in the northwest corner of the map, is the Shopping Complex. It's conveniently placed close to most of the community's residences. So, here, right next to it, are the apartment buildings. And here, just across Maple Avenue from the Shopping Complex, are the single-family homes. Just to the south of these homes is the park, a convenient recreation area for both children and parents. And looking over the park, just to its east, is the school. So, shopping, recreation, and the school are all conveniently close to the residences. And if we look across Green Acres Street from the park, we'll find the library, and just to the east of it, the bank. We've installed traffic lights at all intersections to make crossing the streets safe for everyone.

Narrator: Talk 4

Standing here on the back porch of the mansion, we have a good view of the grounds and can appreciate their beauty and how well everything has been maintained. Directly in back of the house, as you can see, is a marble fountain, which was imported from Italy in the eighteenth century. There are lovely plantings all around it, which include roses, lilies, and other fragrant flowers. To the right of the fountain, just behind that row of pine trees, you can just make out a small building. The gardener's cottage originally stood on that site, but after it was torn down, that small shed was erected in its place and is used to store gardening tools, lawn mowers, and other outdoor equipment. Over to the left of the fountain, you can see a footpath. If you want to walk down to it later on, you'll find at the end a tiny lake filled with goldfish. On the other side is a place where you can sit and rest and enjoy the scenery.

Narrator: Talk 5

OK. Here we all are in the parking lot, and we'll be walking up to our camping area in a minute. We'll walk down this road here though the woods. Just past the woods on the left is where we'll find our tents, all ready and waiting for us. Although we'll be sleeping in the great outdoors, don't worry; we won't be living entirely without modern conveniences. There are showers just across the road from our tents. We'll be cooking all our meals over the fire pits near the tents. Just beyond the fire pits is a nice little pond, so if anyone is up for a swim, that's the place to go. I should warn you, however, that the pond water is not potable. I repeat, don't drink the pond water as it will make you sick. Drinking water is available near the showers, just across the road from the fire pits.

NARRATOR: PRACTICE 3

Narrator: Talk 1

Thank you for visiting the City Museum of History today. Before you leave, you may want to pick up a program brochure in the lobby. Of particular interest is our winter film series, which runs for six weeks, beginning next Tuesday. The theme is "The History of Industry in Film." The ticket price is just seven dollars per film, or thirty-five dollars for the entire series. We hope to see you there.

Narrator: Talk 2

Now that we've enjoyed our tour of the mansion grounds, there's just one more thing I'd like to point out. We've admired the Italian marble fountain in the back, and now, if you'll follow me around to the front of the house, I'll show you the marble statue by the main entrance. This beautiful piece of art was commissioned by Mr. John Grover in 1850 and is made entirely of white marble. OK, if you'd like to wander around the grounds on your own for a few minutes, or just rest here on these benches, our tour buses will be leaving from the main gate at quarter past ten, so that gives you twenty minutes on your own.

Narrator: Talk 3

As you know, the country club members voted to build a new snack bar on the other side of the parking lot. Construction has already begun and will be finished by the end of January. You'll be able to buy food and drink there starting February first. As always, hot and cold drinks will be available, as well as snacks such as cookies and cakes, chips and pretzels. For anyone with a bigger appetite, lunch and dinner are served seven days a week in the club house. And, of course, the new picnic area by the lake is a great place for lunch if you want to bring your own food.

Narrator: Talk 4

Shopping at the Green Acres shopping mall is very convenient. There is plenty of parking there, of course, and it is also easily accessible by bus. Buses run from the mall to downtown every fifteen minutes starting at seven thirty in the morning. Buses leave for the university district once an hour starting at eight. The downtown buses leave from the east entrance. The university line bus stop is located in front of the main entrance.

Narrator: Talk 5

I know you're all looking forward to a weekend filled with exciting outdoor activities here at the campground. We're going to start out tomorrow morning with an early hike. Everyone who is interested in participating in this should meet by the picnic tables at seven-thirty. We'll hike up to the top of Watson Mountain and back. It's not a long trip and should take just about two hours. When we return, you may want to spend some time at the pond as tomorrow's predicted to be quite a warm day. Anyone who wants to take a swim there is welcome to do so, but please remember that fishing is prohibited as we want to protect our local fish population.

Narrator: Section 3

NARRATOR: PRACTICE 1

Narrator: Conversation 1

Woman:	OK, we're discussing your schedule for next semester. I see you haven't included any foreign language courses. I thought you were planning to take Introductory Spanish.
Man:	Well, I was, but then I spent the summer in Mexico and I picked up quite a bit there, so I think I'm past that level.
Woman:	If that's the case, then you should sign up for Intermediate Spanish. You have to take some foreign language class. It's compulsory for all students.
Man:	OK, then Intermediate Spanish.

Woman: Fine. That's Tuesday and Thursday afternoons. Now I see for Monday and Wednesday afternoons you were planning on taking European History.

Man: Right. No, wait a minute. Didn't I put down Latin American history? That's what I meant.

Woman: You put European, but don't worry. It's easy to change it to Latin American, and the schedule is the same.

Man: Good.

Narrator: Conversation 2

Woman: You've started your research project already, haven't you? Could you help me? I'm having trouble getting going.

Man: Sure. What do you need help with? You've chosen your topic already, right?

Woman: Of course. And I've started a list of possible resources, but I haven't done much of the reading yet.

Man: So you already have the professor's approval for your topic.

Woman: Was I supposed to do that?

Man: Uh, yes. You'd better hurry and make an appointment with the professor before you get too much farther into this.

Woman: Yeah, OK, I'll try to do that today. About my sources, am I supposed to include original sources like interviews and stuff? Or are just books and articles ok?

Man: The professor said she wanted us to include at least one original interview, so that's something else you have to do—figure out who you'll ask to do that.

Woman: Hmmm, that's going to take some thinking. I heard some other people talking about taking photographs to include with their written report. Do I have to do that?

Man: I'm pretty sure the professor said that was optional, so I wouldn't worry about it. Also, charts, graphs, any other kind of visual, the professor said it was up to us to decide the best way to present our information. So none of that is necessary unless you want to include it.

Woman: Well, that's a relief.

Man: Yeah, but you better get going. The project is due at the end of the month.

Woman: Oh, that's right. That gives me only two weeks to finish it! I wish I could have until the end of the semester.

Narrator: Conversation 3

Woman 1:   Today I'm going to talk a little bit about Japanese knotweed as an example of an invasive plant. This is a plant not native to our area that has escaped from people's gardens and causes all kinds of trouble in the environment. It is very bad for the local ecology as well as for man-made structures.

Man: If it causes so many problems, why did people ever plant it in their gardens in the first place?

Woman 1:   Well, of course, they didn't realize how destructive it could be. People admired the plant as an ornamental. It has beautiful and fragrant flowers. Beekeepers also like it for that reason. It makes good honey. OK, so knotweed has an extensive root system, which enables it to spread quickly over a small area, crowding out native plants.

Woman 2:   I've heard that the roots are so strong they can damage concrete.

Woman 1:   Yes, that's true. Knotweed roots have been known to cause cracks in concrete and damage sidewalks, parking lots, things like that.

Man: So probably it needs to be controlled with poison.

Woman 1:   Actually, you wouldn't want to use poison or any kind of herbicide as that would harm other plants in the area. The only way is to dig it up by the roots. Then you have to put the roots in plastic bags and take them to the dump. You can't just leave the roots lying around or they'll sprout new plants. They're very tough.

Woman 2:   Can knotweed be used as a medicinal herb?

Woman 1:   I've never heard that, but you can eat it. It's really quite delicious cooked, and you can add it to pies, jellies, and other dishes.

Narrator: Conversation 4

Man: As you know, I like to have a talk with each of my students mid-semester, just to check in and see how things are going.

Woman: I'm really enjoying your class.

Man: Good, good. I'm glad to hear it. And I'm happy to see you haven't missed one class yet. A perfect attendance record.

Woman: I get a lot out of the class discussions. I'd hate to miss even one.

Man: You contribute a lot to the discussions. I really appreciate it. And you've been doing a good job on your written assignments, except for one thing. You seem to have a habit of turning them in late.

Woman: Yes, I know. It's just that I have a very heavy schedule this semester.

Man: Still, you can't continue doing that. I'll expect to see no more late assignments from you this semester. Let's talk about your most recent paper. Overall, it was very well done.

Woman: Thank you.

Man: The way you organized the information worked very well, and you expressed your ideas very clearly. I had a little problem with the way you concluded it though. It wasn't quite logical.

Woman: I really struggled with that part of it. Do you think I should write the whole thing over again?

Man: No, that won't be necessary. You'll have a chance to work more with those same ideas on your next assignment.

Narrator: Conversation 5

Woman 1: OK, so I'm Martha Andrews, and I'm here today to share with you my experience with student teaching last semester since all of you will be doing your student teaching next semester. Overall, it was a great experience. I really got a lot out of it.

Man: So, how did you choose the school where you did your student teaching? Wasn't it hard to find the right school?

Woman 1: Well, it was a little confusing. My plan was to work in an elementary school because when I graduate, that's what I want to do, but, uh, well, I found a middle school that has a great science program, and I'm really interested in science education, so I decided to work there. And I figured, at least it's not a high school so it's not too removed from my goals.

Woman 2: Didn't you find it hard working with kids that age? It must have been hard to keep them under control.

Woman 1: Actually, that wasn't as hard as I'd anticipated. A lot of the time we had the class divided into small groups, and it was much easier to work with them that way. In fact, I think that was the best thing about my student teaching. The kids learned a lot, and I got to know them well. And the teacher did all the lesson planning, so I just had to follow his plan. He kept the kids involved in interesting activities.

Man: What about field trips? Did the kids behave on trips?

Woman 1: We didn't take any trips while I was at the school.

Woman 2: I'm worried about how the other teachers will see me when I do my student teaching. I mean, I don't have any experience, and I'm young. Maybe they won't respect me.

Woman 1: I didn't have that problem at all. Everyone who worked at the school gave me a lot of support. It was a great place to work. I mean, the building was not very modern, and sometimes we didn't have enough textbooks, but everyone who worked there was really great. And I think that's what really matters.

NARRATOR: PRACTICE 2

Narrator: Conversation 1

Man: OK. For the first part of our report, we should go over the structure of a tree trunk.

Woman: OK. Well, on the outside we have the bark, of course. It's like a protective covering for the trunk. Then near the center is the pith.

Man: Wait. We need to mention the cambium layer first, just under the bark.

Woman: Oh, right. And then between there and the center we have the growth rings, and by counting them you can tell how old a tree is and what the weather was like in different years.

Man:	And then the pith.
Woman:	No, first the heartwood. The pith is at the center of the trunk and the heartwood surrounds it. It helps support the trunk and branches of the tree.

Narrator: Conversation 2

Woman:	I have to write about the Great Pyramid in Egypt for my assignment.
Man:	So what exactly is inside the pyramid?
Woman:	I'll show you. Look at this picture. This chamber up here, that's known as the King's Chamber. It was a burial chamber for the pharaoh, you know, the king.
Man:	What's in there now?
Woman:	Oh, hardly anything. The mummy and everything the king was buried with was robbed centuries ago. So this wide area over here is called the Grand Gallery. It's really like a wide part of the passage that leads to the King's Chamber. The ceiling there is nine meters high.
Man:	Wow. What's this room down here below the King's Chamber?
Woman:	Well, it was probably used to hold objects that were for the king, but it's known as the Queen's Chamber, even though no queen was ever buried there. The queens had their own pyramids.
Man:	OK, so if I follow this passage leading down from the Grand Gallery and keep going down here, now I'm below the Queen's Chamber. What's this place down here for?
Woman:	Actually, no one really knows the purpose of that chamber, although there are several theories. So, it's just called the underground chamber because that's where it is.

Narrator: Conversation 3

Woman:	For my project, I'm going to build a steam distiller and then demonstrate how it works for the class.
Man:	But what's it for?
Woman:	It's used for extracting essential oils from plants. It's actually a pretty simple device.
Man:	So how does it work?
Woman:	OK, well, first I get a heater to heat the water. I put a glass beaker, like this, over it and fill it with water.
Man:	To create the steam.
Woman:	Of course. Over the water beaker is another one filled with plant material. So the steam rises through the plant material, and then it goes through this glass tube, the condenser.
Man:	Oh, I see, and then the condensed water collects down here.
Woman:	Yes, but it's actually condensed water and oil. The oil is lighter, so it sits on top of the water. Then all I have to do is skim the oil off.

Narrator: Conversation 4

Man 1:	Today I am going to talk about mountain biomes. You know that as you go up a mountain, the temperature gradually decreases, so you'll find different biomes, that is areas of different plant and animal communities depending on the altitude.
Woman:	But you won't find the same biomes, the same kinds of plants and animals, on all mountains.
Man 1:	That's correct. It also depends on which part of the world you're talking about and other climate factors. I'm going to use as my first example the state of Arizona, and I'm going to compare two different areas of the state. So first we'll look at the northern part of the state.
Man 2:	It's cooler there than in the south.
Man 1:	Yes, and less dry too, so instead of finding sandy desert at the base of the mountain, you'll find grassland. Moving up the mountain, the next zone consists of juniper mostly. Just above the juniper woodland you'll find the pine forest.
Woman:	Then if you keep climbing, you reach the fir forest.
Man 1:	Correct. Then in the area before the top of the mountain is a zone of mixed fir and spruce forest. Finally at the top you have the alpine zone, above the tree line.

NARRATOR: PRACTICE 3

Narrator: Conversation 1

Woman:	I heard you're looking for a job this semester, Jim.
Man:	Yeah, I need something part-time that still leaves me enough time for studying. I went to the campus employment office, and there are a few jobs I'm interested in applying for.
Woman:	What are they?
Man:	Well, there's an office assistant job I'm really interested in because it's at an engineering firm, and you know I'd like to go into engineering.
Woman:	So, have you applied for it?
Man:	I will, but it's not very close to my apartment so I'd have to spend a lot of time just traveling to work every day. So I'm not sure it's the best choice for me. On the other hand, I wouldn't have to work on Saturday or Sunday, so that's a plus.
Woman:	I think you should look for something here at the university. Like in the cafeteria, maybe.
Man:	Well, there is an opening there for a server that I plan to apply for. It doesn't pay very much though. I think I need to earn more than I could get there.
Woman:	I heard they were looking for a cashier at the university bookstore.
Man:	They were, and I wanted to apply, but it turns out they've already hired someone for that position.
Woman:	Too bad. I think it would be really fun to work there.

Narrator: Conversation 2

Man:	As your advisor, Elizabeth, it's my job to talk with you during the semester to find out how your classes are going.
Woman:	I'd say everything's going pretty well, except sometimes I feel overwhelmed with work. Particularly in my economics class.
Man:	So you feel the workload in that class is too heavy?
Woman:	Well, I have about ten books I have to finish before the end of the semester. They're all very interesting, but, you know, it takes a lot of concentration to read about economics.
Man:	What about your other classes?
Woman:	I'm really enjoying my sociology class. I have to write several articles for it. That's a lot, but it's interesting. Anyhow, I prefer that kind of assignment to having to prepare a class presentation. That's something I really don't like to do. So I like that class, but my favorite class is geology.
Man:	Is geology a special interest of yours?
Woman:	Not especially, but the class is really fun because every week we go on excursions to places that have interesting geological features. We get to see these things in real life. It's a fun way to learn.

Narrator: Conversation 3

Man:	I've been doing some really interesting reading about ancient Egyptian art in my art history class.
Woman:	Oh, yes, I was reading something about that recently. The colors all have special meanings, or something, don't they?
Man:	Yeah, the ancient Egyptians used colors to symbolize different things. White, for example, meant purity, and black meant death, though sometimes it represented life, too.
Woman:	That's strange. Anyhow, I thought green symbolized life.
Man:	Well, it does. It represents new life and vegetation, as you might imagine. I mean, that makes sense. There is also this green stone, malachite, that was used as a symbol of joy.
Woman:	It's a really pretty stone.

Man:	Then blue was often used in paintings of gods. I'll have to look that up, but I think it was an association with the sky.
Woman:	It makes sense.
Man:	Victory was symbolized by red, but red had other uses, too. It could mean anger, but also it was just used as a normal skin color.
Woman:	So color wasn't always used in a symbolic way?
Man:	No, not always. I mean, sometimes they just used different colors to distinguish different objects, like if they were painting a row of things or something like that, then they would just alternate the colors.

Narrator: Conversation 4

Woman:	I've been learning some interesting things about the Hawaiian Islands in my geology class.
Man:	Well, the Islands were all formed by volcanoes. That's about all I know about them.
Woman:	Yes, and in fact Hawaii island, also known as the Big Island, is actually still forming. It has several active volcanoes and it's still expanding because of that. It's the youngest of all the islands.
Man:	I didn't realize that. What about Oahu Island? Isn't that where the capital city is?
Woman:	Yes, Honolulu, the capital of Hawaii, is on Oahu. So is most of the population of the state. Unlike some of the other islands, Oahu is not as rural, since it has the city there and such a high population density.
Man:	Yeah, I would've guessed that. But the other islands are quieter and less populated, I would think.
Woman:	Uh huh. Kauai, for example. That island doesn't have any highways or tall buildings. It has a lot of nice beaches, though. That's because it was the first island to be formed, so it's been around for a long time. Ages of erosion have formed miles and miles of beautiful, sandy beaches.

Narrator: Conversation 5

Man 1:	Let's go over the major assignments you'll have in this class this semester.
Woman:	Will there be a final exam?
Man 1:	That's always what students want to know about first. Yes, there will be a final exam, but contrary to what you may think, it isn't mandatory. You don't have to take it. You'll have a choice of writing a final essay instead if you prefer.
Man 2:	What will the essay be about?
Man 1:	We'll be talking about that later on. So some of you will write an essay and some will take an exam at the end of the semester. One thing all of you will do is write a research paper. It's a short one, and you will need to hand it in to me by the end of next month.
Woman:	The end of next month? That's hardly any time at all.
Man 1:	Yes, but remember I said it will be a short paper. The other important assignment you have in this class is the textbook articles. I've put a list of the required ones on the website. Some of them are fairly dense so I recommend finding a classmate to study with. Then you can discuss the material together.

Track 19

Narrator: Section 4

NARRATOR: PRACTICE 1

Narrator: Talk 1

Although in common speech we may use words such as marsh, swamp, and bog interchangeably, these terms actually refer to different types of wetlands with different characteristics. A wetland is an area that is covered with shallow water for at least part of the year. A marsh is a wetland where grassy vegetation predominates. Marshes are often found near still water such as a pond or a lake. A swamp, on the other hand, is a wetland characterized by the presence of woody shrubs and trees. Swamps are also found near rivers. Both swamps and marshes may have either salty or fresh water. Bogs are different from swamps and marshes in that they get all their water from the rain. Plants such as mosses and heaths characterize bogs, and bog water is usually acidic.

Narrator: Talk 2

The ancient Mayans are renowned for the beautiful temples and palaces that they built. Different architectural styles can be seen depending on location and period of history. We've already discussed the Peten style, which developed in the pre-classic and early classic period. The Bec River style developed out of the Peten style, during the late classic period. It is characterized by the use of towers as ornamentation, as well as the use of checkerboard motifs, figureheads, and columns to decorate the building facades, or fronts. The Puuc style was characterized by more complex buildings of many rooms and floors. The walls were decorated with stone carved in geometric patterns as well as carved figureheads. The East Coast style developed in the eastern part of the Yucatan Peninsula during the post-classic period. It was characterized by buildings with flat roofs and main doorways supported by columns.

Narrator: Talk 3

As you might expect, TV viewing habits vary among different age groups. Recent studies have shown that older people, those aged sixty-five and above, spend between six and seven hours a day watching TV. Compare this to teenagers who actually spend the least amount of time in front of the TV, three to four hours a day. Younger adults average five to six hours in front of the TV each day. So the figures clearly show that TV watching increases as we age. And what do the different age groups watch? Although all age groups say that they watch TV for entertainment, older adults actually tend to watch what we might call nonfictional programs, that is news and other types of informational shows. Younger adults watch less news programming and more entertainment shows.

NARRATOR: PRACTICE 2

Narrator: Talk 1

Colorblindness is a misleading term as it sounds like people suffering from this condition cannot see any colors. In fact, this is not the case. Colorblindness is a condition that makes it difficult to distinguish certain colors. The majority of colorblind people have red-green colorblindness, while a small percentage suffer from blue-yellow colorblindness. Colorblindness is usually a genetic condition, passed on from mother to child. However, it sometimes also results from injury or exposure to certain chemicals. Most sufferers are men. Between eight and ten percent of the male population are colorblind, while only point five percent of women suffer from the condition.

Narrator: Talk 2

The llama, an animal native to the Andes Mountains, has been an important part of Inca culture since 4000 BC, when it was first domesticated. The llama is able to survive at high mountain altitudes. It can nourish itself on the sparse vegetation found at higher altitudes and still produce meat and wool. Llama meat was an important source of food for all sectors of ancient Inca society. Llama wool, which is somewhat coarse in texture, was used by the common people to weave into clothing. The upper classes preferred the softer wool of the alpaca, a close cousin of the llama. Later on, the Inca people started the llama as a pack animal. It travels easily over rocky mountain slopes and thus was used to transport goods and maintain connections with distant communities. The llama continued to be important to Inca life for centuries. In the year AD 562, an area of the Andes suffered a drought. This resulted in the deaths of large numbers of llamas due to lack of food and decreased disease resistance.

Narrator: Talk 3

It is common knowledge that most small businesses fail within the first five years. But small businesses don't have to fail, and if you pay attention to a few key points, you can be successful. You can't start a successful small business without a solid business plan. This is where you show what your costs are and how you will make your profit. It is the first and most important step. Another important point is financing. Most people start their businesses with loans. However, even if you do have to borrow some, it's best to start with as much of your own money as possible so that you are not burdened with paying back loans during the first, often unprofitable, years of operation. Another thing to consider is the people that you will hire. Make sure that your employees are qualified for the job. Then they will be able to support the success of your business.

NARRATOR: PRACTICE 3

Narrator: Talk 1

We are all familiar with the sight of colorful dragonflies flying skillfully over ponds and streams. These are dragonflies in the adult stage, which is actually the shortest stage of this insect's life. The dragonfly life cycle, which generally lasts about a year, consists of three stages—egg, nymph, and adult dragonfly. The cycle begins when the eggs are deposited on a plant or below the surface of the water by the female dragonfly. When the eggs hatch, nymphs crawl out. The nymphs live and grow under the water for several months, or up to four years in the case of some species. The nymph stage is the longest part of the lifecycle. When the nymph is completely grown, it crawls out of the water and up the stem of a plant. There it sheds its skin, and the adult dragonfly emerges. The dragonfly lives in this stage for several weeks or months.

Narrator: Talk 2

There are several systems for heating water with the energy of the sun. In a direct system, water is heated as it moves through the solar collector and then is used right away or stored in a tank. This system works well in places where the temperature usually doesn't fall below freezing. The indirect system is used in colder climates. In this system, an antifreeze solution moves through the solar collector. The heated solution is then pumped through a heat exchanger, heating up the water in the storage tank. The heated water is then held in the tank, ready for use by the household.

Narrator: Talk 3

Developing secure attachments is a critical part of a child's emotional growth. Babies are entirely dependent on others for their survival. When a baby's parents or caretakers respond consistently to the baby's physical and emotional needs, then healthy attachments can form. The baby feels secure and loved. Then as the baby grows into a child and then an adult, she learns to handle her own emotions. She is able to develop healthy relationships with others and sees herself and other people positively. When parents respond to their baby's needs inconsistently, the result is usually difficulty in forming healthy relationships or a healthy self-image.

NARRATOR: STRATEGY REVIEW

You will hear a number of different recordings and you will have to answer questions on what you hear. You will have time to read the instructions and questions. At the end you will have thirty seconds to look over your answers and ten minutes to transfer your answers to an answer sheet. The recordings will be played only once. Now look at section 1.

Narrator: Listening Section 1

You will hear a man talking to a woman who works in a rental agency. Take 30 seconds to look at questions 1 to 4.

[30-second pause]

Narrator: On the actual IELTS exam, you would see that an example has been done for you. You would hear the relevant audio for the example. You will not have an example in this review.

Listen carefully and answer questions 1 to 4.

Woman: Good morning. Lakeside Rentals. How may I help you?
Man: Yes, thank you. I'm interested in renting a cottage by the lake this summer.

Woman:	Wonderful. Let's start by taking down your information. May I have your name, please?
Man:	Gregory Thornton.
Woman:	And what is your mailing address, Mr. Thornton?
Man:	That would be Box 7, Hartford, Connecticut.
Woman:	Box 7. Was that Hartford or Hartland?
Man:	Hartford. H-A-R-T-F-O-R-D.
Woman:	F-O-R-D. Wonderful. All right then, Mr. Thornton. What is the size of your group?
Man:	Pardon me?
Woman:	I mean, how many people in your party? How many people will be staying in the cottage with you?
Man:	Oh, right. Just my family. My wife and our two sons and myself. So that's four people all together.
Woman:	Perfect. We have a number of cottages suited for a small group. Now then, when did you want to begin your stay?
Man:	We'd like to get there on July tenth, if that's possible. I mean, it's possible for us, of course, but if you have any vacancies then.
Woman:	Oh, certainly we do. Our busy season really doesn't begin until August first.
Man:	That's good to hear. We were hoping to stay for a couple of weeks.
Woman:	Fine. That'll give you plenty of time to enjoy the area. So I'll put you down for two weeks.
Man:	Yes. I really wish it could be three, but we have to get back to work before the end of the month.

Narrator: Before you hear the rest of the conversation, take thirty-seconds to look at questions 5 to 10.

[30-second pause]

Narrator: Now listen and answer questions 5 to 10.

Woman:	I understand. Let's talk about the cottages we have available. Do you want a two or a three bedroom?
Man:	Either one would be fine.
Woman:	Well, then, Pine Cottage is lovely. It has two bedrooms and features a porch off the living room so you can enjoy sitting outside.
Man:	That sounds nice. What's the rental fee?
Woman:	It's a small cottage, so it's just seven hundred dollars a week. Our other two-bedroom is Maple Cottage. It doesn't have a porch, but it does have a large window in the living room with a spectacular view of the lake. It's a bit larger than Pine, plus it has the view, so it goes for eight hundred fifty dollars a week.
Man:	What about a three-bedroom cottage?
Woman:	Hemlock Cottage has three bedrooms. Are you interested in cooking?
Man:	Not while we're on vacation. We weren't looking for a place with a kitchen.
Woman:	Well, then, I suppose the fact that Hemlock has one wouldn't matter to you. And it is our most expensive rental, at nine hundred twenty-five dollars a week.
Man:	So you do have a cheaper three-bedroom?
Woman:	Yes, there's Spruce Cottage. Actually it has an extra small room downstairs, so we call it a four-bedroom. It goes for nine hundred dollars a week.
Man:	Does it have a view?
Woman:	No, but it does have a nice little garden in the back.
Man:	I'll need some time to think this over. What activities are available at the lake?
Woman:	We rent both water skis and canoes.
Man:	I definitely want to do some paddling.

Woman:	There's also horseback-riding lessons. And we have tennis courts where you can play on your own, and you can also sign up for lessons there.
Man:	I haven't been able to pick up a tennis racket since I hurt my elbow last summer.
Woman:	I'm sorry to hear that. You might want to think about joining some of our guided hikes. There's one every day.
Man:	Sounds great. My wife and I will both enjoy that.

Narrator: Listening Section 2

You will hear a guide welcoming visitors to the City Zoo. First you have thirty seconds to look at questions 11 to 17.

[30-second pause]

Narrator: Now listen carefully and answer questions 11 to 17.

Good morning and welcome to the City Zoo. We are excited to have all you teachers here with us today to learn about the zoo and the programs we offer to school children, and we hope that all of you will plan to bring your classes to visit us during this school year. We're open almost every day of the year, including holidays, with the exception of the last week of the year. We close for that entire week. Other than that, you can plan to bring your classes for a visit any day you like, any time between opening at eight to closing at five. We try to keep our entrance fees as low as possible, and school groups get a discount of fifteen percent when you bring a group of at least ten children. You may also want to take advantage of our free days. We don't charge any entrance fee on the first Monday of each month.

Let's start with a look at a zoo map so you can get an idea of what's available. Here in the lower left-hand corner is the main entrance. Across the pathway to the east of the entrance is the Education Building, where we are sitting right now. Here in the northwest corner is the picnic area, which is a good place for you to plan to have lunch with your class. To the right of it is the cafeteria. Lunch, of course, is available there, too, but most teachers, I find, prefer to have their students bring their own lunches. The picnic area also looks out over the small lake, just to the south of it, which is in the area where our water birds are. So it's a pretty spot. Just to the south of the water birds is the small mammal house, which most children enjoy visiting. If you'd rather see some large mammals, the elephant house is located across the pathway to the west of the small mammal house. Just north of the elephants, you can visit lizards, crocodiles, and turtles in the reptile house.

Narrator: Before you hear the rest of the conversation, take thirty seconds to look at questions 18 to 20.

[30-second pause]

Narrator: Now listen and answer questions 18 to 20.

OK, let's talk about our education programs. At this time, we are set up to serve children from ages six to ten. We hope to have something in place for older children by next winter, for the twelve and thirteen year olds, and I can talk a bit about our plans for that a little later. For high school students, up to age eighteen, we have some plans for them in the works too. Unfortunately, we have nothing for preschool kids, the four and five year old set, at this time.

So, for the primary school kids we have several programs you can choose from. Animals Up Close is a popular one. Kids get a chance to get close to actual zoo animals. While we can't allow the kids to actually pet the animals, they can help with the feeding. And we talk about animal care, keeping the animals clean and healthy, and we give a grooming demonstration. For this, and all our programs, we provide teachers with reading materials to share with the class before the visit. You can also use them as a resource if you plan to test your class on what they learned during the visit. All our programs last one hour, and we do expect you to stay with your class during that entire time.

Narrator: Listening Section 3

You will hear two students discussing their university course schedule. First you have thirty seconds to look at questions 21 to 26.

[30-second pause]

Narrator: Now listen carefully and answer questions 21 to 26.

Man: Hi, Samantha. I didn't see you in biology class today.
Woman: I had to drop it. My schedule is already so heavy. I decided to leave it for next semester.

Man: Yeah, I hear that anthropology class you're in is really tough.
Woman: It sure is. But it's really interesting, too. Now, my economics class, that's another story.

Man: I thought you were in that class last semester.
Woman: I wish I had been. But I have to take it now because it's a prerequisite for the political science class I want to enroll in next semester.

Man: American history is a prerequisite for that class, too, isn't it?
Woman: Yeah, but I've already studied that. Which is a good thing because I don't have any more room in my schedule. I have a ton of homework. I have to read two novels this week for my literature class, on top of everything else.

Narrator: Before you hear the rest of the conversation, take thirty seconds to look at questions 27 to 30.

[30-second pause]

Narrator: Now listen and answer questions 27 to 30.

Man: Wow, Samantha, you do have a busy schedule. But at least you're living closer to campus this semester, aren't you? That should save you some time.
Woman: Yeah, my apartment is just a few blocks away. I can walk to class in five or ten minutes.

Man: Sure beats those long bus rides.
Woman: Uh-huh. I really didn't like it when I was living so far from campus. Oh, I meant to tell you. They hired me at the college bookstore.

Man: That's great. That's got to be better than that boring cafeteria job you were going to take.
Woman: I'm glad I don't have to work there. It sure would be nice to have an office job, though.

Man: Maybe next semester.
Woman: Yeah, I'm actually happy to have such an easy job because this really is a tough semester for me, with all these heavy classes I'm taking.

Man: Between work and class, I guess you don't have a lot of time for fun, do you?
Woman: Fun? What's that?

Man: Ha, ha, you're so funny. Well, there's always summer vacation to look forward to. You can have your fun then.
Woman: I wish. My job lasts until the end of the summer. And I need the money, so I've got to stay at it.

Man: I'll think of you while I'm traveling to the beach.

Narrator: Listening Section 4

You will hear a lecture describing the difference between two marine animals. First you have thirty seconds to look at questions 31 to 35.

[30-second pause]

Narrator: Now listen carefully and answer questions 31 to 35.

Today I'm going to talk about a couple of commonly confused marine mammals—dolphins and porpoises. Aren't they the same animal? you may ask. Many people think they are, and they are very similar to each other. But they are different. Along with their cousins, the whales, dolphins, and porpoises make up the order Cetacea. They are all closely related, and the basic way to distinguish between whales, on the one hand, and dolphins and porpoises, on the other, is size, as whales are much larger than dolphins and porpoises. Additionally, those that are classified as true whales have baleen rather than teeth, which allows them to filter their food out of the water. All dolphins and porpoises, on the other hand, have teeth and, of course, eat a different type of diet. The killer whale, also called orca, is not really a whale, despite its name, but is the largest dolphin. Not a porpoise, but a dolphin. So what's the difference? It basically comes down to size and shape. Although some species of dolphins are on the small side, they generally tend to be larger than porpoises. They can reach up to twelve feet or longer in size, while porpoises are under seven feet in length. You can also determine the difference by looking at the shape of several distinguishing features; for example, the shape of the snout on each animal is quite different. A dolphin's snout, also called its beak, is pointed, while a porpoise's is blunt. So that's one difference.

Narrator: Before you hear the rest of the conversation, take thirty seconds to look at questions 36 to 40.

[30-second pause]

Narrator: Now listen and answer questions 36 to 40.

The form of the teeth is another way to tell the difference. Those of the dolphin are pointed like cones while those of the porpoise are flat and wide like spades. And then there is the dorsal fin, often the most prominent feature when you see a group of dolphins jumping through the water. On the dolphin, this has a curved edge, while that of the porpoise is straight edged, like a triangle. OK, then, in addition to being larger in size, dolphins are also larger in number. While there are something over thirty species of dolphins that we know of, including both freshwater and ocean species, the number of porpoise species is far less, adding up to just six. We might even consider dolphins to be more talented than porpoises, or at least more chatty. Dolphins communicate with each other by making whistling sounds underwater. Researchers believe that porpoises don't do this. Nevertheless, both dolphins and porpoises are highly intelligent creatures.

Narrator: This is the end of section 4. You now have thirty seconds to look over your answers.

[30-second pause]

Narrator: This is the end of the listening test. You now have ten minutes to transfer your answers to the Listening Answer sheet.

Narrator: Speaking Module

Narrator: Part 1

NARRATOR: PRACTICE 1

NARRATOR: FAMILY

Narrator: Question 1

1. I have a large family. There is my mother and father. Plus I have two older brothers and a younger sister.
2. I have a small family, just me and my mother and father. But my uncles and aunts and cousins live very nearby, so we seem like a large family.
3. I recently got married, and my wife and I live alone in a small apartment. But her parents live nearby, and she has lots of relatives. She is very close to her family.
4. I have a twin brother. He is my only sibling, so ours is a quiet family. Most of our relatives live in another city, so we don't see them often. We have some distant cousins who live near us, but I don't know them well.

Narrator: Question 2

1. My brothers and sisters and I all enjoy sports, so we spend a lot of time playing soccer and tennis together. Also, we usually visit our cousins every weekend and have a big meal with them.
2. We all like to read in our family, and we really enjoy discussing books together. We don't always have the same opinions about books, so we argue a lot. It may sound strange, but we think that's really fun.
3. We usually take a big family vacation every summer. We rent a big house at the beach and invite all our cousins to stay with us.
4. Unfortunately, I am usually too busy to spend much time with my family because of my job. But I visit my parents when I can. My mother cooks a nice dinner for me, and we sit around and talk about things. It's quiet and relaxing.

Narrator: Question 3

1. I like spending time with both family and friends. But to tell the truth, I have more fun with my friends. My friends and I share a lot of interests. That's why they're my friends.
2. I have a new baby, so I don't have much time for friends. He takes most of my attention. For now, my friends are my husband and my son. That's fine with me.
3. I really enjoy spending time with my family. My brothers and sisters and I enjoy many of the same activities. We have a lot in common.
4. I have a lot of friends, and I enjoy spending time with them. We go out together in large groups. My friends are like a large family to me. I get along better with my friends than I do with my family.

NARRATOR: FOOD

Narrator: Question 1

1. I like trying all kinds of food. I especially like dishes from foreign countries. I always enjoy trying food that is new and different.
2. I like the meals my mother cooks. She cooks food that is traditional in our country. It's really delicious. Nobody cooks as well as my mother does.
3. I am a vegetarian, so I never eat meat. I prefer food that is prepared with fresh vegetables. I eat a lot of fruit, too.
4. I generally prefer to eat beef or chicken with rice. And I love desserts. I like anything that's sweet. I almost never eat vegetables.

Narrator: Question 2

1. I almost always eat at restaurants because I am out all day. I always have lunch at a cafeteria. When I have to work late, which is often, I usually buy a sandwich to eat in the office. That's my dinner.
2. I always eat breakfast and dinner at home, and I eat lunch at home, too, when I can. But on weekends, I often go to restaurants with my friends.
3. I usually eat at home because it's too expensive to eat at restaurants. I only have a meal at a restaurant when it's a special occasion, for example, someone's birthday.
4. I eat at home because it's more convenient. I have three children, so it's easier for us to eat at home. Also, there aren't many good restaurants in my neighborhood. I think the food we eat at home tastes better.

Narrator: Question 3

1. My favorite restaurant is a small place near my house. It serves the most delicious cakes. It's a great place to go for an afternoon snack. I frequently meet my friends there.
2. There is a very elegant restaurant downtown that has French food. I had my birthday dinner there last year. The prices are high, so I can't go there very often, but I really like it.
3. I like to go to a fast food restaurant near my school. I don't usually have a lot of time for lunch, so it's a good place for me. I can get a hamburger or a sandwich there and eat it quickly. It's cheap, too.
4. My favorite restaurant is a seafood restaurant near my house. I like it because I like fish. It has lots of other kinds of food on the menu, too.

NARRATOR: HOMETOWN

Narrator: Question 1

1. My hometown is very small and quiet. We only have a few stores and one movie theater. It's a peaceful place to live, but it isn't very exciting. The population is small, so everyone knows everyone else.
2. I come from a large city. It's a very busy place. The streets are always crowded. A lot of interesting people live and work there.
3. My hometown is in the mountains. There is a lot of beautiful scenery around it, so tourists like to visit. It's a medium-sized city, but during the summer it fills up with visitors.
4. I come from a suburb outside a large city. It's a pretty place, but there isn't much to do there. Everybody goes to the city to work or look for entertainment.

Narrator: Question 2

1. People come from all over the world to work and live in my city. You can always meet interesting people there. I really like that.
2. My town is a very attractive place. There are lots of gardens and parks. In the spring, it's very beautiful when all the flowers bloom. In fact, my town is famous for its flowers.
3. There are a lot of opportunities for both work and study in my hometown. We have several universities. Also, since it's a big city, there are a lot of businesses and it's easy to find a job.
4. My town is a very quiet and safe place. That's why it's a good place to raise a family. There is very little crime in my town.

Narrator: Question 3

1. My town can be a very boring place to be. There aren't many things to do there. Everything is always the same. Nothing ever changes.
2. I come from a big city, and there is a lot of traffic on the streets. Because of that, the streets are always noisy, and the air is polluted. I don't really like that, but I guess it's the same in every big city in the world.

3. My hometown is in a very cold climate. We have long, dark winters. It can get very depressing. I think I would prefer to live in a warmer place.

4. Everything in my hometown is very expensive. It costs a lot to rent an apartment. It costs a lot to buy food or to ride the bus. If you don't have a good job, you can't afford to live there.

NARRATOR: SCHOOL

Narrator: Question 1

1. I went to a very small high school. When I graduated, there were only forty students in my class. Because the school was so small, we didn't study a large variety of subjects. However, I had some very excellent teachers, and I learned a lot from them.

2. My high school was huge. The classrooms were always crowded. We had a good sports program, and I played on several teams.

3. I went to an ordinary high school. I'm sure it was like most other high schools. We studied the usual subjects and did the same kinds of activities that high school students do everywhere. I was on the basketball team, and I was a member of the computer club.

4. My high school was in a modern building. Everything in the school was new. We had a beautiful gym and a large library. We had all new equipment for our science classes. It was great place to go to school.

Narrator: Question 2

1. I really enjoyed my biology class. I've always liked science, and I think biology is especially interesting. I liked learning about plants and animals.

2. I always liked art classes best. I took an art class every year I was in high school. Maybe I'm not a very talented artist, but I enjoy painting and drawing and things like that.

3. Math was definitely my favorite subject in high school. I wasn't the best student in this subject. In fact, it has always been challenging for me, but I like it anyhow.

4. I liked studying history a lot. I think it's the most fascinating subject. I still read about it often. I like learning about how things were in the past.

Narrator: Question 3

1. They should study hard, of course, and pay attention to their teachers. What students learn in high school is very important for the future, so they should take it seriously.

2. I think high school students should remember to enjoy their youth. When they graduate, they will have a lot of responsibilities, so they should have fun during their high school years.

3. High school students need to start thinking about their future careers. They should study subjects that will help them later on at the university and in their jobs. High school is a time to prepare for the future.

4. I think high school students should study a lot of different subjects. They need to figure out what things interest them. The only way to know is to try out different things.

NARRATOR: TRANSPORTATION

Narrator: Question 1

1. I live in a big city, so we have a lot of subways and buses. People also drive their cars, but the traffic moves slowly because the streets are so crowded.

2. I live in a small town, and we don't have any public transportation. People usually drive their own cars. We have a train station, but that's for long distance travel.

3. In my city, people usually take the bus or use their cars. Also, a lot of people ride bicycles. We have special bicycle lanes on some of the bigger streets.
4. We have a lot of transportation options in my city. We have subways and buses and taxis. If you live and work downtown, you can walk everywhere you need to go. Our downtown sidewalks are always busy.

Narrator: Question 2

1. I usually drive to school because my school is far from my house. It takes me about an hour to get there. I usually give a ride to some of my classmates, so the trip isn't boring.
2. I take the subway to work. The station is about a ten-minute walk from my apartment. It's very convenient.
3. I always walk to school. It takes almost an hour. It's a good way to get exercise, but I have to leave my house early in order to get to school on time.
4. I ride the bus to work. The bus stop is very close to my house. I have to transfer to another bus downtown.

Narrator: Question 3

1. My biggest problem is that I have to spend a lot of money to put gasoline in my car. Also, it takes a long time to get to school from my house. But the only solution to those problems would be to find an apartment closer to my school.
2. I don't really have any problems with taking the subway. It's very fast. The only thing is that the subway fare is high, and it costs more during rush hour.
3. I don't have any problems with walking to school. I really enjoy it. It takes a long time, but I don't mind. For me, it's relaxing.
4. The biggest problems with transportation in my city is the traffic jams. It takes a long time to get anywhere because of that. It doesn't matter if you take the bus or drive a car. Traffic is always a problem.

NARRATOR: WEATHER

Narrator: Question 1

1. In my town we have four seasons, so the weather depends on the time of year. It varies a lot, from very warm to very cold, and everything in between.
2. I live in tropical part of the world, so the weather is always hot in my city. We have two seasons—rainy and dry. During the rainy season, it rains in the afternoons, but the mornings are usually sunny.
3. My city is in the far north, so we have cold weather. The summers aren't cold, but they are very short. The winters are long, and we get a lot of snow.
4. We have a very pleasant climate in my town. The weather is usually mild. The temperature never gets too high or too low.

Narrator: Question 2

1. I love rainy weather. I like to make a hot cup of coffee and get a good book and sit by the window listening to the raindrops on the glass.
2. I feel depressed when the weather is rainy. Everything seems gray and dark and cold. I don't like to do anything when it rains. I just hope that the weather will change soon.
3. This may sound funny, but I like to go outside when it rains. I like to feel the rain falling on me, and I like to walk through the puddles. But, if it's raining hard, I stay inside.
4. I don't do anything special in rainy weather. I don't care about it, except if there's a big storm. If there's thunder and lightning, I feel scared. I don't like that at all.

Narrator: Question 3

1. I would love to live where the weather is always warm because I don't like to feel cold. I like to go outside every day and enjoy the sunshine.
2. I would like to live in a place that has a long winter with lots of snow. That's because I love to ski. I enjoy all winter sports, so I'd like to live where I could do them easily.
3. I like living in a place that has four seasons. Each one offers something different. Spring and fall are very pretty times of year. Summer always has nice weather. I even like the ice and snow in the winter.
4. I don't like rainy days, so I would like to live in a dry climate, maybe even near a desert. I'd like to live in a place where the sun always shines and there are never any clouds in the sky.

NARRATOR: EXERCISE

Narrator: Question 1

1. I play soccer, so that's the main way I get exercise. I also try to run at least a few times a week to keep fit for soccer.
2. I like to ride my bike, but I don't do it very often. I also play tennis sometimes when I can find someone to play with. I guess I'm not a very active person.
3. I like to work out at the gym. That's my favorite way to exercise. Sometimes I swim, also, but the pool at the gym is often crowded and I don't like that.
4. I enjoy yoga. I take classes, and I also practice at home. It's a good way to build up your strength.

Narrator: Question 2

1. When I was in school, I played on several different sports teams. I really enjoyed competitive sports then. I got a lot more exercise then than I do now.
2. I used to walk to school every day when I was younger. In addition, I took tennis lessons, and I also played volleyball. I had a lot of energy then.
3. I played baseball a lot when I was younger. I wasn't very good at it, but I really liked it. I always had a good time, even if my team lost.
4. When I was a child, I spent a lot of time outside with my friends. We didn't do any particular kinds of exercise. We just played a lot of different games. We ran and jumped a lot as part of our games.

Narrator: Question 3

1. I think it's important to exercise regularly. Unfortunately, I don't exercise often enough. I always feel better after exercise, but I get lazy about it sometimes.
2. I try to exercise every day. It's really important for my health. I try to eat a good diet, too. I think that's the reason why I am almost never sick.
3. I think exercise is good, but I am usually too busy for it. I don't have a lot of free time, and when I do have time, I prefer to relax.
4. I don't like exercise at all. I just think it's really uninteresting. I can think of lots of better ways to spend time. I would rather go to the movies or be with my friends, for example.

NARRATOR: PRACTICE 2

Narrator: Family

Question 1: When you were younger, did you spend more time with family or with friends?
Question 2: In the past, did you spend more or less time with your family than you do now?
Question 3: Do you ask your family for help when you have a problem?

Narrator: Food

Question 1: What did you like to eat when you were younger?
Question 2: Who usually does the cooking in your house?
Question 3: Did you eat at restaurants often when you were a child?

Narrator: Hometown

Question 1: Do you think you will live in your hometown later on?
Question 2: What did you like about your hometown when you were a child?
Question 3: How do you think life in your hometown will be different in the future?

Narrator: Work

Question 1: Why did you choose your profession?
Question 2: What do you like most about the job you have now?
Question 3: Do you think you will have a different kind of job in the future?

Narrator: Transportation

Question 1: How did you get to school when you were a child?
Question 2: Will you buy a car when you start working?
Question 3: Do many people in your city ride the buses?

Narrator: Weather

Question 1: What kind of weather do you dislike?
Question 2: How does the weather affect your mood?
Question 3: What was your favorite season when you were a child?

Narrator: Exercise

Question 1: Do you think your exercise habits will change in the future?
Question 2: How often do you exercise?
Question 3: Did you exercise differently in the past?

ANSWER SHEET FOR STRATEGY REVIEWS

#		✓ X
1		✓ 1 X
2		2
3		3
4		4
5		5
6		6
7		7
8		8
9		9
10		10
11		11
12		12
13		13
14		14
15		15
16		16
17		17
18		18
19		19
20		20

#		✓ X
21		✓ 21 X
22		22
23		23
24		24
25		25
26		26
27		27
28		28
29		29
30		30
31		31
32		32
33		33
34		34
35		35
36		36
37		37
38		38
39		39
40		40
Total		

Audio Track Titles

Key Word Strategies

Track 1		Introduction
Track 2		Complete Notes
Track 3		Multiple-Choice Questions
Track 4	Practice 2	Passages 1 through 5

Listening Module

General Strategies

Track 5	Practice 1	Audio 1
Track 6		Audio 2
Track 7		Audio 3
Track 8		Audio 4
Track 9	Practice 2	

Section 1—Conversation

Track 10	Practice 1	Conversations 1 through 5
Track 11	Practice 2	Conversations 1 through 5
Track 12	Practice 3	Conversations 1 through 5

Section 2—Talk

Track 13	Practice 1	Talks 1 through 5
Track 14	Practice 2	Talks 1 through 5
Track 15	Practice 3	Talks 1 through 5

Section 3—Discussion

Track 16	Practice 1	Conversations 1 through 5
Track 17	Practice 2	Conversations 1 through 4
Track 18	Practice 3	Conversations 1 through 5

Section 4—Talk or Lecture

Track 19	Practice 1	Talks 1 through 3
Track 20	Practice 2	Talks 1 through 3
Track 21	Practice 3	Talks 1 through 3

Strategy Review

Track 22	Section 1
Track 23	Section 2
Track 24	Section 3
Track 25	Section 4

Speaking Module

Track 26	Practice 1
Track 27	Practice 2